. . .
. . .
. . .
. . .
. .
. .
. .
. .
. .
. .
. .
. .

P
da

In the Footsteps of Mallory and Irvine

In the Footsteps of Mallory and Irvine

The Wildest Dream

MARK MacKENZIE

JOHN MURRAY

First published in Great Britain in 2009 by John Murray (Publishers)
An Hachette UK Company

1

© Mark MacKenzie and Altitude Films Ltd 2009

The right of Mark MacKenzie to be identified as the Author of the Work has been asserted by him in accordance with the Copyright, Designs and Patents Act 1988.

A CIP catalogue record for this title is available from the British Library

Hardback ISBN 978-0-7195-2482-0
Trade paperback ISBN 978-0-7195-2123-2

Typeset in 12.25/15 Monotype Bembo by Servis Filmsetting Ltd, Stockport, Cheshire

Printed and bound by Clays Ltd, St Ives plc

John Murray policy is to use papers that are natural, renewable and recyclable products and made from wood grown in sustainable forests. The logging and manufacturing processes are expected to conform to the environmental regulations of the country of origin.

John Murray (Publishers)
338 Euston Road
London NW1 3BH

www.johnmurray.co.uk

Contents

Illustrations

Picture Acknowledgements

The author and publisher would like to thank the following for permission to reproduce illustrations: picture 2, Salkeld Collection; picture 3, Alpine Club Photo Library London; picture 4, John Noel Photographic Collection; picture 5, Royal Geographical Society. All other pictures © Altitude Films Ltd.

Prologue

O N THE MORNING of 8 June 1924, George Mallory stepped out from a low canvas tent high on the northern slopes of Mount Everest. It had been a miserable night. The tent he and his companion shared had been buffeted relentlessly by a driving wind that seemed to take a malign pleasure in trying to tear their tiny shelter from its moorings. But it held fast, a small canvas boat resisting a wrathful storm, its anchors straining to their limit on an ocean of ice and rock. Being tall and with long, rangy limbs, Mallory found the tent cramped, barely big enough for two men. The flurries of snow that blasted through gaps in the doors with wearying regularity hardly helped; when the canvas finally became saturated with snow, it froze solid.

Inside the tent, his companion was now stirring, his broad back and shoulders twitching occasionally, as if trying to discourage a fly. When at last Sandy Irvine emerged on to the ridge, his face bore angry red welts, the scars of a losing battle against a sun that, at this altitude, looked like a great, lidless eye. Irvine's lips were cracked and blistered, a discomfort he bore with characteristic good humour but described in his journal as 'perfect agony'.

Below the two men lay the entire world; above them the pyramid of snow and rock for which they would be heading that morning: the summit of Everest. In every direction, the Himalayas rose like islands, a fantastical archipelago upon whose shores washed a sea of cloud. The horizon fell away around them as it followed the curvature of the earth, which, from such a great height, was clearly visible. High above, the bluest of skies deepened to an ecclesiastical purple as it reached towards the heavens.

Though the morning was bright and clear, Mallory knew that in these mountains appearances could be deceptive. The annual monsoon, currently making its way up from India, was racing north to drape over the high Himalaya a curtain of snow that would last for several months. It was yet to arrive, but the clear morning skies would soon give way to afternoon cloud. They needed to get going.

They had reached camp the previous evening – at 26,800 ft, their last stop before the summit. The four porters that climbed with them had deposited the spare oxygen canisters they would need for the ascent, then made their way back down the mountain. The extreme altitude meant the air they were breathing contained roughly a third of the oxygen found at sea level, a result of the hugely reduced atmospheric pressure. The breathing apparatus was vital to counteract the enervating effects of altitude; it was cumbersome and could leak badly, but it could also make the difference between success and failure.

As Mallory and Irvine made preparations to leave, the only sound was the shrill, locomotive shriek of the wind as it raked the mountainside before tumbling into the void below. That and the occasional ring of metal as Irvine checked their oxygen apparatus once again, in a dedication to improving their efficiency that bordered on obsession. Upon waking, Mallory would ordinarily have begun melting snow for drinking water, to combat the harsh thirst induced by the dry air. Yet only the previous day he had, with typical clumsiness, sent their only stove tumbling down the mountainside. They would have to go without. Foul weather had checked the progress of the expedition too often already for them to go back now.

It was more than three months since, dressed in blazers and white linen trousers, Mallory and Irvine had boarded the SS *California* en route to Bombay, watching as the bustling port of Liverpool dissolved into a low, grey seam of English coastline.

More than two months since they had left the Indian hill station of Darjeeling and marched through the gardens and forests of Sikkim – scented oases of hibiscus and bougainvillea which they relinquished reluctantly, trading them for 350 bleak miles of Tibetan plateau that led to their base camp, on the rocky plateau of the Rongbuk Glacier, which now lay more than 8,000 ft below them.

It was the mountain they had come for. The world had not long been liberated from a foul and destructive war, in which Second Lieutenant George Mallory had witnessed with his own eyes a new and mechanized barbarism that cut down young men with pitiless efficiency. But the world survived; he survived, walking out of the mud and stink into a new decade, and the promise of a golden future beyond. And these were bold and exciting times. Man had found his way to both the most northern and the most southern points on the planet. Only the highest still remained unconquered, a cathedral of rock and ice that bestrode the border between Tibet and Nepal. Known to the native Tibetans as Chomolungma, 'Goddess Mother of the World', with its rocky spire standing more than 29,000 ft above sea level it was the last extreme of earth, and for that reason was rightly regarded as the 'Third Pole'.

There had been three British expeditions to the mountain in the past four years, but only George Leigh Mallory had been invited to take part in all of them. By profession Mallory was a teacher – competent, engaging and popular with his pupils. But when released into the mountains he was a different proposition entirely: more than just a climber, possessed of something approaching genius. And this was his mountain, one he had engaged with twice previously, only to return home without a scalp on his belt. This was his last chance. It was the third time he had left behind his dear wife, Ruth, and their young family; the third time he had forced her to endure what he described to his father as the 'fearful tug' of parting. He recognized only too well the brave face Ruth wore whenever he left, and recognized too how much he asked of her in coming here again. 'Darling, I wish you the best I can,' he had written in one of his last letters home, 'that your anxiety will be at an end before you get this, with the best news.'

He almost wished his employers at Cambridge University had denied his request for leave when the invitation came to join this latest foray. Having reached the Himalayas, however, the embers of the torch he now carried for the mountain were rekindled by those immense flanks, that familiar profile trailing a plumage of ice crystals that flapped in the sky like a jib that had slipped its rope. And if he allowed himself to daydream on those days of interminable foot marching across the Tibetan plateau, it might have been of the frenzy of acclaim that would inevitably follow a successful conclusion. As the Antarctic had made Ernest Shackleton, in the years that followed it might be said that this was the mountain that had made George Mallory.

It was sometime between seven and eight o'clock in the morning when Mallory and Irvine at last set off, each man shouldering two cylinders of oxygen for the climb ahead, Irvine undoubtedly flinching as he bit down on the mouthpiece of his oxygen apparatus and pulled tight the webbing straps against his sunburnt face. Taking particular care on the sloping terrain that formed their immediate route from camp, the two men now left the safety of their tent behind. In the weather that could accompany the mountain's foulest moods, 'camp' was something of a misnomer, but a even a small tent could provide vital shelter. As the two friends left theirs behind, the scene inside was chaotic. Gear was strewn across the floor: climbing rope, various parts for their oxygen equipment, all items considered surplus to requirements for the last great push.

When they had did the porters farewell the previous evening, Mallory had sent with them two handwritten notes. One was for John Noel, a retired army captain, who had accompanied them as the expedition's cinematographer. If there was to be a successful summit attempt, capturing it on film would be crucial both to record it for posterity and for maximizing any commercial opportunities that might come their way. 'Dear Noel,' Mallory wrote to his colleague, 'We'll probably start early tomorrow (8th) in order to have clear weather. It won't be too early to start looking for us either crossing the rock band under the pyramid, or going up skyline at 8.0 pm.' He had most probably meant to write 8 a.m.

The 'rock band' that Mallory referred to was a thick seam of cliffs that ran across the entire North Face of the mountain and would be their first major challenge en route to the summit. Around 1,000 ft in depth, it started at the point where the rock changed from grey schist to a lighter limestone, and, with its distinctly yellow hue, it was visible even from Base Camp, thousands of feet below. Mallory and Irvine found climbing up through this 'Yellow Band' arduous work.

After several hours of sustained effort, they at last reached the top of the band, the point at which the upper reaches of mountain opened out. They found themselves on a plateau – a long, sloping shoulder that Mallory had first identified three years previously. It was this, he believed, that would now lead him to the summit; this was the North-East Ridge of Everest.

They pressed on, and, as they climbed ever higher, the simple act of placing one foot in front of the other proved exhausting. Supplementary oxygen could alleviate the worst effects of altitude, but it could not eliminate them. With one of their four oxygen canisters now spent, they discarded it beneath a large boulder. Without water to quench their thirst, dehydration only compounded their discomfort. And the strength of the sun – increasing by roughly 3 per cent for every thousand feet of elevation – served to make Irvine's agony all the more perfect.

Still they went on. If they failed now, the symmetry would be too cruel: a third British expedition; a third failed summit bid. Just a week earlier, Mallory and another climber, by the name of Geoffrey Bruce, had established a camp at 25,300 ft.

They had been well set for a crack at the summit when their porters had succumbed to altitude sickness, and they had been forced to abandon their attempt. Another sortie soon followed. On 4 June, Colonel Edward Norton, the overall leader of the expedition, and his colleague Howard Somervell had made excellent progress on their own plodding course for the top until Somervell, one of the strongest of their number, was forced to retire at 28,000 ft, his body racked by a cough that, exposed to the dry air, had become so violent he had hacked up part of his own larynx. When the offending item became lodged in his airway, ejecting it had been a 'bloody business', Somervell recalled, but it was better than choking to death. Norton continued alone, despite suffering from double vision as he sought to negotiate the treacherous terrain. He climbed for another hour, in which he gained another 128 ft. At the point at which he started his descent, Norton stood higher than any man in history. But it was still nearly 1,000 ft shy of the summit.

As Mallory and Irvine now wound their way upward, they carried with them the final hopes of the expedition. It was up to them – or rather it was up to George, as the expedition's climbing leader. 'It is fifty to one against us,' he wrote to Ruth, 'but we'll have a whack yet and do ourselves proud.'

Mallory knew their prize lay just a few hours away. He also knew that the higher they went, the more tired they would become and the more slender would be the margin for error. Their reserves of energy were as finite as the oxygen they carried on their backs; every footstep took them further from a safe return. As Mallory drove himself on, Irvine battled stoically. Sixteen years younger than Mallory, and lacking his natural talent as a climber, he nevertheless had some experience, and he more than compensated for what he lacked with an immense physical strength and boldness of spirit. The unfettered enthusiasm with which he had thrown himself into every task had been one of the reasons why Mallory had chosen him as a partner. Nevertheless, this was unfamiliar territory.

The second of the two notes brought down by the porters was for a fellow expedition member now climbing in support of the two men. Noel Odell was a highly experienced mountaineer who on the morning of 8 June was a full day behind Mallory and Irvine as he made his way from 25,500 ft, the team's Camp V, to Camp VI, from where the two men had left that morning. 'Dear Odell,' Mallory wrote, all too aware of the chaotic state in which they had left the tent, 'We're awfully sorry to have left things in such a mess – our Unna Cooker rolled down the slope at the last moment. Be sure of getting back to [Camp] IV tomorrow in time to evacuate before dark, as I hope to. In the tent I must have left a compass – for the Lord's sake rescue it: we are here without.'

Odell had spent the morning searching the mountain for fossils. A geologist by profession, he was also the expedition's oxygen officer, and there was some irony in his having spent the previous weeks climbing perfectly well without the need for supplementary air. As he made for the rendezvous with his two colleagues, he had come across some rock specimens he was keen to identify. With him, he carried the compass requested by the ever-forgetful Mallory.

As the morning wore on, the bright start to the day that had so encouraged Mallory and Irvine began to give way, as Mallory had suspected it might. Great banks of mist now rolled in, but Odell climbed on unperturbed; he even thought he detected a certain luminosity in the sky above him. Mallory and Irvine might be heading into better weather.

At precisely 12.50 p.m, Odell looked up to see the clouds part and then, high on the summit ridge, two specks moving beneath a rock outcrop, little more than a notch in the skyline. 'My eyes became fixed', he wrote later, 'on one tiny black spot silhouetted on a small snow-crest beneath a rock step in the ridge; the black spot moved. Another black spot became apparent and moved up to join the other on the crest. The first then approached the great rock step and shortly emerged at the top; the second did likewise. Then the whole fascinating vision vanished, enveloped in cloud once more.'

Odell thought the two climbers somewhat behind schedule, but attributed the delay to possible problems with the oxygen apparatus. All he could do now was wait for their return, hoping that when they arrived they would bring good news. At around two in the afternoon Odell at last wandered into Camp VI. It was at that moment that it began to snow.

Somewhere high above, Mallory and Irvine ploughed onward, the worn gabardine jackets they had come to regard as a second skin now pulled tight against an increasingly biting wind. The older man did his best to monitor the progress of his young colleague, all the while ushering his own exhausted frame forward. The snow began to fall more heavily now – by no means a blizzard, but sufficient to soften the outlines of their footprints as quickly as they were made. The growing softness underfoot also meant that their hobnailed boots now enjoyed far less purchase than they did on icier ground. And soon the light would begin to fade.

And suddenly he was falling. In the blink of an eye, George Mallory was off his feet. He held his breath, hoping it was no more than a slide and that, it would soon come to an end. Instead, he continued downward and, as he fell, the intermittent tug on the rope told him that Irvine was falling with him, making his own course all the more erratic. There was no panic. Mountaineering instincts cultivated over many years of climbing kicked in instantly. Although high altitude could impair cognitive function, Mallory knew immediately that he must arrest his fall, must drive an ice axe, even his hands, into the mountain. And he needed to do it quickly: with the frozen jaws of the mighty Rongbuk Glacier gaping more than 8,000 ft below, he could ill afford to run out of ground.

Suddenly the rope pulled tight, perhaps catching on a boulder or snagging on a finger of rock. Mallory had been in similar situations before. He knew only too well the limitations of the cord cinched in a simple knot around his middle. With he and Irvine pulling in opposite directions, there was every chance that if they loaded the rope with too much strain it would break. It did.

Without Irvine's bodyweight to create drag, Mallory began to gather momentum, the mountain he had coveted for so long rushing up and past him. At some point as he fell, his right foot jammed against something solid. Somewhere close by came a dull cracking noise; it was the sound of his right leg snapping, both the tibia and fibula, at the point at which they entered his boot. With the need to stop ever more urgent, his hands were suddenly empty – he'd dropped his ice axe. His fingers, strengthened by a lifetime of grasping for handholds, began to claw at the slope, and he thrust them repeatedly into the scree. The friction of the rough terrain, combined with the speed of his fall, snatched off his gloves before there was another crack, this time in his right arm, followed by a sharp, stinging blow to his forehead. Slowly, with his heartbeat thumping furiously in his ears, Mallory finally came to a standstill.

He drew a breath. A staccato rattle resonated somewhere in his chest. The burning in his brow began to intensify, and blood dropped in warm, thick gobbets on to the snow in front of his face. His right leg throbbed in agony. In a vain attempt to afford it some protection, he placed his left leg over it. The pain forced his body to convulse. Even in this broken, animal state he was aware of the stillness. The moments turned to a minute, the minutes into an hour. He called out, but the effort merely made the pain worse, his low moan barely audible against the roar of the wind. And where was Irvine?

In the small tent at Camp VI, Noel Odell waited for his friends to return, occupying himself with the discarded parts for the oxygen equipment. When an hour had passed, he began to grow concerned. Descending in such conditions would be difficult for Mallory and Irvine, particularly as a rock ledge above hid the tent from view. He pushed the doors of the shelter aside and climbed into the squall. Making his way upward for several hundred feet, he began whistling and yodelling, as loudly as he was able, praying that his friends would hear him. Periodically he stopped, listening for something, anything, that might sound like a reply. He heard nothing. Returning once more to the tent, he sat out the storm. When at last it subsided, the sun appeared once more and the mountain was bathed in a golden light.

As Mallory's note had reminded him, Odell's role in this latest summit bid required that he return that night to a lower elevation – to Camp IV, at 23,000 ft, where other members of the expedition were waiting. The small, lone tents at the high camps of V and VI were barely large enough for two men, as Mallory would attest, and no man dared risk a night in the open. Reluctantly, Odell left the compass Mallory had requested, and at around 4.30 he set off on the return journey down the mountain.

The night of 8 June was clear and moonlit. Odell spent much of it watching the mountain's great North Face, hoping to spot a lantern. None appeared. The clear weather that allowed Odell to sweep back and forth for signs of his friends also plunged the mountain into impossible cold. Far away in England, Ruth Mallory remained blissfully unaware of events on the great peak.

At dawn, the sun returned – just ambient light at first, edging the clouds, before it spilled across the mountain. With the sun up, Noel Odell prepared to resume what by now was becoming an increasingly frantic search for his friends, and at midday he set off for Camp V accompanied by two porters.

With no indication that the climbers had passed through, the next morning Odell sent the porters back and carried on to Camp VI alone. As he approached the small tent, his heart must have quickened a little. He threw open the tent doors. There was nobody there.

Odell was crestfallen. He peered inside, only to find everything precisely as he had left it two days before – including the compass, which lay undisturbed on the floor. Where *were* they?

If they'd failed to make it back, then they had to be somewhere above Camp VI.

Although Odell began to fear dark things for Mallory and Irvine, he set off to retrace their steps, following a course that he believed represented their most likely line of ascent. For two hours he climbed, trudging upward, his mood sinking the higher he went. Eventually, exhausted by his efforts of the past few days, he was forced to call a halt.

Odell was overcome by despair. Later, he would describe how, as he had climbed on that final, fruitless search, it had been hard to shake the feeling that Everest had been mocking him, an insignificant mortal pitted against the enormity of the mountain. 'It seemed to look down with cold indifference on me, mere puny man,' he wrote, 'and howl derision in wind gusts at my petition to yield up its secret − this mystery of my friends.'

As he began his final descent from Camp VI, Odell looked back repeatedly in the hope that he might catch a glimpse of his missing colleagues. On the face of the mountain he thought he detected some irresistible quality that might have drawn Mallory and Irvine on, as a siren draws sailors to the rocks. 'As I gazed again another mood appeared to creep over her haunting features,' he wrote. 'There seemed to be something alluring in that towering presence ... [such] that he who approaches close must ever be led on, and oblivious of all obstacles seek to reach that most sacred and highest place of all.'

When he arrived back at Camp V, Odell's first task was an unenviable one, to inform the rest of the expedition of the results of his search. He hauled the sleeping bags from the tent and laid them on the ground in a 'T'. It was a prearranged signal to his colleagues waiting at Camp IV below, a black message standing out against the white snow: 'No trace.'

And 'No trace' was how it would remain for a long time thereafter. For many years, what really happened to Mallory and Irvine in those final desperate hours on the upper reaches of Mount Everest existed only in the realm of speculation. The moment when Noel Odell saw his colleagues through a break in the clouds was the last time they were seen alive. They left behind one of the greatest mysteries in the history of exploration: were George Mallory and Sandy Irvine the first men to stand on the summit of the highest mountain in the world?

It would be three quarters of a century before the questions surrounding Mallory and Irvine's disappearance could begin to be fully answered. The remarkable discovery in May 1999 of Mallory's body, lying facedown high on Everest's slopes, caused a sensation around the world and reignited the mystery. On that occasion, the American climber Conrad Anker, a member of an expedition which set out with the specific aim of finding Mallory's body, had strayed outside the designated search area and spotted what he later described as 'a patch of white' on the mountainside. It was the find of a lifetime. And for Anker, that chance encounter with one of the most iconic figures in mountaineering history was also the start of an obsession with the mystery of Mallory and Irvine's disappearance.

Anker finally had the opportunity to walk in George Mallory's footsteps on the Altitude Everest Expedition 2007. Returning to Everest one last time with a group of world-class climbers, including British climbing star Leo Houlding, Anker was able to follow the spirit and last journey of a man who had haunted him for years and investigate for himself whether Mallory and Irvine, with the clothing and equipment they had available in 1924, could have stood on the summit of Everest twenty-nine years before Edmund Hillary and Tenzing Norgay. It was in its own right an epic expedition. Anker and Houlding's ascent of the North East Ridge Route of Everest gave them a unique insight into Mallory's own perilous route to the summit, not least on the rock outcrop on which Noell Odell had last seen them, a feature known as the Second Step. Few climbers have conquered the North Face without using a ninety foot fixed ladder attached to this sheer rock wall just a few hundred feet below the summit. Virtually every modern climber uses this ladder, making this deadly stretch a simple five minute haul. Mallory, of course, didn't have this luxury. After long negotiations with the Chinese government, the expedition received permission to remove the ladder for a very short window of two days. During this period Everest was restored to the pristine and far more terrifying peak which confronted George Mallory and Sandy Irvine in 1924.

In 2007 the savage, instantly changeable weather five miles high would make Anker and Houlding's assault on Everest a genuine race against time, with the monsoon season fast approaching as they attempted their historic 'free climb' of the Second Step. It was a timely reminder of the power of the mountain that more than eighty years earlier had exerted such a hold over George Mallory. In a golden age of exploration, Mallory had been the pioneering adventurer who dared to reach into the world's last great untouched wilderness. A genius, a visionary, an extraordinary man, Mallory's abilities went far beyond his age and era. He stood higher, quite literally, than anyone before him. His story was one of supreme courage, utter dedication and enduring obsession.

I

Walking off the Map

ONE DAY IN 1873, George Mallory was sent to his room for misbehaving. Being seven years old at the time, he felt a deep sense of injustice. When it was deemed that he had done his penance, another member of the family came to fetch him. On opening the bedroom door, George was nowhere to be seen. The only clue to his whereabouts was an open window and a curtain flapping gently in the breeze as the errant boy scampered on the roof above.

George Leigh Mallory was born in the Cheshire village of Mobberley on 18 June 1886. His father, Herbert, was rector at St Wilfrid's, the parish church, and he and his wife, Annie, were loving parents who did their best to foster independence and self-reliance in George and his two sisters, Mary and Avie, laying down basic rules on discipline without quashing their children's independence of spirit. Young George had his own interpretation of 'the rules'. Invariably it involved climbing, and invariably somewhere dangerous. If this gave his parents cause for alarm, his friends and siblings recognized something that his mother and father did not: that, when it came to climbing, George was different. His peers would look on in awe as George scaled all manner of obstacles with a feline ease. As his sister Avie recalled, for example, he would climb 'the downspouts of the house with cat-like sure-footedness'. George's appetite for adventure sometimes left his playmates with some explaining to do. 'His mother ...' his school friend Harold Porter once recalled, 'quite unaware of our activities, rushed in to find me paying out rope as George sped over the roof to a known route of descent on the far side.'

In 1894, when Mallory was eight, the family moved to Birkenhead, where Herbert Mallory became Vicar of St John's.

The young George was a bright student and enjoyed his studies. At the age of 14 he won a scholarship to Winchester College, a renowned school in the English city of the same name. George was a handsome child, raised to be courteous and to volunteer help whenever possible – something with which the Winchester motto, 'Manners Makyth Man', chimed nicely. He was, to use a popular expression of the time, 'a dear'. He worked hard and wrote home often, keen to let his mother and father know how he was getting on. Where extra-curricular activities where concerned, however, he exercised sound editorial judgement. Into his letters, for example, went the results of a 'footer' match played one weekend, along with an 'apology' for running up his parents a hefty book bill in the course of his lessons. Left out, on the other hand, were details of an outing to the town of Romsey, where he climbed the tower of the ancient abbey.

It was the English public-school system that ensured that these early inspections of church architecture became something more enduring. Highly physically capable, George had a natural flair for gymnastics, something that couldn't fail to be noticed by one of his schoolmasters. Graham Irving believed greatly in the redeeming qualities of exercise and was passionate about a pastime that was proving increasingly popular among the middle classes: the sport of mountaineering.

The common practice for those now travelling regularly to climb in the Alps and the Dolomite mountains was to employ the services of a local guide such as a shepherd – someone who knew the topography of the area intimately and would know where was safe to climb and where was not. It was an approach endorsed by the most famous mountaineers of the era. But Irving, much like George, preferred to be different, and would often indulge in what was a new and controversial practice: climbing without a guide. For a young man keen for adventure, scaling great peaks without anyone holding your hand offered the same kind of liberation as shinning illicitly up a rectory drainpipe, only in the mountains it was a freedom multiplied a thousand-fold. Irving took young Mallory under his wing, and the boy soon flourished. He became one of the founding members of the school's climbing society, the Winchester Ice Club, and from his first climbs it was clear that the flair that had revealed itself in childish games could enable George to achieve extraordinary things on bare rock.

In 1905, Mallory left Winchester to read history at Cambridge University. This too was to prove a revelation. To someone raised within rectory walls, Cambridge was a hotbed of new ideas and thinking. By day Mallory studied history, yet it was time spent outside the tutor's study that ignited the spirit of a passionate and idealistic undergraduate. Greatly excited by the progressive social issues that were fast becoming the causes célèbres of the liberal intelligentsia, he joined the Fabian Society, an organization that championed the gradual introduction of socialism into British society. He was an advocate of female suffrage, and soon began to favour agnosticism over the traditional Christian doctrine of his childhood. He rebelled in more traditional ways too, growing his hair long and wearing black. Among those who began to explore this new exciting new intellectual landscape with him were the future surgeon and author Geoffrey Keynes and Rupert Brooke, who would go on to become a celebrated poet. Together they discovered new horizons, discussing the latest developments in art and literature, the lanterns of their youthful zeal often burning deep into the night. The friendships formed in those inspired hours would prove long-lasting, and the young Mallory would come to value friendship above almost everything else.

Among the friends he made at Cambridge were members of the Bloomsbury set, an elite group of artists and thinkers whose orbit was held by the flamboyant writer Lytton Strachey. With his imposing physique and handsome good looks, not to mention his appetite for perilous ascents, Mallory made for an exotic, muscular flower in such bookish company. An Adonis in their midst, to an intellectual circle steeped in the classics, he was a gift directly from Mount Olympus. After his first meeting with Mallory, Lytton Strachey could barely contain himself. 'George Mallory ...' he wrote to friends:

> My hand trembles, my heart palpitates, my whole being swoons away at the words – oh heavens! heavens! ... he's six foot high, with the body of an athlete by Praxiteles [a renowned Athenian sculptor], and a face – oh incredible – the mystery of Botticelli, the refinement and delicacy of a Chinese print, the youth and piquancy of an unimaginable English boy. I rave, but when you see him, as you must, you will admit all – all!

For the artist Duncan Grant, a fellow 'Bloomsberry', Mallory made a perfect model, posing for his friend on numerous occasions. Grant adored him almost as much as Strachey did, once confessing that he would happily pay to keep Mallory as his 'mistress'. For the young boy from the rectory these were heady times, and Mallory seemed to revel in the attention of this gilded elite, a group that thrived on what they perceived as an intoxicating tension between the classical virtues of platonic love and the need to explore the human appetite in all its forms – including sexual. Sex was regarded as both an artistic and an intellectual rite of passage, and Mallory had the briefest of affairs with James Strachey, Lytton's younger brother.

If Graham Irving spotted Mallory's talent in the bud, it was a more celebrated mountaineer who recognized the moment when it reached fruition. Geoffrey Winthrop Young was already a mountaineer of some standing when he first met George Mallory, at a Cambridge dinner in February 1909. Though Mallory couldn't know it then, Young – some ten years his senior – was destined to become one of the greatest influences on his life, a mentor to whom he would turn in moments of darkness and light and with whom he would consult on all the major decisions in his life.

From a country house he owned at Pen y Pass, a Welsh town popular with turn-of-the-century climbers, Young would lead groups of friends to take on bold and challenging ascents, among the peaks and crags of nearby Snowdonia. These groups included some of the finest climbers in the country, and the patrician-like Young came to refer to them as his 'hill company'. Young was well connected, and the social gatherings he hosted during the evenings at Pen y Pass were peopled by those whose achievements in politics or the arts mirrored the lofty heights of the surrounding topography. His guest list included future Nobel Prize winners and Cabinet ministers, a roster of the great, the good and, in Mallory's case, the extremely good-looking – something that would not have been lost on Young, who had a series of homosexual relationships both before and after his marriage in 1918.

On Mallory's first visit, Young recognized his virtuosity as a climber at once, noting how he seemed to move over rock with 'wave-like ease'. His relationship with it, Young observed, was so intuitive it allowed him to operate outside the usual rules, just as he had as a boy. His success on any given ascent had an air of inevitability. 'Whatever may have happened unseen … between him and the cliff, in the way of holds or mutual adjustments,' wrote Geoffrey Young, 'the look, and indeed the result, were always the same – a continuous undulating movement so rapid and powerful that one felt the rock must either yield or disintegrate.'

Often, what shook lesser climbers left George Mallory unperturbed, and this coolness under pressure was to become his trademark. In 1909, the year he met Young, the two men were climbing in the Alps on the south-east ridge of a mountain known as the Nesthorn. At 12,545 ft, it offered some challenging climbing, and, while attempting to scale an overhanging rock, Mallory fell. He did so, Young recalled, 'soundlessly, a grey streak flickered downward and past me, and out of sight'. Coming to a stop some 40 ft later, suspended over the icy expanse of the glacier below on a thin cotton rope holding his full weight, Mallory was unnerved by the fall so little that he still held his ice axe in his hand.

For Mallory, climbing was a physical expression of the rich intellectual life he enjoyed elsewhere. It was an aesthetic experience, artistic almost – made all the more so by his exceptional gifts. 'Climbers ...' he told the Climber's Club Journal in March 1914, 'endanger their lives. With what object? If only for some physical pleasure, to enjoy certain movements of the body and to experience the zest of emulation, then it is not worthwhile.' For Mallory, mountaineering existed 'on a higher plane than mere physical sensation'. There was, he wrote, 'something sublime [in] the essence of mountaineering. [Mountaineers] compare the call of the hills to the melody of wonderful music, and the comparison is not ridiculous.' In the early years of the twentieth century, Mallory was fast becoming one of the sport's greatest virtuosos.

But there was an off note, the hint of a flaw in an otherwise polished diamond. Not all those who gathered at Pen y Pass – among them some of the great climbers of the age – were as complimentary as Geoffrey Young. When the renowned Austrian mountaineer Karl Blodig spent a day climbing with Mallory, he concluded that 'that young man will not be alive for long.' While his talent was beyond doubt, even Mallory fell on occasion, as his experience on the Nesthorn could testify, and what Blodig saw was the lack of a piece of armour vital to climbers: the ability to acknowledge risk. The charge of recklessness would be laid at Mallory's door more than once, though his ever-loyal friends would state the case for the defence. Mallory was, according to his friend and long-time climbing partner Cottie Sanders, 'prudent according to his own standards, but his standards were not those of the ordinary medium-good rock-climber. The fact was that difficult rocks had become to him a perfectly normal element; his prodigious reach, his great strength, and his admirable technique, joined in a sort of cat-like agility, made him feel completely secure on rocks so difficult as to fill less competent climbers with a sense of hazardous enterprise.'

In 1914, George Mallory fell again, this time deeply in love. On graduating from Cambridge, he had spent a year deliberating on his future career before finally settling on teaching. In 1910, he had been given a job as a tutor at Charterhouse, another public school, based in Godalming in Surrey. He taught a mixed curriculum with vigour, and was popular with his pupils, forever seeking ways to broaden their interests with the latest works in art and literature. Among his students was the future poet Robert Graves, whom Mallory also introduced to mountaineering. It was while taking part in a play nearby that Mallory met a local architect. Thackeray Turner owned Westbrook, a large house on the outskirts of Godalming, where he lived with his three daughters. His middle daughter was quiet and pretty, qualities that masked a bold spirit. Her name was Ruth. George Mallory was a regular visitor to the house, and at Easter 1914 he was invited on a holiday that the family was taking in Italy. He had already confessed his interest in Ruth to a friend, Will Arnold-Foster, and, by the time the holiday party reached Venice, George and Ruth had fallen very much in love. They had a good deal in common – not least an enjoyment of the countryside and the outdoor life. They were soon engaged, and Mallory wrote to his mother with the good news. 'I'm engaged to be married,' he told her. 'What bliss ... Ruth Turner – she lives just over the river from here in a lovely house and with lovely people, and she's as good as gold, and brave and true and sweet.'

Soon after returning from Europe the Turner family promptly disappeared again, for a holiday in Ireland, and this time without George. It was now that he and Ruth began the almost daily correspondence that would come to define their often long-distance relationship: in ten years of marriage, they were destined to spend almost half that time apart. For the young lovers, letters were far more than communication. They were an almost physical connection, dispatched so frequently they seemed to bridge both time and space. Ruth carried George's letters with her constantly, reading them time and again, as if to ensure she extracted every nuance of meaning. Mallory even used them to woo her at a distance, telling her that the loops of his hand-writing were his kisses, and the tall strokes of individual letters his arms that would embrace her. 'Life with you is going to be very perfect,' she wrote in reply.

After leaving Cambridge, Mallory had started work on a book on James Boswell, the author of *The Life of Samuel Johnson*, and in 1912 this was finally published. If *Boswell the Biographer* received mixed reviews, in commercial terms it was an unequivocal flop. Yet Mallory persevered with the idea that his future was to be a writer, rather than a humble schoolteacher. For George Mallory was nothing if not a dreamer, and the classical idealism that had first stirred at Cambridge would inform much of the rest of his life.

Though Ruth had been educated at Prior's Field, a progressive school which championed the arts, she considered herself somewhat intellectually inferior to her husband. Nevertheless, George was emotionally articulate, able to express to her his most intimate thoughts, and it was this poetic streak that Ruth found so beguiling, convincing her they were two halves of one whole. 'I am glad there is a lot of growing to do with you,' she wrote to him. 'I would rather grow old with you than anyone in the world. I think you have made me grow a good lot already.'

Now that Mallory was to be married, he would have to focus on such prosaic concerns as supporting his future wife. Whereas Ruth had a private income of her own, her husband-to-be had to rely on the modest wages of a schoolmaster. His chivalrous assertion to his future father-in-law that he couldn't possibly marry a girl if she had her own income was met with the withering response that he couldn't possibly marry her if she hadn't.

They married on 29 July 1914, three months after the Turner

family holiday in Italy and only days before the outbreak of the First World War. The newly-weds would move in with Ruth's parents, but with Europe in turmoil there was little hope of first honeymooning abroad. Which was just as well. Mallory suggested to Geoffrey Young that he and Ruth might visit the Alps, taking in a little climbing on the way. It was a suggestion with which his friend, who acted as best man at the wedding, was less than impressed. In a letter to Mallory, he seemed to echo the words of Karl Blodig three years previously. Being a great climber and being a leader of men, or in this case women, were separate skills and ones that Mallory had yet to acquire. 'The consequence of your ... extraordinary physical brilliance in climbing', Young wrote, '[is] that you ... have not held back from allowing yourself to sweep weaker brethren, carried away by their belief in you, to take risks or exertions that they were not fit for, and which had the crisis come, neither you nor any man in climbing could have the margin to cover for both.' Mallory was upset by the criticism and opted instead for a hiking holiday in southern England.

As the conflict in France grew worse, Mallory considered it his duty to sign up, even if his liberal sensibilities balked at the jingoistm of some of the British press. Yet his headmaster at Charterhouse, a well-meaning man by the name of Frank Fletcher, refused him permission to leave, exercising his right to release staff for war duty only at his own discretion. Another schoolmaster, Fletcher said, simply couldn't be spared, and Mallory struggled with the comfortable life that he and Ruth were living. Detailed accounts of the atrocious conditions under which Mallory's peers laboured were now beginning to filter back, and the burden of guilt weighed heavily on his shoulders. 'It becomes increasingly difficult to remain a schoolmaster,' he wrote to Geoffrey Young, who by now had joined an ambulance unit in France. 'I read this morning the dismal tale of wet and cold which makes my fireplace an intolerable reproach.' To take his mind off things, before the autumn term of 1914 began at

Charterhouse, Mallory took Ruth to the Lake District, and it was here, on the crags above Wasdale, that he introduced her to climbing.

In the spring of 1915, George and Ruth Mallory moved out of Westbrook and into a home of their own, a large house in Godalming known as The Holt. The following September, Ruth gave birth to their first child, Clare. Under any other circumstances this should have been a time of unconfined joy, but the regular news from France now began to include the death notices of friends and acquaintances, and Mallory's sense of obligation only increased.

When at last his release to join the army was granted, Mallory began his basic training before being commissioned into the Royal Garrison Artillery as a second lieutenant in December 1915. But it was not until he arrived in France, the following May, that he even learned how to fire a revolver. 'If I saw a German 20 yards away,' Mallory commented, 'and he gave me plenty of time to aim, I might hit him.' He was eventually posted to Armentières, a town on the Western Front in northern France. Mallory was by all accounts a competent soldier, and coped well with the hardship of life in the trenches. As a young boy, he had conditioned himself not to feel the cold, sleeping with only one blanket in winter. It helped that he was also blessed with that most admirable quality possessed by the English middle classes: the irrepressible ability to make do and get on.

To make life more comfortable, he instructed Ruth to send regular parcels of provisions. There were deliveries of potatoes, cheese and copies of the *Times Literary Supplement*, of rat poison, and even of a set of velvet curtains for the officers' mess (though admittedly when the war was coming to an end). And he sent his cleaning and mending home to Ruth, who duly obliged and posted it back, good as new. There was no hiding from the grim realities of trench warfare, but Mallory was possessed of a strong will and that coolness under pressure he had displayed on the Nesthorn with Geoffrey Young. In his hour of need, amid the arbitrary brutality of war, his nerve did not desert him. In conditions and sights appalling enough to send others mad, Mallory displayed remarkable fortitude. 'The gruesome enters in a good deal,' he wrote to Ruth. 'Happily my nerves are quite unaffected by the horrible – not so my nose: but oh! the pity of it! I very often exclaim when I see the dead lying out; and anger I feel too sometimes when I see corpses quite inexcusably not buried.'

When his duties permitted it, he corresponded with Ruth more frequently than ever, though doing his best to shield her from the worst of trench life. Back home in England, Ruth found the sense of powerlessness hard to bear. 'There is an awful feeling of futility sometimes when I pray for you and that you may not be killed,' she wrote to her husband. 'Every one out there has someone passionately praying that they will not get killed and yet one knows some must and certainly will ... But I must. It's all I can do, and I must.'

And there was good reason to ask for divine protection. In the trenches of the Western Front, the close calls that were a daily occurrence paid no heed to rank. On one occasion, a bullet passed between Mallory and another man walking directly in front; on another, he was making his way along a trench while behind him two comrades laboured under a heavy roll of trenching wire. When they came under attack from a German shell, only Mallory was left walking.

In summer of 1917 Mallory was sent home for an operation on an ankle damaged in a climbing accident some years earlier. During leave the previous Christmas Ruth had become pregnant again, and on 16 September she gave birth to another daughter, Beridge.

For all his natural optimism and forbearance, the war left George Mallory a changed man. How could it do otherwise? Of the bells that tolled across Europe, those that rang from the chapel of Winchester College were particularly mournful. Of its senior alumni, many of those in their twenties and thirties had been slaughtered on the battlefield and the extent of the carnage was something that troubled Mallory deeply. He had been delivered back to Ruth and their two daughters, and yet so many young men with whom he had shared the rites and adventures of boyhood now existed only in neatly penned columns in the school archives. It was to prove a turning point. 'Life presents itself very much to me as a gift,' he wrote to his father. 'It is surprising to find myself a survivor, and it's not a lot I have always wanted. There has been so much to be said for being in the good company of the dead.'

That 'good company' included many of the best climbers of the age – members of Geoffrey Young's glorious 'hill company' among them. War had torn the heart from the climbing community just as much as from every other section of society. There was a sense, among those who survived, of an obligation to honour their fallen comrades by grasping life. Ruth Mallory always knew that while her place in her husband's affections was assured, she would have to share it with his fascination for mountains. Walking away from the horrors of the trenches would have been enough for many men, their lives fulfilled by a family to raise and a garden to tend. But George Mallory wasn't one of them. So when, in 1921, he was summoned to a lunch in Mayfair to discuss a proposed expedition to the Himalayas there was a certain inevitability to what followed.

The quest to be the first to stand on the summit of Mount Everest began in the early 1800s. Lieutenant Colonel William Lambton was a British soldier who, having failed in the effort to hang on to the rebellious British colonies in the Americas, was dispatched with his regiment to India, in 1796. Being a mathematically minded sort of fellow, he was appointed superintendent of the Survey of India, a project established to map British territory in the region. Of its various undertakings, perhaps the one that is best remembered is the Great Trigonomic Survey, begun by Lambton in 1802 and concluded by his successor, now afforded the title of Surveyor General of India, in 1852.

Until then, it was commonly held that the highest point on the planet was Nanda Devi, in what is now the northern Indian state of Uttarakhand. Standing a lofty 25,479 ft, this is part of the Himalayan range, which runs for 1,500 miles and has close to 100 peaks. But in 1852 a young surveyor called Radhanath Sikdar, a notably talented mathematician in an organization brimful of them, suggested that another mountain in the region might be a contender for Nanda Devi's title. With the borders of Tibet and Nepal closed by heads of state wary of Western intentions, the usual protocol of awarding the mountain a local name was out of the question, so instead it was referred to by a title hardly likely to stir the soul – Peak XV. After years spent checking and double-checking the calculations, it was eventually awarded an altitude of 29,002 ft – more than 4,000 ft higher than Nanda Devi. The figure was a startling testament to the skills of Sikdar and his fellow surveyors, based as it was on calculations made from hundreds of miles away and 120 years before satellite technology would later reset the altitude at 29,035 ft. Changing the name of the peak to give it more of a flavour of Empire was the doing of one Andrew Waugh, the second Surveyor General of India, who suggested it be named in honour of his predecessor, George Everest (pronounced Eve-rest).

Half a century after Everest was confirmed as the apex of the planet, few travellers from the West had managed to come close even to its base, let alone its summit. Mont Blanc, the Alpine peak which, at 15,774 ft, is the highest mountain in western Europe, was 'conquered' for the first time in 1786, by two Chamonix-based climbing enthusiasts, Jacques Balmat and Michel-Gabriel Paccard. A British 'alpinist', Alfred Wills, climbed another notable summit, the 12,113-ft Wetterhorn in the Swiss Alps, in 1854. Three years later, in 1857, a national body was established in London to bring together like-minded 'alpinists', and named the Alpine Club.

By the time a climber named Edward Whymper made a celebrated first ascent of the 14,692-ft Matterhorn, in 1865, many of the major Alpine summits had been tackled by this new breed of 'mountaineers'. These were heady times for a nascent sport, an era that would come to be known as the 'Golden Age' of mountaineering. Whymper's success had even brought him a certain amount of notoriety. One of Ruth Mallory's early presents to George was a copy of Whymper's popular account of his early mountaineering career, *Scrambles Amongst the Alps*.

Yet, compared with the high Himalayas, Mont Blanc and the Matterhorn were but foothills. The first person to suggest an ascent of Everest was Charles Granville Bruce, of the 5th Gurkha Regiment, a man with considerable experience of the region and its people. On the receiving end of that proposal, in 1893, was a well-known explorer and diplomat of the time, Francis Younghusband. In 1903 Younghusband was dispatched to the Tibetan capital, Lhasa, with a well-armed military escort after rumours began circulating that China, which nominally controlled Tibet, was about to turn it over to the Russians. Younghusband was a consummate negotiator and a man used to getting his way. His arrival in Lhasa would see him effectively dictate a settlement treaty to the Tibetan authorities, but on the way he and his troops met resistance in the town of Gyantse. The siege of the town's magnificent hill fort ended with the death of more than 1,300 Tibetans, but not all of the men under Younghusband's command were involved in the slaughter: two of his officers made their way to the Everest region, and when they returned, having made their way to within 60 miles of the mountain, they suggested that a route to the summit might exist along a northern ridge.

The fiftieth anniversary of the Alpine Club, in 1907, renewed the call for an expedition to Everest, and this was to grow louder through the events of the next few years. In April 1909 the American explorer Robert Peary made the first visit to the geographic North Pole. Two years later, in 1911, Norway's Roald Amundsen notched up a similar feat at its southern counterpart – an achievement greeted with only muted enthusiasm in

Britain, where the public were busy grieving the man he pipped to the post, Robert Falcon Scott. Ernest Shackleton would help to reignite the public's appetite for exploration, thanks to this daring exploits in Antarctica, which culminated with the loss of his ice-bound ship, *Endurance*, in 1915, and his subsequent escape from Elephant Island the following year. It was therefore only a matter of time before Everest came to be regarded as one of the greatest challenges left to man.

In 1913 another army captain, one by the name of John Noel, robed himself in the attire of a local tribesman and made a covert sortie into Tibet, intent on reaching the great rock cathedral. He came within 40 miles before the Tibetan authorities caught wind of this unwelcome incursion; with a party of irate border guards in his slipstream, he was forced to make a run for it.

The outbreak of the First World War put a check on ambitions to climb the mountain that now assumed greater importance than any other, yet, such was the nature of the prize, it was unlikely that interest would stay dormant for long. Efforts to send a first British expedition to Everest resumed soon after the end of the war. In 1919 Francis Younghusband became president of the Royal Geographical Society (RGS), an organization already well established in supporting expeditions to remote parts of the world, including those of Charles Darwin and Dr David Livingstone, and synonymous with the highest ideals in the field of exploration. In an address to the RGS, Younghusband expressed his belief that a successful summit bid would help 'elevate the human spirit and give man ... a feeling that we really are getting the upper hand on the earth, and that we are acquiring a true mastery of our surroundings'.

And so it was that two years later, in 1921, the RGS and the Alpine Club formed a joint body unified by a simple yet august title: the Mount Everest Committee (MEC). After much discussion, it was agreed that an expedition would be executed in two phases: the first would send a team of geographers to produce maps of the mountain, while a climbing party would accompany them on 'a reconnaissance', assessing possible routes to the top, with a summit bid to take place the following year. The committee set about organizing a climbing party, gathering under their banner the finest mountaineers in the land. The first to be approached was George Mallory. What they found was, according to Younghusband, a rather confident young man, 'conscious of his own powers … and [with], in consequence, a not obtrusive but … quite justifiable pride in himself as a mountaineer'. Mallory's dream of being the first man to stand on the summit of Everest had begun.

As plans for Mallory's first visit to the mountain began to come together, it was the opinion of Sir Francis Younghusband that it was only fitting that General Charles Bruce, the original proposer of an expedition to Everest, lead the charge. The old soldier had recently been diagnosed with a heart condition, however, so leadership of the expedition fell instead to Charles Howard-Bury, an old Etonian but also formerly of His Majesty's armed forces. In charge of the climbers would be Harold Raeburn, a highly experienced Scots mountaineer who had reached 21,000 ft on Kanchenjunga, on the border between India and Nepal, and who would be aided by his fellow countryman Dr Alexander Kellas, a physician with an unparalleled knowledge of high-altitude travel.

Raeburn and Kellas were no spring chickens: at 56 and 53 respectively, it was clear that their best climbing years were behind them. The climbing duties, certainly the more dangerous ones, were therefore likely to fall to the two young thrusters of the party: George Mallory and George Ingle Finch. Finch, an Australian, was regarded as something of a renegade in the bluff and bluster circles of the MEC. He wore his hair long and cared little for social graces, but he was an excellent climber – the perfect foil for Mallory on this first reconnaissance of the mountain. Or at least he would have been had not his official medical tests revealed that he was anaemic and losing weight. While relatively little was known about the effects of high altitude, experience in the Alps and elsewhere made clear that, in the punishing atmosphere and extreme cold they were likely to experience at high altitude, the climbers would need to retain all the muscle mass they could. Finch's participation was out of the question, but it wasn't long before a replacement was found in Guy Bullock, a Winchester friend of Mallory's then employed by the Foreign Office.

Geoffrey Winthrop Young, undoubtedly one of the more eminent mountaineers of his generation, might well have been considered as a potential leader of the climbing expedition but he had lost a leg in the war. Even so, he took a keen interest and corresponded with Mallory on almost every facet of the expedition. Young advised Mallory that the celebrity that was sure to come with an expedition to Everest could only help in his ambitions to become a writer. The general public would see the enterprise as nothing but heroic, Young counselled. It would mean leaving behind his wife and three children (in 1920, Ruth had given birth to a son, John), but Mallory needed no more convincing.

In April 1921 a small party of climbers boarded the SS *Caledonia*, moored at Tilbury in Essex, to sail for Calcutta. Other expedition members were already in India, including Kellas and the party of geographers whose job it would be to map the mountain. From Calcutta, Mallory's group took the train to Darjeeling, where they gathered supplies for a route that would over the next three years become a familiar, if wearisome, friend. With the kingdom of Nepal still closed to the west, there was little choice but to head north, for Tibet, whose border with India was now open following the British invasion and subsequent treaty of 1904. Their journey took them through the succulent forests of Sikkim, crossing into Tibet at Phari and then, by way of the snow-walled Chumbi valley, moving up on to the Tibetan plateau. All told, it would be a month's march – 350 miles, and much of it across what Mallory described in a letter home as a 'flat desert of gravel'.

Mallory found his fellow adventurers a mixed bunch. The

expedition's leader, Charles Howard-Bury, for example, he found 'too much the landlord with not only tory prejudices, but a very highly developed sense of hate and contempt for other sorts of people than his own'. Harold Raeburn, who led the climbing team, irritated him too, prone as he was to dispensing advice which Mallory listened to but steadfastly refused to take. Far more appealing was Raeburn's compatriot, Dr Kellas, of whom Mallory became quite fond, finding his shambolic demeanour and absent-mindedness quite endearing.

But on 5 June, two and a half weeks after they set out from Darjeeling, Kellas, who had spent the weeks leading up to the expedition engaged in work in other parts of the high Himalayas, died of enteritis. He had became increasingly sick, following the main party with the help of the porters, and often arriving into camp long after the rest of the expedition. For a deeply compassionate soul such as George Mallory, Kellas's death was deeply disturbing. It troubled him that a fellow expedition member had passed away 'without one of us anywhere near him', and his first thoughts were to reassure Ruth, who he knew would be troubled by reports of a death in their party. 'My sadness at this event', he wrote to her, 'makes my thoughts fly to you. I know it is no use saying "Don't be anxious", because anxiety is unreasoning and comes upon us unbidden. You mustn't let this event increase your anxiety in general.'

They buried Kellas in the small village of Kampa Dzong, committing his soul to God with a reading from Corinthians. It was shortly after this that the leader of the climbing team, Harold Raeburn, also withdrew, suffering extreme dehydration brought on by diarrhoea.

It was a depleted team that left Kampa Dzong a few days later, but it was now that Mallory, looking west, glimpsed something in the far distance. The triangular profile was vast, even though it still lay more than 100 miles away. 'There was no mistaking the two great peaks in the west: that to the left must be Makalu, grey, severe and yet distinctly graceful, and the other way to the right – who could doubt its identity?' 'It was,' he recalled, 'a prodigious white fang excrescent from the jaw of the world.' It was Everest.

In that moment, George Mallory's life changed for ever. Now, as he marched ever closer, the mountain began to bore into his consciousness, almost by stealth, as he glimpsed it between far-off ridges or from high mountain passes. By the time they reached the valley of the Arun River, still 40 miles or so from the mountain, Mallory hoped he might at last get a clear view. Edging ever closer to the mountain, they were soon to reach the extent of the charts available for the area. 'We're just about to walk off the map,' Mallory wrote to Geoffrey Young. 'We've had one good distant view of Everest ... I hope we shall see him from 30–40 miles off.'

But in the land where cloud often lay low in the valleys for days on end, Everest remained hidden, obscured by mist. It was only when, some time later, Mallory and Guy Bullock left the main group to climb another small ridge that he got what he was looking for. It was now that the broad silhouette of the mountain began to reveal itself more intimately:

> Mountain shapes are often fantastic seen through mist; these were like the wildest creation of a dream. A preposterous triangular lump rose out of the depths; its edge came leaping up at an angle of about 70° and ended nowhere. To the left a black serrated crest was hanging in the sky incredibly. Gradually, very gradually, we saw the great mountain sides and glaciers and arêtes, now one fragment and now another through the floating rifts, until far higher in the sky than imagination had dared to suggest the white summit of Everest appeared. And in this series of partial glimpses we had seen a whole; we were able to piece together the fragments, to interpret the dream.

Two and a half weeks after the death of Alexander Kellas, they reached Tingri Dzong, a small village set on a wide floodplain across which danced small twisters as the wind whipped the topsoil into miniature vortices. In the distance, the flatland rose to form the curved bulkhead of another mighty Himalayan peak, Cho Oyu. It was from Tingri Dzong that Mallory and Bullock, all that now remained of the climbing team, set off to discover a route to their target. Accompanied by a cook and a small platoon of porters, they made their way to the Rongbuk valley, the main approach to the mountain from the north. Everest now rose up before them like a great guardian. 'There is no complication for the eye,' Mallory wrote. 'The highest of the world's mountains, it seems, has to make but a simple gesture of magnificence to be lord of all, vast in unchallenged and isolated supremacy. Other mountains are visible ... not one of their slender heads even reaches their chief's shoulder.'

The mountain lay a further 16 miles away, but they were close enough to see for themselves the nature of the challenge, and Mallory relished the prospect of what might lie ahead. 'Suffice it to say it has the most steep ridges and appalling precipices that I have ever seen,' he wrote to Ruth. 'My darling, this is a thrilling business altogether, I can't tell you how it possesses me, and what a prospect it is. And the beauty of it all!'

While the base of Everest remained just a short march up the valley, getting on those great flanks would be a different matter. By far the most obvious route to the summit appeared to be one via the mountain's northern face; the only problem lay in the fact that this face also happened to plunge for thousands of feet on to the main Rongbuk Glacier. 'Conscious of his own powers' as a mountaineer though Mallory might have been, his climbing on ice had been limited to high but accessible ridges such as those found in the Alps; a direct ascent of such a monstrous face as this was well beyond his experience. A more obvious solution seemed to be an approach to a saddle of rock that appeared to join Everest to a neighbouring peak. From here, a number of ridges seemed to rise up, offering a number of routes to the top. This saddle, then, was clearly the way to go. Mallory called it the North Col. However, the direct approach to it from where they were seemed precipitously steep. The two friends therefore spent the next few days criss-crossing a landscape that, for all their Alpine experience, must have felt like another planet. This was a land of yawning crevasses and wide lakes of glacial meltwater, watched over by vast towering ice pinnacles.

No matter how hard they searched, time and again Everest seemed to conspire with its neighbouring peaks to thwart them. To the west, a possible route that looked to start from what would later become known as the South Col was soon ruled out for the drop of more than 1,500 ft that separated it from their approach. They named this vast, glacial basin the Western Cwm; later expeditions came to know it by another name – the Valley of Silence. Next, Mallory turned his attentions east, in the hope that a route along an adjacent channel, the Kharta valley, might provide a passage to the North Col. But when Guy Bullock, accompanied by a team of porters, set off to investigate he found his way blocked by yet another ridge, one that ran north to south. It was then Mallory had an epiphany.

It occurred to him that behind the ridge that had halted Bullock's most recent investigation might lie another glacier, one smaller than the main Rongbuk Glacier, an eastern 'fork' of the glacier upon which the precipitous and spectacular drop of the North Face terminated. The idea came from a sketch map provided by Major Edward Wheeler, one of the geographers the Mount Everest Committee had hired to map the mountain. The chart in question had recently arrived at the camp that Mallory and Bullock had established in the Kharta valley. Given that they had already identified a number of inaccuracies in the map, they had assumed that a glacier Wheeler had drawn parallel to the Kharta valley was simply another mistake. It wasn't. From the Kharta valley, this secondary glacier could, the map suggested, be accessed through a small gap in a wall of glacial debris or 'moraine', an opening that both Mallory and Bullock, for all the intensity of their searching, had missed. If Mallory had described the approach to Everest as 'walking off the map', Wheeler was about to put them back on it.

With Wheeler in tow, they decided to follow his sketch, and on 18 August they set out for another high col, the Lhakpa La, which stood at 22,200 ft. It was from the top of this high pass that they hoped to see what, until now, they could only assume might be there. It wasn't long before the small party were given a rude introduction to some of the more unusual hazards that Everest could present. 'We were enveloped for the most part', Mallory wrote to his wife, 'in thin mist which obscured the view and made one world of snow and sky – a scorching mist, if you can imagine such a thing, more burning than bright sunshine ... One seemed literally at times to be walking in a white furnace.'

Labouring in intense heat, the altitude draining their energy, they now travelled through terrain as spectacular as any they had yet come across. They passed beneath the mountain's prominent eastern wall, the mighty Kangshung Face, a climb so treacherous it would not be conquered for another sixty years. When they eventually reached the Lhakpa La it gave them what they had hoped for. Obscured by cloud at either end, it was impossible to see where it began or ended, but here lay the very glacial tributary that Wheeler had suspected was there all along. It was the eastern fork, an East Rongbuk Glacier. And, crucially, it showed them a route that would at last deliver them to the North Col, the starting point for an assault on the mountain. In his next letter home, Mallory could hardly contain his sense of achievement. 'I fairly puffed out my chest with pride and the consciousness of something well done,' he told Ruth, and 'this success brings our reconnaissance to an end.' He signed off boldly: 'We have found the way and we're now planning the attack.'

On 23 September they set up camp on a wide plateau of snow, the final approach to the low saddle of rock from where they hoped to identify their route to the top. The welcome the mountain gave them as they prepared to march on the North Col was less than warm – quite the opposite of the furnace-like mist of previous weeks. Throughout the night, strong winds hammered the tent, and the next day proved more taxing still. They arrived at the North Col at noon, utterly exhausted. Of the three of them, it was Wheeler who was in the most distress. He had lost feeling in his lower legs, and it was only after some concerted rubbing from Mallory that it returned.

The wind they experienced the previous night had been just a foretaste of what was to come, and now whipped itself into a violent tempest. 'From top to bottom the ridge was exposed to the full fury of a gale from the northwest,' Mallory later wrote. 'By inclining the head at an angle away from it, it was possible to breathe even in the strongest gusts. But it was strong enough to leave no shadow of doubt in any of our minds ... I question whether anyone could have survived in it more than an hour or so.'

On reaching the North Col, they had made 23,000 ft. George Mallory returned to England convinced he had seen a way to the summit of the highest mountain on earth. Though the peak sat more than a vertical mile above the North Col, the route had now been established for any man who dared to dream of following it. That man would be him. The 'reconnaissance' of the mountain had been a success, now it was time to launch an all-out assault.

2

The Quiet American

THE CB RADIO crackled and whined, sifting through the soup of transmissions as the small receiver sought to lock on to one of the signals floating up from the valley floor. In the winter season of 1989, the Denali National Park, in Alaska, was playing host to a record numbers of climbers, the fourth yearly increase in succession, and the result of a series of increasingly mild summers. Conrad Anker rolled the dial between his thumb and forefinger. Mostly he caught conversations between truckers, using the open channels in an effort to stay awake as they hauled goods along the George Parks Highway, the winding snake of asphalt connecting the Alaskan cities of Anchorage and Fairbanks. Every so often he would pick up exchanges between the residents whose houses dotted the wooded valley below – 'the voices in the forest' Anker called them. Their talk was day-to-day stuff – 'If you're going to town I need 20 lb of flour' or 'How's the garden coming along?' – but as Anker and his climbing partner sat marooned, high above the ground, it was a good way to pass the time.

It had been three days since the snowstorm had started, seventy-two hours in which they had moved no further than the six or so square feet of nylon on which they now sat. A portaledge is essentially a hanging tent – a collapsible base with a waterproof shelter above it, which can be anchored to a rock face with metal pegs. For those who derive an income as a professional climber, living on what they refer to as 'the vertical plane', such accommodation can prove surprisingly comfortable, even in bad weather – and this *was* bad weather. Outside the portaledge, 1,500 ft of rock separated them from the ground – roughly the same distance that lay between them and the summit. With visibility down to a few yards, there was little option but to sit tight.

Anker and his climbing partner had flown into their expedition base camp, on Alaska's Kahiltna Glacier, the previous week, chartering one of the small Cessna aircraft that, each season, were wheeled from their corrugated-tin hangars at the Talkeetna airstrip and launched into skies above the Denali National Park, the remote wilderness which is home to the highest mountain in North America. With twin peaks rising above folds of elegant ridges and heavily glaciated slopes, at 20,320 ft Denali is considered by many to be the definitive 'big mountain'. It was originally named Mount McKinley, in honour of William McKinley, the twenty-fifth president of the United States of America. But since 1980 the state of Alaska has recognized it as Denali, a name which means 'High One' or 'Great One' in the Athabaskan language of the native Americans indigenous to the area.

On Anker's flight in, the pilot had coaxed his aircraft as it bucked and bobbed in the aggressive localized weather systems unique to mountain flying, relying as much on intuition as on the dashboard gauges. Nobody knew better than the 'bush pilots' that the unseasonably favourable weather wouldn't last for ever. The noise of the engine that filled the cockpit had precluded any small talk, but, on touching down, the airman had bade his two passengers farewell and they had set off, travelling light in what climbers referred to as 'alpine style', carrying with them everything they would need: their ropes, gear, food and water.

The Alaska Range that was home to Denali offered numerous challenges for the vertically mobile. Anker and his partner were headed for a sheet-like expanse of rock and ice which, at 3,000 ft, was considerably lower than Denali, but nevertheless offered plenty of climbing routes both dangerous and demanding. The Eye Tooth might have been named in honour of some vengeful deity that sat in residence at the summit. Now, as the two friends sat out the storm in their shelter, there was little chance they would get to find out any time soon. From their base camp on the glacier they had started strongly, making good progress to a point half way up the Eye Tooth. It was around that time that the weather decided to break. As the first flakes of an 8-foot snowfall began to dance on the wind around them, they had been left with little choice but to 'make camp', to bed down for the night on the mountain's terms.

In a tight spot, the climber Anker now shared the portaledge with was a good man to have around. Terrance Stump had made pioneering ascents across North America, including a daring climb of the Moose's Tooth, a neighbour of the Eye Tooth, and renowned for its long 'ice couloirs'. Bounded by walls of rock on either side, in winter these steep, narrow gullies would routinely fill with snow or ice. Often the most direct way to climb them was straight up the middle, and so being able to judge the stability of the snowpack, the layers of snow that accumulated during a winter, was crucial. If a climber miscalculated and an avalanche occurred, you could find yourself with nowhere to run. The storm that hung above the Eye Tooth gave Stump similar cause for concern. The more snow that fell, the more the slopes between the foot of the climb and their base camp on the glacier were becoming loaded with snow. In the hours immediately afterwards, this made them susceptible to avalanche. By far the safest option was to allow things to settle before attempting a descent, but first it had to stop snowing. Stump was unfazed. He considered 'just hanging' to be as integral to the experience of climbing as anything else.

The two men had first met six years before, in 1983. Stump was fully twelve years older than Anker, and their backgrounds might suggest they had little in common. Stump was charismatic and had been a former star of the college football circuit – the sort of guy to whom cheerleaders give their loyalty, and a lot more their fathers would rather they didn't. With big hands and a generous, open face, he had run, jumped and caught his way to minor celebrity in his youth, playing for Pennsylvania State University. The green shoots of a highly promising career were fed and watered by the guiding influence of Joe Paterno, a legendary figure of the college game. But, in a sport in which being regularly floored by 300 lb of testosterone-fuelled muscle was all in a day's work, Stump was forced to step down with his honour intact but his knees in pieces. This premature retirement left him bitter and resentful towards a game he had loved. If football had proved a brief, intense affair, however, when he turned instead to climbing he found a lifelong soulmate, and soon became one of North America's most well-known and respected climbers.

To Middle America, intensively reared on baseball, basketball and football, the professional climber was something of an alien species, a breed apart. It was a stereotype to which Conrad Anker conformed. Tall, gangly and high-minded, he was well read and studious in most things he did. Born in 1962, with his sharp intellect he could seem, to those who didn't know him, a little intense – a characteristic which would often manifest itself as earnestness. He and Stump – known universally as 'Mugs' – had first met in Salt Lake City, where Anker had been an undergraduate, and they had clicked instantly. Successful climbing partnerships are as much about complimentary personalities as they are about identical ones, and many are the stories of climbers who would share a windswept ledge in an emergency, but wouldn't share a beer. Stump's particular forte was 'technical climbing', complex ascents of bare rock on which even the entry level was set at sheer. The younger Anker had been a keen and willing student, and before long the two of them were sharing a house.

Once under the same roof, Stump extended the terms of his charge's apprenticeship: out climbing, it was Anker who shouldered the heavier loads; at home, Anker who did the cooking. In return, Anker's climbing skills developed quickly, and pretty soon the two of them were climbing as peers, Stump regularly impressing upon Anker his own vision of what climbing was about: boldness and independence, always pushing the limits of nerve and technique. Guiding less talented climbers – something many professional climbers did to supplement otherwise modest incomes – was a necessary evil, but Stump left Anker in no doubt that he considered it a debased form of the climber's art.

Of all sports, nowhere is the importance of mentors more pronounced than in climbing. Being shown the ropes by more experienced, and invariably gnarled and muscle-knuckled, hands is a concept that has run around the globe and down the years for one simple reason: the more you learn, the better you get; and the better you get, the greater your chances of living to climb another day. Which was precisely why, holed up in their in their nylon eyrie on the Eye Tooth, both Stump and Anker thought it best to stay put. As the days turned to a week, their food supply began to run low and they were forced to ration what they ate. And still the snow kept falling.

The fate of others in the park that month only emphasized the wisdom of waiting out bad weather. On the nearby peak of Mount Johnson, two climbers from Anchorage, Jim Sweeney and David Nyman, had been attempting to climb a huge, vertical wall of ice known as the Elevator Shaft when a part of the wall had collapsed and they had plunged 100 ft, Sweeney fracturing his hip in the process. In a remarkable act of survival, the two men not only endured a week on the mountain but were peppered by eight separate avalanches before being rescued by military helicopter. Others were not so lucky: on Denali's West Rib, three British climbers died when they were trapped by the storm; and on the mountain's West Buttress, another popular route for climbers, a four-strong Japanese party disappeared and were never heard from again.

But a week without moving was a long time for men so physically active, and pretty soon, with supplies of food and water dwindling further, their energy reserves began to drop to dangerous levels. When they were too weak even to screw a gas cartridge into the small portable stove they carried with them to allow them to warm food to fend off the cold, they decided it was time to make a break for it. Which was roughly the time the weather decided to give them a break. After eight days and seven nights, the snow finally stopped and the two friends abseiled to the ground, lowering themselves by feeding rope through a simple friction device attached to a climbing harness.

Tough as it had been, Anker would remember his time with Stump on the Eye Tooth with only affection. It was in trying circumstances such as these, when bad weather or injury forced climbers to test both their experience and their forbearance to the limit, that the bonds of friendship were made stronger than ever. Such ascents were a vital part of climbers' CVs, and it was with no small relish that they were referred to as 'epics'. For Anker, the presence of Stump in the portaledge beside him had all but guaranteed their survival, and the experiences of less fortunate climbers had helped to bolster his friend's aura of invincibility.

Conrad Anker had begun his climbing career in a world far removed from icy behemoths such as Denali. Big Oak Flat, built during the gold-rush era of the 1850s, was a one-tree kind of town in California's Yosemite valley. It was here that Anker had been raised. Before he could walk, he would be shouldered in a backpack on the regular hikes his family made into the vast, open spaces of California's Yosemite National Park. If you had a taste for the outdoor life, the 760,000 acres of Yosemite was the place to indulge it, and even as early as the nineteenth century, when the majority of North America was still pristine wilderness, the forests and mountains of Yosemite were regarded as the Elysian Fields by the increasing number of outdoor types attracted to the area.

With its jaw-dropping views and rich fauna and flora – it was home to more than half of California's indigenous plant species – Yosemite boasted scenery of Arcadian splendour, swathes of redwood forest broken intermittently by granite monoliths that thrust into the sky through the top of the forest canopy. It was a topography which, by the 1960s, meant Yosemite had come to be regarded as a sun-kissed Mecca for one outdoor pursuit in particular: rock climbing. And Anker's parents were only too happy to indulge the obsession their son soon developed for the outdoor life.

Walter Anker had met Conrad's mother, Helga, in her native Germany. As a 12-year-old girl growing up in Torgau, on the banks of the river Elbe, she had watched one dark night in 1945 as an unending swarm of Allied aircraft had droned in echelon overhead, making for the city of Dresden some 80 miles to the south-east. Two days later the city once regarded as the 'Florence of the North' lay in ruins, and among the tens of thousands of civilian dead was much of Helga's extended family. And somewhere beneath that smouldering wreckage her belief in all-loving, benevolent God lay buried too. When the American military joined the huge reconstruction effort that took place in Germany after the war, Walter Anker, a musician, arrived with them.

He eventually returned with his new bride to Big Oak Flat, where they were to have three children. Every summer, Walter would load up a mule and lead the family into the high sierra, to walk and camp in the mountains for weeks at a time. Conrad spent his summers living an idyllic American childhood that verged on cliché. With a fishing rod in hand, he would watch small boats twist their way down mountain streams, or climb trees, or be spooked by bears. At school, it didn't take the young boy long to realize that team sports weren't for him, that the repetition of throw, chase and score meant little compared with the raw, unpredictable fare available in the woods. At night, he dosed up on the stories of Jack London, drawn in by such titles as *The Call of the Wild*, concentrated hits of what-it-says-on-the-tin adventure, and with a distinctly American flavour. He gulped them down melodrama and all, for it was a world he recognized. He knew what it felt like to be outdoors, the pleasure he got from damming a stream, what it felt like to be cold. And if occasionally the ending was tragic, he knew also that nature was to be treated with respect.

One day in the early 1970s the Ankers were on one of their regular hikes into the valley on a golden Yosemite morning when the young Conrad felt a sudden urge to forge ahead on the trail. Arriving at the top of a ridge, he decided there and then that living and working in the mountains was what he wanted to do. For most children, epiphanies come and go like acne, but by the time Anker was 14 he was learning to rock climb. By the time he was 18, almost every decision he made, short of what to have for lunch, involved a coil of rope and a very long way down. When it came to college, in the early 1980s, he searched long and hard for a course of study that might allow him to combine academic interests with climbing ones. None did, but, while a degree in 'commercial recreation' was hardly the stuff of Ernest Hemingway, the University of Utah at least provided him with decent climbing nearby.

Of the many things Mugs Stump taught Anker, one was that, in climbing, accidents were part of the deal. As a young man, Anker had always regarded climbing accidents as something that befell only the inexperienced or naive – the 'bumblees' he and Stump would call them: the kind of climbers whose crampons – the specialist spiked footwear used to negotiate icy terrain – wore them, rather than the other way round. So when a guided party happened upon trouble on Denali on 21 May 1992, it seemed at first glance another incident of incompetence to be logged in the annual report compiled by the National Park authorities. On that day, a party of climbers were descending the mountain's South Buttress when they came to a halt, waiting for their guide to negotiate a crevasse. Suddenly the snow bridge the guide was using to cross the void gave way, plunging him into the depths of the crevasse. His body was never recovered. The incident changed Anker's view of the mountains for ever. Gone in an instant was the idea that climbing – his sort of climbing – was somehow safe; that the levels of technical excellence he aspired to offered some sort of immunity from danger; that only novices fell prey to such random acts of misfortune. For the guide on that fateful day on Denali was Mugs Stump.

It was the first time Anker had lost a friend to the mountains, and that it was Stump was almost beyond his comprehension. Had Mugs fallen while wrestling some immense, craggy beast, Anker might eventually have reconciled himself to a sense of natural law, but for him to die guiding climbers much less competent than himself seemed cruel – perverse even. What Anker struggled to cope with more than anything was the arbitrary nature of his friend's death, and he spent the next year in a deep depression. Climbing in the bold, purposeful manner that he and Mugs had practised had defined his life, and it was a life whose parameters they had set between them. During the next twelve months, if Anker climbed at all he did so with body rather than heart, convinced the chances of meeting another partner like Stump were slim. He began to resign himself to never again climbing with someone who endorsed his own philosophy so wholeheartedly – certainly not one who possessed the same prodigious technical gifts as Stump. But he did.

If Stump's death offered a sharp reminder of the risks that exist at the sharp end of Conrad Anker's chosen sport, there were plenty prepared to take up the torch. Alex Lowe was one of them. Like Anker, Lowe had grown up on the edge of the wilderness, following his own father into the mountains of his native Montana. For men like Anker and Lowe, going vertical was a natural progression, the logical next frontier once they had hiked their way over the challenges available at ground level. Lowe had been born a generation after the so-called 'great peaks' – those fourteen mountains dotted around the globe that stand above 8,000 m or 25,246 ft – had been all been conquered. He therefore looked to climbing mountains that were once considered impossible – more so than Mugs Stump; more so than anybody.

From the moment Anker first met him, it was as if the connection he had enjoyed with Stump had been remade. He and Lowe were, they were fond of telling people, 'like brothers from different mothers'. At around 6 ft 2 in, they were the same height, they were the same build, and they even had the same size feet. But whereas Stump had inspired quiet confidence, Lowe was a volatile mix of noise and energy, the latter of which he possessed in huge reserves and which he topped up with vast quantities of caffeine, taken, it was once remarked, 'like a diabetic takes insulin'. Anker, reserved, considered and softly spoken, provided a perfect foil, a far more quiet American. To those who didn't know him, Lowe's enthusiastic encouragement for others to join him climbing could prove overwhelming. Such was his talent that being invited to climb with Lowe was 'like Michael Jordan calling you up to shoot hoops', said one regular climbing partner.

Examples of his prowess were legion. In 1988, in the Tetons mountain range in Wyoming, Lowe had climbed a route known as the Grand Traverse, made up of eleven separate peaks. The previous record for crossing this series of great stone spires was twenty hours; Lowe did it in less than nine. In 1993 he made a solo ascent of Khan Tengri, a 23,000-ft peak on the border of Kyrgyzstan and Kazakhstan, his time of 10 hours and 8 minutes beating the previous best effort by four hours. By the late 1990s Lowe was widely acknowledged as one of the best, if not the best, all-round climbers in the world. In the specialist climbing press he soon began to assume superstar status, although he did his best to play it down. 'People referred to [him] as the Secret Weapon,' Alison Osius, then president of the American Alpine Club, told *Outside* magazine. 'When other climbers found out he was going along on a first ascent, the response would be: "That's cheating."'

If few could keep up with Lowe out climbing, on the home front it was he, rather than Anker, who wore the proverbial slippers. In 1983, the year Anker had began his friendship with

Mugs Stump, Lowe had married, and five years later he and his wife, Jennifer, had their first child, Max. A second son, Sam, came along in 1992, and a third, Isaac, in 1996. As Lowe juggled the demands of climbing with family life, Anker remained a committed bachelor, spending nine months of every year on expeditions.

By 1999, seven years after Mugs Stump's death, Anker and Lowe had racked up six major excursions together on some of the most challenging terrain on the planet, as well as sometimes just heading off somewhere less demanding together. For the second time in his career, Anker knew he owed a climbing partner a great debt, that Lowe had restored his faith in climbing. Together, the two friends soon booked themselves a rolling reservation at the top table of American climbing. It was a position which meant they could take their pick of jobs and look forward to the next phase of their careers, being the first to make highly technical ascents on some of the most remote and challenging peaks in the world.

3

A Patch of White

H E SCANNED THE mountainside again. The snow cover was only patchy, but there was still every chance that they would miss what they were looking for. If Everest had kept the bodies of George Mallory and Sandy Irvine hidden for the past seventy-five years, there was no reason for it to co-operate in a handover today. It had been six weeks since Conrad Anker and a small party of climbers had arrived on the mountain, and that morning, 1 May 1999, the members of the Mallory and Irvine Research Expedition had again left their camp, just shy of 26,000 ft, and spread out.

If Anker was doubtful of success as they lined up to make a sweep beneath the limestone cliffs of the Yellow Band, the thoroughness of the search appealed to his natural sense of fastidiousness. From his position roughly 100 ft below his teammates, he began to run his eye back and forth across the slope, tapping the spiral-bound document in his pocket as he did so. Condensed to just a few pages inside this 'research manual', as he and his colleagues called it, was what amounted to the life's work of a young man who now waited anxiously lower down the mountain. Jochen Hemmleb was a German mountaineering student for whom the disappearance of Mallory and Irvine had become all-consuming.

In the years since Noel Odell had last seen the two men, pushing for the summit of Everest, a number of subsequent expeditions had stumbled across clues that hinted at where their bodies might be – an ice axe on one occasion; an empty oxygen canister on another. Hemmleb had diligently collated them all, using their locations to plot the small search area in which Anker now found himself and which Hemmleb felt sure might contain one, if not both, of the two Englishmen. Even to a casual reader, the disappearance of Mallory and Irvine, high on the slopes of Everest, was a poignant and romantic tale – Mallory the complex and dashing adventure hero, a bright light helping to further illuminate the glory of the British Empire. To a student of mountaineering history, finding the body of Mallory or Irvine would be like discovering the Holy Grail perched on top of the Ark of the Covenant.

As Anker made his way across the upper reaches of the mountain, the extra effort demanded by the thin air made his movements slow and deliberate. It was his first visit to the rarefied atmosphere of Everest and, having never needed supplementary oxygen before, he was keen to see how well his body coped without it. He traversed west along a route that took him towards the Great Couloir, an immense ice gully that had formed part of the summit attempts of numerous climbers. Rheinhold Messner, a legendary Tyrolean mountaineer, was one of them. In 1980 Messner had become the first person to reach the top of Everest solo and without oxygen. His success in pushing the human machine to a level of endurance few thought possible had attracted worldwide acclaim. Anker regarded the feat as little short of astonishing. It was partly a curiosity to see for himself the route that Messner had chosen that led him towards the very edge of Hemmleb's designated search area. When he got there, his natural inquisitiveness got the better of him; he decided to step beyond it.

As he walked across the snowfield, nearly 27,000 ft above sea level, he ran his climber's eye over the topography, noting how the slope of the rock formed a catchment area, a bowl that funnelled any falling material. Intuitively, he knew it was as good a place as any to search, and it was as he crested a small rise, his prescription dark glasses throwing everything into perfect relief, that he spotted a body a short distance beneath him. Immediately he began to descend towards it, the extreme elevation giving him little choice but to take his time. Bodies high on Everest were hardly rare, and, as he approached, it didn't take long to realize that these were the remains of neither George Mallory nor Sandy Irvine. If the modern fabric of the purple climbing suit that clung to the corpse wasn't proof enough, the crampons still attached to the climber's boots only confirmed it. While the 1924 expedition had used crampons at lower elevations, these were of a much more contemporary design. Of the man's head, only the skull remained, goraks, the raven-like scavengers that patrol even the highest slopes of the high Himalayas, having long since eaten away his eyes and the soft tissues of his face. The right arm was thrust towards the sky at an angle grimly incongruous with the rest of the body, which pointed downhill. Anker's experience in 'search and rescue' – that euphemism employed by mountaineers to describe the recovery of bodies – suggested the man had probably been dead, or at least unconscious, when he came to a stop. With the head and upper torso far heavier than the legs, it was nothing more complicated than a consequence of gravity.

Anker's radio sparked into life. It was Andy Politz, the climber in charge of the search party that morning. Anker, Politz pointed out, had strayed outside the search area, and the request that he return to it immediately was polite but firm.

It was as he was taking the call from Politz that Anker noticed another body, roughly 100 ft below him again. The pallid skin had escaped the attentions of the goraks, but still suggested that the corpse had been lying there for a number years. When he drew closer, though, it was modern equipment that again confirmed the casualty as a relatively recent one. The trunk of the body was almost doubled over, and the jumble of arms and legs suggested a long fall – perhaps one made all the more violent by repeated collisions with the mountainside as the falling man accelerated into great, bounding arcs.

As they set out that morning, Anker had thought that their search would constitute little more than a reconnaissance of the mountain's upper slopes, and this was beginning to look all too prescient. He sat down to take on some fluid – a frequent necessity in the parched atmosphere – before removing the crampons from his boots. Confident he could cover the next patch of ground without them, and with his throat now soothed, he stood up and looked to his right, towards the summit of Everest. It was then that something else caught his eye, an object with an unusual quality that caused it to stand out from the snow. In contrast to the sheen of the snowfield around it, this object, although also white, appeared matt, seeming to absorb the light rather than reflect it. It looked, as Anker would recall later, in *The Lost Explorer*, his gripping account of the expedition, 'like a piece of marble'. In a state of considerable curiosity he began to climb towards it.

Closing the distance between himself and the oddly coloured snow was laborious work, but as he came within a few feet of it, his eyes focusing on the approach, he now found himself looking at a small knob not unlike a white pebble. It was the heel of a foot, one that was naked save for the tongue of a leather boot wedged between the toes. The toes themselves pointed down into the rock, and the foot to which they were attached was joined, in turn, to a leg whose withered calf muscles gave it an elongated appearance. Anker looked down in quiet amazement on the remains of a body that lay fused to the mountain, face down, by years of advancing and retreating ice. What, if anything, remained of the face he couldn't be sure, buried as it was, but strapped to the head was a leather helmet of the kind used by airmen in the early twentieth century. Sprouting from beneath it, a tuft of hair was clearly visible.

Anker's brain almost tripped over itself as it did a quick calculation. In 1960 the Chinese government had sponsored a massive expedition in an effort to secure a first summit from the north side of Everest. What clothing remained attached to the corpse suggested that this was a climber of a far older vintage. Only two climbers had disappeared on these slopes before the successful Chinese assault – and this was one of them.

At first he thought that he would carry on walking, keep the find to himself and allow the figure now before him to retain what remained of his dignity. Had he done so, life for Conrad Anker might have been very different. But he banished the idea. A secret like that would be impossible to keep. Even if he managed to get himself down the mountain and hide the discovery from his teammates both at Base Camp and on the long journey home, it was sure to come out eventually – perhaps one night lying in a tent beneath a canopy of stars, chatting with a fellow climber before drifting off to sleep, or by his fireside back home, after supper with friends, the stories flowing as generously as the post-prandial Scotch. In the years that followed, barely a day went by when he didn't reflect on what he did next. In a state of rising excitement, he got on the radio, notifying his teammates that he was calling a 'mandatory group meeting' – disguising the nature of his find with this coded message so as not to alert the other teams on the mountain, all of whom received the same radio traffic.

For the next twenty minutes he sat there alone with the body, the remains of a man who had last been seen heading for the summit of Everest three-quarters of a century earlier. As he waited for his teammates to arrive, Anker studied the condition of the corpse. The patch of white he had seen from roughly 100 ft away was in fact the large muscles of the man's back, well preserved in the dry, frozen atmosphere. The clothes that had once covered them had long since been torn away, though fragments remained around the shoulders. Other muscles showed more pronounced signs of weathering: long since devoid of blood and water, they had what Anker would later describe as a 'stringy' consistency. A hole in the right buttock looked large enough for a single gorak to come and go as it pleased. Around the man's ribs, the skin still bore a deep-blue bruise, presumably where the rope that remained wound about the man's middle had pulled tight before snapping.

Though the left foot was naked, the right remained cased in an old hobnail-style boot. The right leg, at the point where it entered the boot, appeared broken and, though the skin had not been punctured, the leg lay at an awkward angle. Though he couldn't be sure, it appeared to Anker as if the left leg had been deliberately crossed over the right, as if, in one final conscious act, the man had vainly tried to protect his injured limb. What struck Anker more than anything were the man's arms. The right one looked broken but, along with the left, was stretched up above the head. The naked fingers, strong and tanned, showed no sign of frostbite. Given that frostbite affects only living tissue, this suggested that the man had died soon after he came to a halt. Most noticeable of all, the fingers appeared to be thrust into the rocky slope. Clearly the man had been attempting to stop his fall, but, locked as the fingers were, it was almost as if he had refused to relinquish his grip on the mountain. The ordered nature of the limbs and the relatively minor extent of the man's injuries suggested that the fall that had led to his death had been a controlled affair, at least compared with those of the poor souls whom Anker had found earlier that morning. Violent falls – the grotesque cartwheeling type commonly associated with mountaineering accidents – invariably resulted in far more severe wounds, and in extreme cases some victims were decapitated.

One by one, Anker's teammates began to arrive, whispering in hushed tones out of respect for the fallen climber. As they assembled around the corpse, the consensus was that here lay the remains of Sandy Irvine. It was a conclusion which stemmed from a reported sighting of a body almost a quarter of a century previously. In 1975 a climber named Wang Hongbao was part of a large Chinese expedition high on the north side of Everest. With his team camped at around 27,000 ft, Wang decided to take a walk. Wandering away in such a manner was a decidedly dangerous thing to do, but Wang claimed that after twenty minutes he stumbled upon what he described as an 'English dead', the body of a mountaineer wearing clothing from the early twentieth century. For four years he kept the find to himself, until in 1979 he reported his discovery to Ryoten Hasegawa, the leader of a Japanese team on Everest that Wang was assisting that year. Wang's sighting had never been verified, but the story passed into Mallory and Irvine lore nevertheless, securing its place thanks to the unfortunate fate of Wang himself, who perished beneath the rushing mass of an avalanche shortly after confiding in Hasegawa.

That Wang's 'English dead' might have been Sandy Irvine was supported by another clue to Mallory and Irvine's disappearance. In 1933 a British expedition to the mountain was being led by the well-known mountaineer Percy Wyn Harris when, making their way towards the shoulder of Everest's North-East Ridge, one of Harris's team noticed something glinting in the snow. Closer inspection found it was the steel head of an ice axe, a long-handled variety popular among climbers of Mallory's and Irvine's era. In good condition, it appeared the axe hadn't fallen far. The head still bore the manufacturer's name, and the shaft was marked with three curious notches. Before Harris's ascent, only George Mallory and Sandy Irvine had made it to that part of Everest, so the axe had to have belonged to one or the other of them. Similar notches had been found on equipment left behind by Irvine – he had used them to distinguish his gear from that of his teammates. 'Irvine's axe' was one of the clues that made Anker and his colleagues all but certain that the body they now stood over was Irvine's.

It was then that a climber by the name of Jake Norton began prising back the layers of clothing which clung to the shoulders of the corpse. Inside the remnants of a cotton shirt he found a label embroidered with a name. During their weeks of preparation in and around Base Camp, the team had become so familiar with the personal histories of the two men that they now referred to Mallory and Irvine by their first names. The label Norton now revealed read, 'G. Mallory'. This wasn't Sandy at all. It was George.

The ice around the body had had decades to sink its fingers into the man's remains, and when the climbers tried to lift the corpse they found it was gripped by the mountainside, as if in the embrace of some vast rock succubus. They set to digging it out, chipping away the larger chunks with ice picks and then, as the excavation became more delicate, using the pocket knives they carried with them. When they had trimmed away enough debris, they at last prised the body from the mountain – just a little, so as not to cause damage to the fragile structure, but sufficient to retrieve a number of items still lodged in the chest pockets of the man's jacket. Separated from the mountain at last, as it rose the corpse made a noise which Anker recalled in *The Lost Explorer* as sounding like a wet log being lifted from the ground.

What they found confirmed what the label peeled back by Norton had suggested. This was George Leigh Mallory. In addition to everyday ephemera of expedition life – an embroidered handkerchief initialled G.L.M., a tin of 'meat lozenges', some mint cake – other articles seemed to provide new evidence of Mallory's final battle on the mountain's upper ramparts. A pair of goggles in one pocket indicated that perhaps darkness had fallen while the two men were still climbing. Or perhaps Mallory had removed them to see his footing better as he guided Irvine through the treacherous cliffs of the Yellow Band. Then again, maybe they were just a spare pair. They found also an altimeter, calibrated at between 20,000 and 30,000 ft. With its dial smashed, there was no evidence of what altitude Mallory and Irvine might have reached before they fell. Lastly, there were two letters: the first addressed to Mallory's brother, Trafford; the other to a mysterious 'Stella', later revealed as Stella Cobden-Sanderson, a friend of the family. Its envelope bore two columns of numbers: one a detailed inventory of every oxygen cylinder carried by the expedition party; the other the pressure contained in each bottle.

The last task in their excavation was the most grisly. To confirm beyond doubt that this was George Mallory, they would need to check the man's DNA. Having sought permission from the families of both Mallory and Irvine in the event that they found a body, Anker began to saw a small square of skin from one of Mallory's forearms. It was a far from dignified job. After years exposed to sun and frost, Mallory's skin had taken on the texture of thick leather, and cutting it was tough work. Anker stuck to his task all the same, only too aware how crucial it would prove.

When they had retrieved as many items as they could carry, at least without damaging them, they gently laid the body back in the snow and covered the remains with a small pile of rocks as a rudimentary memorial. In a brief but dignified committal service, Andy Politz read from the Bible, Psalm 103, a passage that had been requested by the surviving family of Sandy Irvine. If his body was still out there, its whereabouts known only to the mountain, there was something affecting in the relatives of one of the two climbers paying tribute to the other.

As Anker listened to the words of the psalm, he wondered what might have entered Mallory's head in his final moments high on Everest, if he had indeed been conscious as the position of his body suggested. Perhaps, cocooned by the onset of shock, he had imagined he might still walk off the mountain. Perhaps he thought that Noel Odell, his colleague climbing in support, would yet reach him, bringing hot tea as he had so often done before. It would be a welcome restorative before the journey back to Base Camp. Then on to Darjeeling, Bombay and home – to Ruth and the children. Instead he had been left alone, with only the goraks for company.

In the week that Anker and the team spent following their return to Base Camp, word of the discovery leaked to the world's press. In the blink of an eye, Conrad Anker went from being a relative unknown, at least outside climbing circles, to being headline news. He had found one of the most iconic figures in the history of modern exploration, the 'lost son' of Everest. But not everybody was as thrilled at the find as he and his team had been. A number of well-respected names in the climbing world now accused him and his colleagues of trespassing on consecrated ground and, in retrieving Mallory's personal effects, of high-altitude grave robbery. The criticism was only exacerbated by the photographs of the body that circulated in newspapers around the globe. When they did, celebrated mountaineers such as Chris Bonington and Sir Edmund Hillary lined up to voice their disapproval. Even Mallory's own grandson, George Mallory II, joined the detractors, saying that the recovery of the artefacts was 'like digging for diamonds without having to do any of the digging'. A strongly principled man, Anker was deeply hurt by the comments.

Nevertheless, a little over a fortnight later, on 15 May, the search team found themselves high on the mountain once again, to conduct a second search for any item they might have missed. Perhaps the most poignant item that Mallory was believed to have carried with him on his final visit to Everest was one that Anker's team didn't find. Before departing, Mallory had promised Ruth that, were he to make it to the summit, he would leave a picture of his wife there in her honour. When the team had searched what remained of Mallory's belongings, such a picture was nowhere to be found. Could it be that Mallory had made it to the top: that he had laid the image in the snow – a final act of communion with his beloved Ruth before it was ripped free by the wind?

In the weeks since finding Mallory's body there had been heavy snowfall, and locating the corpse once more proved difficult. Eventually, it was one of Anker's teammates, Thom Pollard, who found it. Like Anker before him, Pollard found himself overcome with a sense of awe as he sat in the snow next to the remains of the legendary explorer. Before touching the corpse, he muttered a quiet prayer – then turned over Mallory's head. The Botticellian face that had so enraptured Lytton Strachey now displayed a more prosaic reality. After seventy-five years of high-altitude weathering, the features were skewed. Mallory's eyes were closed, and Pollard noticed some stubble sprouting from his chin. There was a deep puncture wound over the left eye, and around it a ring of dried blood. Joined now by Andy Politz, the two of them searched the body again. There was no sign of the photograph. In a trouser pocket, however, they found a wristwatch. Only the hour hand remained, but this suggested that it had stopped sometime around 1.30 – whether morning or afternoon was impossible to say.

When members of the expedition had set off to find Mallory's body on that second occasion, Conrad Anker hadn't been among them. Since the discovery of Mallory's final resting place, his role had changed. His initial inclusion in the expedition had come in recognition of his skills as a technical climber, and now Anker and a small climbing party planned to make their own bid for the summit. What made their ascent different from the countless other summit bids that would take place that season was their choice of route.

One of the principal arguments around whether Mallory or Irvine might have been the first to reach the summit of Everest centred on the rocky outcrop on which Noel Odell claimed to have seen the two men in that moment when the clouds parted, at 12.50 p.m. on 8 June 1924. Odell believed he had seen the two men on a feature that the expedition of 1924 came to refer to as the Second Step, which is located at around 28,230 ft. This is one of three such features that must be negotiated on a summit approach via Everest's North-East Ridge, and is by some distance the most challenging. It has a face roughly 90 ft high, the final few feet of which consists of a section of overhanging rock which represents the most difficult part of the climb – what climbers refer to as the 'crux'. At sea level it would constitute a relatively easy challenge, but the enervating effects of climbing in rarefied air mean that, at altitude, it is a far from a straightforward proposition. Whether Mallory could have climbed it without the technical aids that modern climbers take for granted – safety gear known as 'protection', used for securing a climber to the rock face – had been the subject of much debate.

Anker planned to replicate Mallory's experience: to scale the Second Step using a technique known as 'free climbing'. He would use just his hands and feet to carry him upward, and his safety gear would be used only to catch him in the event of a fall. It was the way he had learned to climb as a child, naturally and relying on instinct – the way Mallory had learned to climb when he scurried over the rooftop of his Mobberley home.

In the years since Mallory's disappearance, various theories had emerged on the best way to climb the Second Step. The Chinese team of 1960 that recorded the first confirmed ascent via the North-East Ridge claimed to have negotiated it by using something known as 'combined tactics', a rudimentary technique in which a climber stands on the shoulders of a colleague in order to reach better holds that might exist higher up an ascent. Fifteen years after the first summit from the north, in 1975, the Chinese party of which Wang Hongbao had been a member when he came across his alleged 'English dead' decided to end the conversation on how best to tackle the Second Step by bolting a small metal ladder to its face. It was a device used by virtually every summit party on Everest's northern slopes thereafter; if Anker wanted to 'free' the Second Step, he would have to go round it.

On 16 May the expedition's six-strong summit team stared out across the vast peaks of the Himalayas, the sun bathing the mountain in the golden light of evening. With their final push scheduled for the following morning, Anker was confident their summit day would bring them success. Sharing a tent with him that night was Dave Hahn, a long-time friend who had climbed Everest before, and who had first suggested that Anker join the expedition. Camped alongside them were two other Americans, Jake Norton and Tap Richards, and the team's two strongest Sherpas, Ang Pasang and Da Nuru, had come up from the North Col earlier in the day in order to help out.

After an indifferent night's sleep, on the morning of 17 May they set out around 2.30 a.m. The Sherpas were, uncharacteristically, slow to rise. The temperature was sufficiently cold to cause the bulb in Anker's headlamp to break. He had little option but to stop and replace it: a minor inconvenience, but in such temperatures any delay that occurred before sun-up could have deleterious effects on a climber's body temperature.

They left camp beneath a clear sky, and made their way up through the cliffs of the Yellow Band. When they reached the top, Conrad Anker found himself on the very shoulder of rock where Mallory had last been seen alive, the North-East Ridge. The wind was getting up now, and as he traced a line to the summit he saw that clouds had begun to form on the mountain's apex. The weather was changing. They decided to take a break, seeking shelter from the wind behind a large rock. Dave Hahn began to voice reservations about continuing, and for the next three-quarters of an hour they discussed whether or not to turn back. Norton and Richards were equally unsure and, of the six-man team, only Anker seemed determined to continue.

It was he who finally led the team out, guiding them over the first obstacle in their path, the short scramble of the First Step, where two limestone bands come together to form a prow of rock. Having climbed it quickly and easily, they began the traverse to Anker's principal target, the Second Step. The ground was treacherous, with pockets of deep snow hiding sharply angled slopes. Lose your footing here and you might find yourself on the express elevator all the way down to the Rongbuk Glacier, more than 8,000 ft below.

After forty-five minutes of concerted effort, Anker came to Mushroom Rock, a limestone bollard that acted as a waymark for climbers on a northern ascent of Everest. He waited for his colleagues. It had been hard and dangerous climbing, and by the time his teammates reached him he could see the anxiety etched into their faces. He knew what was coming. Both Norton and Richards were both vastly experienced climbers, but somewhere on that traverse they had both come to the same conclusion – they were turning round.

It had been an emotionally draining few weeks. Since their team had arrived on the mountain, a climber from another party had died, and finding Mallory's body had affected the team in ways some of them had yet to fully appreciate. In Anker's published account of the ascent, Richards would later describe how 'a feeling of death was blowing in our faces.' As he joined Richards on the descent, Jake Norton was in tears.

When Anker and Hahn at last reached the base of the Second Step, nearly eight hours after setting off, the situation grew worse still. It was now that both Sherpas, first Ang Pasang and then Da Nuru, decided that, for all their strength as climbers, they too had had enough. The climbing party was now down to two.

It was a small mercy that Anker's one remaining teammate, Dave Hahn, had enjoyed a noticeable upturn in his spirits, but, as Anker now surveyed the 90 ft of cliff face above them, he saw almost immediately the nature of the problem. The Second Step consists of two plane faces which come together to form a 'dihedral', like an open book. The small metal ladder put up by the Chinese almost four decades previously occupied a central position on the right-hand face, so as to provide climbers with a route past the most difficult part of the ascent. Climbing around it would be extremely difficult. The obvious place to begin the ascent was to the left of the ladder, at the point where it was fixed to the mountain and where a large crack traced a line up the face.

The mask of the breathing apparatus made it difficult for Anker to see his feet; he had little choice but to remove it. Speed would be of the essence. The lactic acid in his muscles would build quickly, and if he took too long in negotiating the lower part of the climb he might find himself compromised long before he reached the crux. Even to an experienced climber like Anker, the exposure beneath him was massive: 8,000 ft of nothing but bitingly cold fresh air, terminating on the icy slopes of the Rongbuk Glacier. He began to climb, inserting pieces of protective equipment as he went, removing one after another from the belt of his climbing harness secured about his waist.

Climbing on, Anker cast his gaze left and right, searching for the best holds as he kicked his feet into cracks wide enough to accommodate the bulky toes of his boots. Despite his best efforts to the contrary, he found himself moving inexorably towards the ladder. Soon the gap between his right foot and the ladder's left edge was reduced to a matter of inches. The success or failure of Anker's free climb – an ascent of the Second Step as Mallory had encountered it – rested on the decision he was about to make.

The obvious place for his right foot now lay directly between the ladder's rungs. Stepping through them would be risky. If he placed a foot on the ladder, he would be using an 'artificial' aid, and the free climb would be over. Then again, he didn't have too many options. Cautiously, he moved his foot between the two pieces of metal. Rising fatigue and the heaviness of the boot caused his leg to twitch, like that of a marionette controlled by some puppet master above, and it was only a matter of seconds before he bowed to the inevitable. When his foot finally touched the ladder, Anker fired a fusillade of expletives into the freezing atmosphere. In the moments that followed he paid for the expenditure of energy, breaking his curses to suck down huge lungfuls of air.

For all his frustration, he couldn't afford to hang around. Anker completed the climb skirting round the ladder. When Hahn followed, he took advantage of each and every rung. Then, from the top of the Second Step, they both climbed on across the broad expanses of Everest's uppermost slopes.

Having scaled the Third Step, the last of the great rock outcrops, as they approached the summit itself Hahn indicated to Anker that something was wrong. During the final stages of the ascent, Hahn had been forced to suffer the indignity of a sudden and violent attack of diarrhoea, a common complaint in the far from sterile environment of high-altitude expeditions. To add to their problems, he was also out of oxygen. With his reserves of energy diminishing rapidly, Hahn had tried to alleviate his flagging fortunes by running the last of his oxygen cylinders at its maximum rate of flow – and now it was empty. When they finally reached the summit, at 2.50 p.m., their moment of victory was brief.

The descent that followed was an anxious one. Hahn's physical condition had begun to deteriorate so quickly that on several occasions Anker feared he might come to a complete standstill. Back at Base Camp, the expedition leader, a highly experienced mountaineer by the name of Eric Simonson, berated Hahn for having allowed himself to run out of oxygen. Anker felt the criticism a little harsh, but chose – wisely as it turned out – to keep out of the fray. The air of ill-feeling between Hahn and Simonson, two good friends, lasted for several days.

Anker spent the time pondering the events of the previous few weeks. He thought about Mallory. There was something about the body – something timeless and undisturbed – that had made him wonder, in those weeks that followed, if he might be desecrating consecrated ground. He also thought about the Second Step. When he had been forced to abort his free climb, he had radioed Base Camp immediately. His attempt had failed: it was as simple as that. The outcome irked him, but as he prepared to head home he might have been forgiven for thinking that was an end to it – that his business with a 90-ft stretch of rock high above the earth was over. In the account of the climb that he wrote soon after, he concluded as much: the last great obstacle that had lain between George Mallory and a first ascent of Mount Everest was for others stronger than himself. He was wrong.

4

Shishapangma

FOR MOST OF his professional life, Conrad Anker had never been all that taken with the highest mountain in the world. Whether you climbed on its southern slopes, in Nepal, or on the northern side in Tibet, Mount Everest had been pretty much 'done'. In the decades since Edmund Hillary and Tenzing Norgay became the first men to summit Everest, in 1953, the mountain had seen at least one groundbreaking achievement on each of its great flanks. In 1963 Anker's countryman, Jim Whittaker, had become the first American to stand on the summit, and he was followed just weeks later by Willi Unsoeld and Tom Hornbein, who together became the first men to overcome the treacherous West Ridge. In 1975 Japan's Junko Tabei became the first woman to reach the top. Five years later Rheinhold Messner had made the oxygenless ascent which, thanks to Anker's innate curiosity, had contributed in its own small way to the discovery of the last resting place of George Mallory.

Anker had been an unusual choice when Dave Hahn had thrown his name into the mix. Just as in Europe, the climbing scene in North America has its own unique cliques and codes. Eric Simonson, the expedition's leader, was, in Anker's words, a 'Rainier climber' – a regular on Mount Rainier, a peak in Washington State whose permanent snowfields and glaciers make it a popular training destination for those with Everest ambitions. The prevailing ethic when climbing there is, as with Everest, of 'expedition-style' tactics: climbers make their ascents with the use of well-rehearsed logistical support, with camps positioned in semi-permanent locations and a gangway of fixed ropes or 'lines' secured year-round to the mountain. Anker, in contrast, had learned his trade in the Yosemite valley, the US heartland of technical climbing, where climbers favour the fast and light tactics of 'alpine-style' ascents. Unencumbered by the cold, you took only such gear as you could carry. Nevertheless, Anker had read widely around the subject, and took a keen interest in the history of the sport. The basics of the Mallory and Irvine story had been on the periphery of his professional radar for as long as he cared to remember. It was a great yarn, but no more than that. When he was invited to join the 1999 expedition he was young and flattered to be asked, and Hahn was a good friend, so he went. That May morning in 1999 changed his attitude completely.

As a professional climber, Conrad Anker made his living in a variety of ways, which included film projects, magazine articles and public speaking at a wide range of engagements. Whether called on to inspire the senior executives of large corporations or on a promotional tour for one of his many sponsors, his tales of a life suspended high above the earth would leave audiences enthralled. Corporate audiences in particular liked to 'smell the fear', to prod and probe this strange, willowy creature for details of a life less ordinary – one that didn't start with a latte and end falling asleep in front of a computer screen. While he referred to these presentations, rather disparagingly, as 'the petting zoo', he was good at them. He had a certain aura, a detached sense of difference, that became more strikingly obvious the more conservative the company he was in. It was something common to many climbers, for whom the line dividing life from death was one walked daily. It was only to be expected that, in 'the real world', they might find their mind wandering occasionally. In Anker's case, it might appear to those who didn't know him that he was often not quite in the moment, a touch aloof. But when the subject being discussed was climbing, a certain look would cross his face, a glint spark in his eyes, and his own particular intensity return.

Since 1 May 1999, one subject that began to feature in his lectures with inevitable frequency was the life of George Mallory. He was now for ever connected to the man who, three-quarters of a century ago, had been enveloped by the mists, high on Everest. Mallory had been the great lost explorer and Conrad Anker the man who had found him – it was as simple as that. In the aftermath of his discovery of the body, he had given countless interviews to the world's press. He had read widely about Mallory, such that he now knew the official accounts of the three expeditions in which Mallory had taken part pretty much by heart. He had come to see Mallory as a man of many parts: as the passionate idealist; the innovative climber; and the ambitious and fiercely independent spirit, one who used climbing to push the limits of human experience. It was a similar philosophy to that which he himself had shared with Mugs Stump, and which he had rediscovered with Alex Lowe. But somewhere in those long hours of study Anker had also come to know George Mallory as a loving family man, a husband and father who, time and again, had left behind his wife and children for the dream of Everest. That it would eventually claim his life, that he was destined never to see them again, resonated with Anker deeply. Just how deeply he had yet to discover.

On 8 May 1999, nine days before he had stood on the summit of Mount Everest, a group of three Ukrainian climbers had launched their own summit bid. They were a strong group – strong enough to make the ascent without the use of supplementary oxygen. But at some point during their final push a storm had blown in. It hadn't simply hit the mountain and run, but had given it a prolonged hammering, and the Ukrainians soon found themselves in serious trouble. Anker had been at Base Camp, responding to interview requests after the great discovery. Despite being a relative newcomer to extreme altitude, the valuable search-and-rescue experience he had gained on

Denali in Alaska meant that, when a rescue party was assembled, it was only natural that he join it. When the rescuers reached the Ukrainians, only one of the team had survived unscathed. Another had suffered severe frostbite to his nose and extremities; the third man was never found, having walked off the mountain's East Face and been enveloped by the storm. Anker knew the Ukrainian team had made a poor judgement call. The weather simply hadn't been good enough, they had tried to go too fast, and the storm had found them out. In the days that followed his own summit bid, another climber went missing, this time from a Brazilian party. In both cases, what affected Anker almost as much as the fate of the lost climbers were the responses of the dead men's teammates. Shock and confusion were a common reaction when safe from danger at last. But it was the burden the survivors carried of reporting back to a dead man's family that Anker found truly frightening. Mugs Stump's death on Denali had been an equally tragic occurrence, and losing his close friend and mentor had left Anker shattered. But there had been small mercies, such as the fact that Stump didn't have kids.

Despite, or perhaps because of, the responsibilities that came with a wife and three sons, in Anker's partnership with Lowe it was Lowe who was always, in Anker's words, the 'Alpha guy'. It was Lowe who was always the one to push harder, and it was Lowe who was the one to climb faster – appetites reflected in his ever-increasing list of nicknames: 'the White Knight' spoke of his skills on ice; 'the Lung with Legs' emphasized his phenom-enal fitness and endurance. Those ascents considered impossible by other climbers, Lowe considered merely a matter of time. 'We're all at this one level,' Anker once told *Outside* magazine, 'and then there's Alex.'

Mountaineering history is littered with double-acts: Edmund Hillary and Tenzing Norgay were one, George Mallory and Sandy Irvine another. Such relationships are often primarily about complementary strengths, and Lowe knew full well that Anker was not only a friend he could rely on utterly, but one who never once felt like a straight man, never once felt a dull second to Lowe's flashing blade.

Just five months after finding Mallory's body on the upper reaches of Everest, Conrad Anker found himself in the Himalayas again. Of all the earth's fourteen peaks above 8,000 m, the last to fall to the ambitions of climbers was Shishapangma, in northern Tibet. At 8,013 m (26,289 ft), among elite mountaineers it is regarded as one of the easier of the great peaks, though its twin spires were not conquered until a Chinese expedition made an inaugural summit in 1964.

Anker and Lowe had long eyed it with a certain relish – not because it would represent an easy scalp to add to their list of climbing achievements, but because the South Face of the mountain was home to an aesthetically pleasing ridge – one that Lowe, who applied the same bold sense of ambition to going down as he did to going up, intended to ski down. When the Mallory and Irvine Research Expedition had drawn to a conclusion, the trip that Anker and Lowe had been planning to Shishapangma hoved back into view.

Despite being an accomplished skier himself, Anker was not convinced that his technique was sufficient for the 'fall and you die' runs they would inevitably encounter on the descent of such a peak; and yet he and Lowe were friends. So when Lowe first raised the prospect of the expedition, Anker had thrown his hat into the ring willingly. Not only would his climbing expertise help get his friend to within striking distance of where he needed to start his run, but, as they planned to record Lowe's efforts on film, Anker had enough rudimentary production experience to make him a viable secondary cameraman. On 13 September 1999 the two friends left the United States and flew to Nepal to begin a round of acclimatization. A few weeks later they found themselves at an advanced base camp at the foot of Shishapangma.

Early on the morning of 5 October 1999, a team of seven expedition members set out to investigate possible ski runs on the mountain. Anker and Lowe, along with fellow US climber

David Bridges, were ahead of their teammates when they came to an avalanche run-out zone – a wide apron formed when an avalanche has spent its energy and the material it has gathered on its route down the mountain comes to a standstill. It was the sort of terrain they had encountered numerous times before. The upper reaches of the mountain were heavy with snow, but the three men were vastly experienced on this kind of terrain and, as they prepared to cross the apron, they surveyed the condition of the snowpack above for any signs that it might be unstable.

Anker had spent most of his adult life studying how avalanches behave – why they mowed down some trees with ruthless abandon but left others standing, where they deposited material, and so on – accumulating a vast well of knowledge that he would tap into intuitively when working in the mountains. Confident that all was well, they had begun to traverse the area when, halfway across, they stopped to catch their breath. It was then they saw the avalanche.

In ski resorts around the world, relatively small powder avalanches account for the deaths of hundreds of skiers every year. This was different: a massive Himalayan ice avalanche triggered by the collapse of a serac, a giant ice cliff, and moving a good deal faster than any resort equivalent.

To begin with, none of the three men regarded themselves as being in any real danger. They were a safe distance away, and as the serac moved down the mountain they even took the opportunity to photograph it. Yet with each passing moment it gained more momentum, more speed, more mass; pretty soon, Anker would later recall, it was travelling well in excess of 100 mph. At some point in its descent, recalls Anker, 'we all looked up and thought: "Oh shit."' In a bid to get clear, Lowe and Bridges decided to run downhill – a decision that meant they were effectively trying to outrun the rushing mass of snow and ice. Anker opted for a different course: one that took him obliquely across the avalanche's path.

As Anker ran, he turned back once then twice to track the advancing snow as it drew closer. When he checked its progress for a third time, he knew there was nowhere to go. He laid down and made himself as small as possible, driving his ice axe into the snow to brace himself for the impact. In the split second before the speeding torrent struck, Anker later remembered, he felt buffeted by a strong wind, generated entirely by the approaching mass. The leading edge of the avalanche hit him with tremendous force, wrenching his grip from his axe and throwing him about 70 ft. He didn't remember landing – only that, as he was transported beneath the snow, he felt as though someone had covered him with a thick blanket and was pounding his body with baseball bats. He was convinced that his career built climbing on some of the most dangerous rock faces in the world was about to end with his being buried beneath a vast rubble of snow and ice.

When he finally came to a rest, however, he realized that he lay under only a foot or so of debris. Kicking himself free, he emerged to an eerie scene. The 'windblast' that had preceded the avalanche had been so powerful that a fine mist of snow hung in the air. Apart from the quiet, the main thing that struck him was how utterly still everything was. He began to gather his equipment, his mountain-rescue training telling him the most likely time to find survivors after an avalanche was within the first fifteen minutes of it occurring. Concussed, and with a badly cracked rib, he began scanning around desperately for a glove, a ski stick, a boot, something, anything, he could dig towards. There was nothing.

Badly shaken and beaten up, he was helped back to Advanced Base Camp by the teammates who had been following his group, and spent the rest of the day convalescing in his tent as the rest of the team combed the avalanche run-out zone for signs of life. As the day wore on and the temperature began to drop, the consistency of the snow began to change from heavy and wet to a texture resembling concrete, freezing solid everything beneath it. By 8 p.m., twelve hours after the avalanche had struck, they were resigned to what they had already known for several hours: Lowe and Bridges were gone. To this day Anker can still recall the reaction of the Sherpas who were climbing with them in support. It was the look in their eyes as much as the few words they were able to share that told him that they understood the loss of two close friends. Given the mortality rates among climbing Sherpas in the Himalayas, it was very likely a grief they had experienced themselves. When he thought of Lowe's family back home, he was overcome with guilt. After all, he was the freelance guy – the one living a simple life, doing whatever pleased him, without the responsibility of a wife and children. Why was he the one to survive?

That evening, Andrew McLean, the expedition leader, had the grim task of contacting Lowe's wife, Jenni, by satellite phone. He dialled the number. The moment she answered she knew it was bad news: from the tone of McLean's voice, he wasn't about to tell her they had missed the aircraft home. In the next few days the survivors wrapped up the expedition, aware they would now have to return home and face the dead men's families. Before they left Base Camp, they built a memorial cairn for their fallen friends, whose bodies would never be recovered.

Back in the US, word spread through the climbing community like a lightning strike. The death of Alex Lowe, widely regarded as the most influential climber of his generation, snatched from the incredibly close-knit climbing brotherhood at the youthful age of 40, was as bad as it got. Two weeks after the tragedy, a memorial service was held at Spring Hill cemetery on the outskirts of the town of Bozeman in Montana, where the Lowe family had their home. It was the first time Anker had seen Jenni and the boys since the accident. It was only then that the magnitude of what had happened hit home. Everything had changed. He remembered when the boys had been born, and how often he had played with them in the garden at home. Anker had always regarded 'survivor's guilt' as a bit of a cliché, a self-indulgent reflex, but he now began to experience it for himself.

In all the time they had spent together, he and Lowe had done a good deal of talking – about the state of the world, mostly, or the nature of humanity. One subject they never broached was their own mortality: what might happen, heaven forbid, should one of them die. It was their equivalent of 'the Scottish play', and Anker had always been pretty sure that it didn't need to be said that, if one of them failed to return from an expedition, the other was honour-bound to look after the family back home. Purely by chance, Alex Lowe died on a mountain in Tibet – a country where, in some regions, it is customary that, when a husband dies young, a brother will step in to assume responsibility for the dead man's family. It is a sense of duty rarely seen, much less understood, in the West. So what happened next was remarkable.

Anker and Lowe's family began to see more of each other. He spent time as much with the boys as with Jenni, and it began to nag at him that as they grew older, as they began to steer a course through life, they would need some sort of a father figure. Over the course of the next year, Anker and Jenni Lowe began to fall in love. Two years after the tragedy on Shishapangma, they married. Anker knew he would never fully understand the effect their father's death had had on Max, Sam and Isaac, whom he began to refer to simply as 'the boys'. He wasn't their father, and didn't try to be: he just did his best to provide what love and support he could. 'Children are very resilient,' he said. 'Put enough love and support into the equation and eventually they come back.' The care and nurture he provided in the wake of their father's death had much to do with their 'recovery'.

Rather than uproot the family during a difficult time, Anker moved himself, and his life, to Bozeman. Photographs of Alex Lowe, Conrad and Jenni now sat there alongside each other. Instead of seeing his and Jenni's relationship as something strange, Anker began to see it as a continuum – an interesting philosophy, and especially remarkable given the number of climbers whose attitude towards even their biological kin can be ambivalent at the best of times.

In just a five-month period in 1999 his life had changed beyond measure. On 30 April he had been plain old Conrad Anker, a hardworking, if relatively anonymous, professional climber. A few days later he was headline news, his name woven into the fabric of Everest legend for ever. And yet, while he had made the great discovery of the last resting place of one of the great icons of the twentieth century, the grief that had enabled it had been borne by others. In losing Alex later that year, it seemed as if, by a perverse quirk of the 'natural order', he was being made to confront what that meant. It was as if the mountains were calling in a contract he had not been a party to signing, as if the yielding up of one great climber had to be paid for with the sacrifice of another. The new life he had found with Jenni and the boys had helped to make some sense of it all, but it was impossible to shake off the feeling that somehow the events of those tumultuous few months had all been connected: finding Mallory; failing on the Second Step; and then Alex Lowe dying.

In the spring of 2004, a film-maker called Anthony Geffen was enduring a particularly long stopover in Washington DC's Reagan Airport as he made his way home to London from the United States. Browsing around the selection in the airport terminal's bookshop, Geffen found himself in a section that included books on mountaineering. Ten minutes later, he left with a copy of *The Lost Explorer* – the gripping account Anker had written of his 1999 Everest expedition with the help of respected climbing writer David Roberts – tucked under his arm. As he waited in the airport terminal long into the night, Geffen began to leaf through the pages of Anker and Roberts's book and it wasn't long before he was hooked, consuming the text in one sitting.

Geffen began his career as a graduate trainee at the BBC where he became one of their leading filmmakers. Several of his films had a huge international impact revealing new insights and understanding into world famous figures. *Hirohito: Behind The Myth* uncovered the Japanese Emperor's participation the Second

World War, despite Japanese and American claims that he was only a marine biologist. This was followed by *The Rise and Fall of the Ceausescus*, filmed in the aftermath of the Romanian dictator's downfall and *The Faces of Arafat* in which Geffen tracked the Palestinian leader for a year.

After eleven years at the BBC, Geffen left in 1992 to set up Atlantic Productions. Now one of Britain's leading independent production companies, Atlantic specialises in producing high-end documentaries for some of the world's top broadcasters. These films are regularly seen by audiences in Britain, the United States and as many as forty countries around the world. At Atlantic, Geffen's work has won many of the industry's leading awards, and he has produced more than a hundred and fifty films, including the landmark series *The Promised Land* about the Great Black Migration across America and *The Greeks: Crucible of Civilisation* as well as drama documentaries, such as *Richard The Lionheart* and *Saladin: Holy Warriors*.

Geffen had long wanted to make a film about Mallory and Irvine. Between leaving Oxford University and joining the BBC, he worked for Frank Wells, then Vice Chairman of Warner Brothers. At the time, Wells had set himself the goal of climbing the Seven Summits, a feat which involves scaling the highest mountain on each continent, in a year and introduced Geffen to the world of mountaineering. Geffen knew that the disappearance of Mallory was one of the most dramatic episodes in the history of adventure, and often thought about the potential for a film – the combination of the golden era of exploration, Mallory's personality and the mysterious disappearance made an intoxicating mix. Now, as he read through Anker's account of the 1999 expedition, the outline of a film began to form in his mind. From the airport lounge he got on the phone to a contact in New York. Moments later, in the back of his newly purchased book, he pencilled Anker's telephone number.

Anker was at his desk, scrolling through his email as was his early-morning habit, when the call from Geffen came. As a 'name' climber, he was used to regular enquiries about his availability: Would he be interested in a magazine feature? Did he have calendar space for a documentary? More often than not he declined, too polite to say flatly that he wasn't interested, preferring to let people down gently when they proposed yet another trashy, made-for-TV mountain drama. When he picked up the phone to Geffen he was naturally cautious. Enquiries about climbing projects were one thing: enquiries about Mallory were something else entirely.

The idea that Geffen had in mind was a re-creation of something of the lives of Mallory and Irvine, culminating with their final days on the mountain. Using a team of modern-day climbers, he wanted to reenact directly their experiences, and – the devil was in the detail – he wanted to do it on Everest. In conversation with such an accomplished mountaineer, he deferred to Anker's experience, but he wondered if it might be possible to retrace the precise route the two men had taken, and to do so in period clothing. He didn't know what, if any of it, was possible, but he had been in the film business long enough not to let that stop him.

That the enquiry came from a British film company was important to Anker. His own climbing philosophy traced its lineage back to the early days of the sport in England, when climbers risked their lives scaling walls of sheer rock only to report their achievements with modesty and sobriety. He was also impressed with Geffen's ambition for the project. Sensing the widespread appeal of the mystery inherent in Mallory and Irvine's story, and knowing that mounting an expedition to Everest would in itself be an epic undertaking that could captivate the audience, Geffen was planning to produce a film for theatrical release. It would be the biggest project that he had ever undertaken, and would serve as a fitting testament to two of the most significant figures in the history of mountaineering.

When the call ended, Anker began to mull it over. There were good reasons not to get involved. In the years since George

Mallory had first tackled Everest, the nature of the climbers who visited its slopes had changed considerably. In 1985 a wealthy American named Dick Bass had reached the summit of the mountain with the help of a talented young climber and guide named David Breshears, who is today an Everest veteran of some standing. Having been guided to the roof of the world, Bass became the first man to achieve the Seven Summits. But, among elite climbers, the Texan's success was not viewed as a creditable addition to the annals of mountaineering history. Rather, it was regarded as a turning point, giving rise to a phenomenon that many feel has diminished Everest's mighty reputation ever since. To some, the commercially guided expeditions that now run on both sides of the mountain enable high-spending novice mountaineers to reach the summit all too easily.

But, following his experience in 1999, Anker knew that getting to the top was far from a cakewalk even with the help of modern logistical support. After finding Mallory's body, the summit he had made with Dave Hahn had been something of an afterthought, but he still recalled the sheer effort required to get there. For each heaving step he took upward he had needed to suck down eight or nine lungfuls of air. It had been, he recalled, 'a pretty intense moment', but it had also been miserable one. There were no amber fields of grain at the top; he had expected an epiphany on top of the world, but instead, brutally cold and with his head pounding, he had to make do with a small patch of snow and the struggle to breathe. Most important of all was what he might be asking of his family in returning to the Himalayas again. Jenni and the boys knew only too well what it meant to lose a husband, a father, to the mountains, and Everest was a dangerous place. He discussed the project with his wife. Given the family's history with the region, it was only natural that she expressed a distinct sense of unease.

The longer the conversation with Geffen had gone on, however, the more Anker realized that re-creating an ascent of the mountain as Mallory and Irvine had experienced it in 1924 represented a unique opportunity. It was a chance for George Mallory, that man he had sat alone with in the snow five years ago, to be honoured by his own, by fellow climbers – for Anker, as a man, to pay homage to the figure, or at least the legend, of one who had become an integral part of his life. For Anker the climber it meant something else: if they were to follow Mallory's route to the letter, they would need to tackle the Second Step. For some, a five-year separation from a 90-ft stretch of rock high above the earth might have been sufficient time to move on. But Anker, like any climber worth the name, had ruminated on his failure, and in the intervening years had often thought about how he might have done things differently, had sequenced every hold and wondered if there was an alternative outcome to be had.

It had been the ladder that had contributed to his failure on the Second Step in 1999. If they were serious about reaching the roof of the world in similar conditions to those which had faced Mallory and Irvine, they would have to remove it. If they did that, it would set man against mountain just as it had been all those years ago, and just possibly it might answer a question that had vexed historians for the best part of a century: Could George Mallory have climbed the Second Step unaided? It would offer Anker a unique opportunity to answer the question that had been haunting him for five years. He knew that another opportunity might not come along. Despite her anxiety, Jenni gave him the go-ahead. He called Geffen back, and began to build a team.

As a prominent and well-respected expedition leader, Anker had some of the most stellar names in the exploring business in his contacts book. He had been to Antarctica, to the Karakoram range in Pakistan, to Patagonia, and always with the very best for the job. So when it came to choosing men for Everest, Geffen knew better than to interfere. He left it entirely to Anker to put forward names for the team, knowing that, if they were to have any chance of conquering the Second Step, sound climbing ability would be the minimum requirement. An established track record in working at high altitude would be essential for the crew. But as Anker began to assemble a team of seasoned Everest specialists around him, he also wanted to ensure that the expedition would include someone with enough technical climbing ability to join him in attempting to free climb the Second Step, but who, like Sandy Irvine in 1924, would be experiencing Everest for the first time. Conrad Anker knew just the man.

5

The Stone Monkey

A s he scurried earthward beneath the giant riveted arm, the young blond boy knew he would have to be quick. The police patrol cars were getting closer, and it wouldn't be long before all six of them would be haring up the approach road. If one of his friends had remembered to take a photograph in the first place, as his slim frame had rocked back and forth beneath the great rusted overhang, there would have been no need to climb back up a second time.

The Angel of the North, the vast, winged iron sculpture that acts as a lookout for the city of Newcastle, wasn't exactly a difficult climb, but it was a very public one. Boasting he could do it wearing merely sneakers had been a touch arrogant, but then, in 1998, he had been just 18. His escape had depended on being sufficiently convincing in the role of nonchalant bystander. It was a part Leo Houlding was never going to win. The arresting officer had been perfectly polite. Houlding had even taken a perverse pleasure in the repeated attempts to record his fingerprints at the station. The weeks he had spent just previously, climbing in Finland, had worn his fingers smooth; if they could find any prints worthy of the name, they were welcome to them.

Beneath Houlding's thick mop of blond hair lay boyish good looks; beneath those, a self-confidence of granite. A wicked sense of mischief developed as a child now found an ally in the physique of a man. The result was a muscular Puck who was only too keen to demonstrate his talents – the less appropriate the circumstances the better. It didn't help that he surrounded himself with equally precocious and risk-averse individuals. In ordinary young men, a cocktail of youth and recklessness is a volatile mix that invariably blows up in someone's face. But risk, Houlding had learned from an early age, was relative to ability – being good at something inherently dangerous meant people always assumed you were in greater peril than you were.

Leo Houlding and his friends were used to the response their antics often provoked, as if Superman had just flown past the window. For example, there was that day in the summer of 2001 on the Aiguille Midi, the precipitous traverse that must be endured by any skier wishing to access the high runs of the Vallee Blanche above the town of Chamonix in France. When skiers have been brought smoothly and securely from the valley floor in a cable car, nothing prepares them for the raw sense of exposure they get at the top, roping up to cross the sharp blade of snow, the windows of Chamonix winking in the winter sunshine some 10,000 ft below. Houlding could see how it might have looked, some kid balancing on the rope handrail that spanned the traverse as it swung violently beneath him, out over the abyss, back, and out again. But it was merely a glorified piece of 'slack lining', a variation of tightrope-walking that climbers use to amuse themselves all the time. It was just more customary to sling a rope between two trees.

The episode had found its way into the press, and an interview for Britain's *Observer Sport Monthly*. It was a journal more used to chronicling the lives of mainstream stars from the worlds of soccer, tennis and athletics. For a climber to make their pages, and a kid climber as he had been back then, he needed something special. He took the opportunity to explain his theory of risk and relativity, working through the various misconceptions that people had about him. It was an occupational hazard when your star was on an even steeper ascent than the vertiginous climbs for which he was becoming famous. His marijuana use was vastly overhyped, he explained, particularly as the drug would prob-ably be legalized in the near future. He was forthright, some might say mouthy, but then, as the interviewer, a well-known climbing writer called Ed Douglas, had commented in the resulting article, Leo Houlding 'could make Robbie Williams seem self-conscious'.

On newspaper and magazine pages more accustomed to hosting combustible chefs or the latest It girl, Houlding ticked boxes that for years had been left empty by what most people thought climbers to be: bearded, taciturn men – and it was usually men – who inhabited an insular and arcane world in which the mainstream press were viewed with deep suspicion. Houlding, in contrast, was young, handsome and articulate. If he was a bit cocky, then so much the better: it merely served to bolster the aura of this already exotic show pony. The headline writers hardly burnt the midnight oil, introducing the world time and again to a new 'Rock Star', or referring to his brand of 'Punk Rock'. Still, they were epithets he could live with.

Mountaineers like to animate their enemy, depicting peaks as great, angry beasts, ultimately unconquerable, but which occasionally sheath their ire long enough for you to make a darting scramble to the top. For a kid climber in a hurry, that sounded tantamount to apologetic. As one of the world's leading 'speed climbers', Houlding had a simple modus operandi – all-out attack. When moving over rock, he was fluid and gymnastic and could knock off complex ascents in a fraction of the standard time, one that accounted for safety as well as difficulty. Carrying little more than a chalk bag filled with the fine white powder that climbers use to improve their grip, from a distance he appeared a tiny fragment of humanity cast adrift on seemingly boundless expanses of rock. But to watch the machine working up close, shirtless and tanned, the muscles of his back sliding beneath the skin, was to witness a determined soldier ant. With fingers probing like antennae, he would stop only rarely, to check a hold before resuming his charge. Getting the job done as quickly as possible was a speed climber's mantra: safety in speed.

Speed climbing is a series of continual victories – precise, split-second judgement winning out over the sort of dithering common sense that can get you killed. The biggest of 'big walls', those on which climbers must confront their own insignificance as sheer, flat rock stretches away in all directions, are triumphs of the unremitting stubbornness of geological processes measured in millennia. But Houlding was an agile, unpredictable opponent: for every route he found blocked he merely opened another, unpicking the mountain's resistance as the rock face stared proudly skyward. As he climbed, the logical left side of his brain logged possible holds, calculated potential lines. But he was also an artist: all the while, the creative right hemisphere would be saying, 'What if?' As the synapses fired in opposition to each other, should the two sides at any point falter in their series of ongoing negotiations he would fall. But then Leo Houlding was good at even that. Forced to react in the time it took his rope to pull tight against the protective equipment he had wedged into the mountain, he would relax his body as he estimated where and how the fall would end. When it did, he simply took the opportunity to rest before recalibrating his senses and pressing on, stretching what was possible in the relationship between gravity and the human body.

His talent stemmed in part from a fortuitous design: a conformation with a high ratio of muscle to body fat and which combined the static strength of a weightlifter with the reflexes of a sprinter. But whereas the runner flowers explosively and briefly, a climber must develop sustained reserves of power to be called upon when the need arises. For arise it will, and often. In continually assessing not just where they are going but how they might get there, it is crucial for climbers to possess a highly evolved sense of what sports scientists call 'proprioception': the awareness of the position of one's body in space – where your feet are when you can't see them, where your hands are, and hence where the next hold is coming from. It is a sense that any climber hoping to survive on daunting terrain must possess innately.

When it came to climbing, Leo Houlding – born in 1980 – had grown up with geographical advantages as well as physiological ones. The Lake District, that part of England credited as being the birthplace of climbing, was just twenty minutes' drive from the Houlding family home. It is an area popular with walkers, and in 1886 one Walter Parry Haskett Smith, the son of a local landowner, is said to have invented technical climbing there when he scaled a pillar of rock known as Napes Needle not to gain the summit, but for the sake of the ascent. Thus, the 'sport' of climbing was born.

The area had been a hub for climbers ever since, so it was relatively inevitable that Mark Houlding, Leo's father, had a number of friends there who knew a bit about the sport. It was one these, Malcolm Cundy, who took father and son to a small cliff face called Burrell's Brock one day in 1989 and introduced them to the rudiments of climbing. There was a lot to learn: managing the ropes; how to place 'protection', the various pieces of gear that climbers wedge into cracks before securing their ropes, and thus themselves, to the face; and how to make a 'belay', a simple friction device created by running a rope through a metal loop to allow a climbing partner on the ground to arrest the fall of a climber above. Houding learned fast – even as a child, he was hardwired to do things quickly – and just six months after his lessons with Cundy began, he joined his father on their first 'serious' ascent.

In Britain, the difficulty presented by a particular climb is graded by an adjectival system that runs from 'easy', a scramble requiring some use of the hands, to 'extreme', a category covering the most challenging terrain. The Old Man of Hoy is an intimidating sandstone stack, 450 ft high, off Hoy, one of the Scottish islands of Orkney. It is regarded as an extreme climb, albeit a less challenging one, and known therefore as an E1. But to a 10-year-old boy such classifications are relative. Following Cundy up the ascent in inclement weather, it was comforting to have his father along, but it was, Houlding recalled later, 'a long way from football in the park'. The coastal location meant it was usually raining, and the most difficult part of the climb – the crux – took the climber through a daunting overhang. On the descent, Houlding had needed to be lowered on a rope, and in a gusting wind. He remembered it as the last occasion when he had been scared on a climb.

On those weekends Houlding spent climbing with his father and Cundy, the young boy would be regaled with the stories of those who had gone before – tales of bygone eras and of unorthodox characters whose legends extended well beyond their talent on rock and ice. Men like Doug Scott, the first Briton to climb Everest, in 1975, who spent the night in a bivouac near the summit. Bedding down on Everest alongside him that evening was Dougal Haston, a dark, brooding character among whose great achievements was a first ascent, in 1972, of the south face of another Himalayan peak, Annapurna, known universally as the 'killer mountain'. Accompanying Haston on Annapurna was a climber who came to be seen as the greatest iconoclast of them all, a hard-drinking brawler by the name of Don Whillans, known simply as 'the Villain'. Through his stories, Cundy opened a door on to a world of blue-collar heroes, climbers often from Britain's industrial heartlands, Wales and the north of England. The areas that had once supplied coal, steel and textiles to the world were also home to some of the best climbing crags in the country. For climbers working in manual jobs, it was the only place to be when the shift siren sounded. As he listened wide-eyed, the young Houlding couldn't have been more entranced.

At some point on his climb of the Old Man of Hoy, Leo Houlding decided to ask Cundy the sort of question only a child can, one utterly devoid of context or qualification. Which climb, in his opinion, was the hardest in the world? Cundy replied without blinking: the Indian Face. Located on the Welsh peak of Clogwyn d'ur Arddu – widely considered one of the best, which is to say most challenging, climbing cliffs in Britain – the Indian Face was an ascent so technically demanding that it held a grading of E9, then the highest for a British climbing route. Over the years, it had treated the efforts of some fine practitioners of the climber's art with disdain. Houlding's next question was as straightforward as it was predictable: 'And who's the best climber?' Today it would be an almost impossible question, and twenty years ago it was still difficult enough. It was fortunate then that Malcolm Cundy had an answer: Johnny Dawes.

When it came to free climbing, negotiating an ascent using equipment only to catch you in the event of a fall, Leo Houlding was destined to become a master of the art. He had by then learned from one of the best. By the time Leo Houlding first met Johnny Dawes in 1990, the Derbyshire-born climber, then 26, was already regarded as an enigmatic genius by the rock cognoscenti. Houlding's Hoy climb led to an appearance on a children's television programme, *Motormouth*. Appearing on the same bill was Dawes. Despite the sixteen-year difference in their ages, the two got on well. They stayed in touch, and when Houlding was 13 he began to travel regularly to Dawes's home town of Sheffield, an industrial city synonymous with its primary material: stainless steel. For climbers, its outlying regions are home to another precious resource: 'grit'. A variant of sandstone, gritstone is a sedimentary rock that was once the tool of choice in Britain's flour mills. Climbers prize it for other reasons: the coarse grain offers excellent traction even on the subtlest features, and it is perhaps for this reason that it is known as 'God's own rock'. Though barely a teenager, Houlding would spend weekends with Dawes's thirty-something crowd, learning the finer points of gritstone climbing, his self-belief growing all the while. Among Dawes's key attributes was his vision, seeing routes that others thought impossible, and it was some of this which rubbed off on his young apprentice.

The high point of Dawes's celebrity came in 1986, when he became the subject of a documentary film. Shot by the film-maker Alan Hughes, it aired on the then relatively new Channel 4, a television station that in the mid-1980s was a byword for eclectic and alternative culture. It was also an era when great leaps were made in technical climbing.

Hughes's film burned itself into the memory of many who saw it, climbers and non-climbers alike. Part of the reason was that it seemed to capture the essence of an elegant, acrobatic athlete, leading one reviewer to compare Dawes's physical virtuosity to that of Rudolf Nureyev. His grace and movement were obvious; you didn't have to be a climber to appreciate them, just as you didn't have to be a boxer to appreciate Muhammad Ali. Equally memorable was the film's title.

Stone Monkey seemed to capture perfectly Dawes's near-primal talent and his highly developed sense of mischief. Just as Houlding would later climb the Angel of the North, Dawes scaled Nelson's Column in London, only to be met by the wagging finger of the law on his descent. That 'monkey' became a term of endearment between fellow climbers was at least in part a result of Hughes's film, and the word was used frequently in reference to Houlding. The year that *Stone Monkey* first aired also saw confirmation of Cundy's answer to Houlding's questions on that Hoy climb. In April 1986 Johnny Dawes became the first man to free climb the Indian Face.

In 1993, the year he had first climbed with Dawes, Houlding passed yet another milestone. Climbing in Tremadoc in Wales on another E1 route, the Plum, his father, Mark Houlding, was leading the climb as he always did when he took a second fall on a particularly tricky section. With some concern, he agreed to let his son try for himself. It was the last time Leo Houlding ever followed his father up an ascent. A year later, in 1994, Houlding was just 14 when he visited the offices of Animal, a small company based in Dorset in England's West Country. Then only a suggestion of the global brand it would become, it manufactured watch straps for surfers tired of losing their timepieces in the swell, but was slowly beginning to expand into new areas of clothing and equipment. Though still only a teenager, Houlding could see that this was a company on the up. Investors were piling in on

Britain's relatively untapped surf scene, hoping to exploit what they saw as the sport's cool cachet and aware that the lifestyle that surfing promised offered a host of other revenue streams. As Houlding saw it, climbing was just as cool as surfing, was just as much about lifestyle as it was about conquering summits. There and then he made up his mind: if he played his cards right, it was climbing that would become his livelihood.

But the problem for any child prodigy is that God-given talent gets you only so far. To really improve, you must put away at least some childish things and play with the big boys. In the summer of 1995 Houlding travelled to the town of Llanberis in North Wales. He planned to spend six weeks camping in an area which offered some of the best climbing in Britain – Snowdonia. He spent the weeks before his departure trying to convince school friends to join him. When none was interested, he simply set off on his own. What he found when he got there was a pretty informal gathering, but one where 'young' meant climbers of 19 or 20 years of age.

He climbed well – well enough to want to return the following year for what was to prove a summer of life-changing experiences. He hooked up with friends he had made twelve months previously, among them Tim Emmett, himself a rising star at the age of 22. Together they began to climb dangerous routes 'on sight': without planning their moves first, and without a safety rope. While on-sighting is a common practice among climbers, it was a rare skill in one so young, and particularly on routes that had challenged some of Britain's best when at the peak of their powers. Among those routes was Master's Wall, a climb with a fearsome reputation on Clogwyn d'ur Arddu – the peak that is also home to the Indian Face. Houlding's success on Master's Wall was the first time he would see his name in print. Headlines telling how 'Leo Houlding on-sights Master's Wall' stroked his ego, even if they brought a swift end to his under-age drinking at The Heights, the local pub. No matter, there was always a party to be had somewhere else on long summer nights where even by midnight the sun had not fully set. The tent he had taken with him as accommodation had the pleasure of his company for just one of those nights, the wooden floors of Llanberis providing as much comfort as a 16-year-old off the leash required.

After his second summer in Llanberis, in 1996, Houlding returned to his home town of Appleby to discover he'd out-grown the pond. His friends had misspent their summer in much the same way as he had, with girls and underage drinking, but he sensed that, for some of them, that might be the limit of their ambition. Determined not to go the same way, he enrolled in a college course; but when that didn't work out his parents bowed to the inevitable, giving him a year to see if he could make it as a professional climber. It was long enough, but only just. Nearly twelve months later, he got what he would look back on as 'the dream phone call'. Berghaus had been a highly successful brand of mountaineering equipment in the 1980s, but was now having to do battle with an ever-increasing number of rival manufac-turers. What they needed was someone to freshen the brand, someone to appeal to an emerging youth market, but someone with sufficient credibility among the serious climbers whose business they still relied on. A down payment of £5,000 was a lot of money when you were 17 years old, and the young Leo Houlding was on his way.

A year after signing for Berghaus, Houlding celebrated this first major deal with his debut ascent at a venue whose import-ance to climbers is hard to overstate: Yosemite National Park. His earlier observations of the similarities between climbing and surfing were to prove prescient. Just as legendary breaks are revered by surfers around the world, the routes that exist on the granite towers of Yosemite have a similar reputation among climbers. And rising above them all is a 3,000-ft tower that is home to some of the most renowned climbs on earth – El Capitan. Of all the routes on 'El Cap', none is more celebrated than the Nose.

e summit awaits: Mount Everest as seen from Base Camp, May 2007

George Mallory with his wife Ruth. They were married on 29 July, 1914, just six days befo
the outbreak of the First World War

Right: George Mallory climbing in the Alps, August 1909. This photograph was taken by Geoffrey Winthrop Young, Mallory's climbing mentor, as they descended the Peuterine Ridge of Mont Blanc

Below: The 1924 Everest expedition group photographed by John Noel at Base Camp. *Back row, left to right*: Sandy Irvine, George Mallory, Edward Norton, Noel Odell and John Macdonald; *front row, left to right*: Edward Shebbeare, Geoffrey Bruce, Howard Somervell, Bentley Beetham

The last photograph of George Mallory and Sandy Irvine alive, taken by Noel Odell at North Col on 6 June 1924 as they prepared to launch their summit bid

Base Camp, at 17,000 ft, on the north side of Everest. From this tent city on a gravel plain by the Rongbuk Glacier, expeditions prepare for their summit bids

e Altitude Everest Expedition 2007 team with their Sherpas. *Back row, left to right*: Josef
auer (sound recordist), Gerry Moffatt, Ken Sauls, Anthony Geffen, Conrad Anker, Leo
ulding, Kevin Thaw, Peter Allibone (cameraman), Mark Kahrl (Base Camp technician),
e Hayns (cameraman); *middle row, left to right*: Candice Martin (location producer),
my Chin (in grey top)

nrad Anker and Leo Houlding in full concentration during an expedition planning
eting at Base Camp

Conrad Anker and Leo Houlding at the 'puja' ceremony performed at Base Camp by mon
from the nearby Rongbuk Monastery

Anthony Geffen directs high-altitude cameraman Ken Sauls at North Col

An evening inside the dome tent on the North Col. *Left to right*: Gerry Moffatt, Anthony Geffen, Kevin Thaw, Leo Houlding and Ken Sauls

Conrad Anker and Leo Houlding wearing replica 1924 kit. Their clothing included six laye of wool and silk with a gabardine over suit and leather hobnailed boots

The first ascent of what is now unquestionably the most iconic rock climb in the world came fifty years ago, in 1958, when a US climber by the name of Warren Harding led a pioneering team up what was then uncharted territory. They climbed by means of a series of bolts and pitons, essentially rope anchors driven into the rock – a technique known as 'aid climbing' – and in the process established a series of semi-permanent bases or 'camps' en route to the top. With his teammates making countless shuttle runs up and down the face to collect supplies, only Harding remained for the duration, continuing to hammer aids into the rock face while a revolving cast of fellow climbers came and went. When he reached the top, Harding had spent an astonishing forty-five consecutive days effectively living on the rock wall. Journey times on El Cap have come down markedly since Harding's pioneering ascent, although an average climb of the Nose still takes around five days.

Life on 'the vertical plane' offers a unique view of the world. Being 'clipped in', attached to a climbing harness for weeks at a time, even when you sleep, can do strange things to your sense of perspective. Flipping the world through 90 degrees can mean that days after coming off the mountain a climber might still wake in the night clutching at where his or her harness had been until recently. Cooking, eating and sleeping thousands of feet from the ground can take some getting used to, although incidences of climbers freezing in panic, unable to go on, are rare – the chances are that such paralysing vertigo will find you out long before you reach such technically challenging heights. On the biggest of big walls, such as the 20,000-ft Great Trango Tower in Pakistan, the sense of exposure can be so immense as to be almost beyond comprehension.

Most climbers make their debut on El Capitan on relatively easy routes and using similar aid-climbing techniques to those employed by Warren Harding. Leo Houlding wasn't most climbers. On El Cap, the Nose was only one route famed for its difficulty. El Nino was another: high, complicated and dangerous.

Not only did Houlding plan to make his big-wall debut on El Nino, he also planned to free climb it. Should you be under any illusion as to the difficulty of the task, fewer than 100 people have 'freed' routes on El Capitan. In 1998, the year Houlding introduced himself to Yosemite, that figure was fewer than 10.

The initial problem for the young Briton was a shortage of kit. More specifically, a portaledge, which, at several thousand dollars, cost several thousand more than he had left from his cheque from Berghaus. A chance conversation with two big-wall veterans at the Yosemite Lodge Hotel solved his problems. Conrad Anker was headed for Antarctica the following morning, but his house guest, a British climber by the name of Kevin Thaw, would return with the portaledge the following day. It was the first time Houlding and Anker had met, and the result was what Houlding called with characteristic immodesty 'one of the best ascents El Cap has ever had'.

The view of the world that El Capitan provided him with would become increasingly familiar. 'It always amazes me when you're on a big wall,' Houlding would say later, 'sat on a ledge the size of a dressing table with a friend, talking about arbitrary stuff. You look down and there's 3,000 ft of air between your legs, or a golden eagle comes soaring past or a cloud forms before your eyes.' If you need evidence that technically proficient climbers are granted access to places on the planet beyond the reach of lesser mortals, big walls such as those found in Yosemite are Exhibit A.

In the climbing world, Houlding's ascent of El Nino was headline news, a typically bold piece of technical climbing such as was fast becoming his trademark. On the countless climbs Houlding made thereafter, Kevin Thaw had become a regular partner. The two of them worked well as a unit, despite the thirteen-year difference in their ages, a balance of naked talent and pragmatic experience. They endured bad times as well as good, occasions when the intimations of a climber's mortality seemed clearer than usual. In October 2001, for example, Houlding, Thaw and a climber by the name of Alan Mullin had set their sights on Cerro Torre, a celebrated 10,000-ft granite spire in Patagonia, the mountain's imposing North Face being made up of nearly 5,000 ft of highly technical climbing.

A first conquest of the mountain had been claimed by an Italian climber in 1959, when a man by the name of Cesare Maestri reported how he and his climbing partner, Toni Egger, had made an audacious ascent of the treacherous North Face. The fact that Egger had been swept to his death by an avalanche as the two men descended after a heroic unsupported assault on an ice-encrusted summit only added credibility to what, at the time, was heralded as a revolutionary climb. But in 1968 a highly talented team of British climbers made a two-thirds ascent of a route on Cerro Torre that many considered far easier than that claimed by Maestri. On their return, the British team described a challenge so arduous that many in the climbing community began to review the Italian's account. The row over whether Maestri could have made such a difficult climb rumbled on until, in 1971, the now increasingly bellicose and eccentric Italian grew tired of defending himself and returned to the mountain with a mechanical drill. Sinking hundreds of bolts into the rock, which future climbers would use to secure themselves to the mountain, Maestri reduced Cerro Torre's technical rating at a stroke, provoking outrage over what many in the sport regarded as sacrilege.

Since Maestri claimed his first ascent, a number of climbers on Cerro Torre had found other clues, including discarded bits of Maestri's gear, that seemed to cast further doubt on his claims. That his descriptions of the mountain's upper reaches proved wildly inconsistent with the experiences of those who came later only fanned the flames of controversy. One of the more fascinating truths of mountaineering at high altitude is that the evidence a climber leaves of his or her presence is likely to remain undisturbed for many years, preserved by dry air and freezing temperatures. Eventually, however, remote though the locations often are, there is a reasonable chance that someone will find it.

It is a variation of Locard's Law, the basic principle of forensic science, which roughly states that 'every contact leaves a trace.' The Maestri row continues to this day, a protracted, internecine conflict that has made enemies of former friends and, with its numerous twists and turns, has become mountaineering's equivalent of *Jarndyce* v. *Jarndyce*. It was a debate that found its mirror in George Mallory and Mount Everest.

Once they had landed in Buenos Aires, Houlding, Mullin and Thaw had made for the small town of El Calafate, from where they could pick up a bus that would take them to within a four-hour march of Cerro Torre's base camp. With an advanced base camp (ABC) a day beyond that, the plan was to free climb as much of the North Face as possible.

From their ABC, Houlding had been leading the climb when, roughly 1,000 ft up, he was forced to choose between two routes. One flowed with glacial meltwater, making it dangerously slick; another would allow him to continue free climbing, but it was a route fraught with danger. Unsurprisingly, Leo Houlding chose to do things the hard way.

Then 21, Houlding had recently returned from a trip to the Yosemite valley during which he had, even by his own standards, pushed himself hard. So hard, in fact, that more than once he had thought that he might be climbing close to his limit. It was a dangerous place to have been, not least because, having returned unscathed, his sense of his own youthful invincibility remained intact. Having negotiated the worst of the difficult stretch he had chosen, Houlding was approaching the easier stretch of rock that existed beyond it when he slipped. The basic theory of free climbing is that, disregarding any slack in the rope, a climber can only ever fall a maximum of twice his or her distance above the last piece of protection placed in the rock. In Houlding's case that meant 70 ft. He made a grab for the rope in an attempt to slow his fall, but the resulting rope burns were so severe that they cut almost to the bone. And on the way down his right foot caught a ledge and was pushed violently upward.

By the time he reached Thaw and Mullin, whom he had passed in the fall, shock was taking hold and his foot was beginning to swell alarmingly. The only way down was to abseil, a descent he would have to make with raw, burnt hands. It was agony. Back on the glacier, he made his way back to their advanced base camp by sliding on his bottom. When he got there, having only a basic first-aid kit to call upon, the night that followed was a painful one. The next morning Houlding taped up his raw, rapidly blistering hands and improvised a splint by forcing his swollen foot inside a walking boot not designed to accommodate disfigured feet.

If his judgement on the mountain had been poor, he had plenty of time to contemplate his error as Thaw attempted to carry him to back to Base Camp. On the loose terrain they encountered, it proved all but impossible for Thaw not to drop his friend time and again. Eventually, every step Thaw took only made the pain worse. When their jolting progress became unbearable, Houlding took matters into his own hands. He chopped up his sleeping mat, bound it to his knees with tape, and made the rest of the journey on all fours. Crawling along the moraine, dragging his injured foot behind him, the journey took eight hours.

His return home to England was no less painful. An orthopaedic surgeon diagnosed a crushed talus, the bone in the upper foot that acts as a pivot between the foot and the leg. Houlding would be lucky if he ever climbed again. Worse news was to come, for such was the nature of the injury that there was even a chance it would develop into avascular necrosis, a highly unpleasant condition in which damaged bone effectively dies and, in the worst cases, must be amputated. In the event, Houlding was spared that particular agony, but the diagnosis still meant six months on crutches, a major operation, and nine months away from climbing. Enduring 270 dark nights of the soul, he wondered if he would ever set toe on a rock face again. Some doubted he'd get back to his best – but he did: back to those places on the planet where he could focus with absolute clarity, a tiny figure charting its course across an ocean of rock.

As if to prove the extent of his recovery, in 2004 Houlding renewed his acquaintance with Cerro Torre, this time making it all the way to the summit. A year later, he and Thaw were back in Patagonia again, scaling the Cazzarotto Pillar, a treacherous route on the peak of Mount Fitzroy in the Andes. Cazzarotto appealed to them for similar reasons to Cerro Torre – almost a vertical mile of climbing. They climbed well and quickly, and came unstuck only when a freak storm overtook them on their descent. In winds approaching 80 mph, they abseiled down as far as they dared until they came to a tiny ledge. The weather that hammered the mountain was, Houlding later recalled, 'enough to rip the roof off a house'. Hidden inside the hoods of their jackets, they hunkered down, crouching low as the wind roared past like a freight train. They hadn't eaten or drunk any water for twenty-four hours, and even speaking with faces just inches apart they could barely hear one another. They took the only course open to them, and howled with laughter. It was just Mother Nature – nothing personal.

When Leo Houlding had spent those teenage summers in and around Llanberis, exploring the early boundaries of his fledgling talent, the fact that the town was a stone's throw from Pen y Pass had meant very little. The elegant soirees that Geoffrey Winthrop Young had hosted there early in the century had doubtless been more sophisticated affairs than Houlding's teenage exploits, but they had something in common: the presence of a rare climbing talent. Houlding had first heard the name of George Mallory while at primary school, when a teacher had set him an assignment about two English climbers who had disappeared high on the slopes of a faraway mountain many years ago. She drew pictures of the peak, named Mount Everest, and marked the positions of the various camps the climbers had established on their way to the summit. Before they vanished, she told the class, some believed they might have got all the way to the top. Shortly afterwards the young Houlding was set the task of writing an essay on a historical figure he considered to be a hero. Somewhat ironically, given his future career as a technical climber, he chose a mountaineer. Perhaps prophetically, he chose Sandy Irvine.

When the call from Conrad Anker inviting him to Everest had come, towards the end of 2006, Houlding had been surprised. His rock-climbing ability was the stuff of legend, but his experience at high altitude was limited. Yet the opportunity to tackle Everest with 'the man who found Mallory' was too good to pass up. Once he had committed to the expedition, he discovered Mallory's reputation as a formidable climber, and it was this that held his interest.

In the months leading up to his departure for Everest, he persuaded his father, Mark, to join him on Great Gable, the peak above Wasdale in the Lake District. Great Gable was one of the peaks where, in 1914, Ruth Mallory had seen for herself her husband's extraordinary ability to scale smooth sheets of near vertical rock not just with ease, but with a fluid elegance. As Leo Houlding knocked off one route after another with his father, the difficulty of some of them surprised him. The climbs represented a key part of the Mallory story in a language he understood, and, as a result, Houlding began to develop a growing regard for the man he had first come across at primary school.

From his office in London, Anthony Geffen also put Houlding in touch with Julie Summers, the great-niece of Sandy Irvine who went on to become his biographer, and they had talked regularly on the phone. He visited Merton, the Oxford college where Irvine had been an undergraduate and which still held some of his possessions. Looking over Irvine's belongings, leafing through his journal, the effect had been a strange one. When Irvine had last handled them, he too had yet to see Everest. For Houlding, it helped to bring to life the man about to depart for adventure in a land that was unfamiliar and alien.

Conrad Anker's choice of such an accomplished talent as Houlding had had several motives. For one thing, allying himself to such a skilled rock technician could only improve his chances on the Second Step. But, for all Houlding's prodigious ability, it was something else that led Anker to choose the young Briton. Part of his growing respect for Mallory's tragic story stemmed from the part played by his climbing partner that June day, the inexperienced but seemingly fearless Sandy Irvine. If they were to recreate the Mallory and Irvine climb with any authenticity, he needed a partner with limited knowledge of high altitude and to whom he might offer the benefit of his experience. To date, the highest Leo Houlding had climbed was around 16,000 ft. Everest was almost twice that.

For all the god-given genius Houlding might offer on the Second Step, Anker knew there was one factor that might render his talent obsolete. When it came to coping with the demands of altitude, Mother Nature had a trick up her sleeve which, put simply, meant that success was arbitrary. Near the summit of Denali, Conrad Anker had witnessed 'real thin guys, heavy smokers, doing real well. Other guys that looked like an advert for a body-toning studio would double over at 14,000 ft.' Acclimatization was largely a matter of biological programming, something that would apply as much to Houlding as to anyone else. When it came to high altitude, Leo Houlding had more than a little in common with the blond, wide-eyed boy who in February 1924 had boarded the steamer SS *California* en route for Mount Everest.

What Anker didn't know, however, was that Leo Houlding had an Achilles heel, which the thin, frozen air of Everest was guaranteed to locate – he hated the cold. Trussed up in a down suit, the highly insulated yet highly cumbersome clothing that all high-altitude mountaineers are obliged to wear on Everest's upper reaches, there was every chance that this particular stone monkey, for all his gifts, might find his guns well and truly spiked.

6

Oxygen

WHEN THE SECOND British expedition to Mount Everest arrived at its base camp at the head of the Rongbuk valley in 1922, it did so with just one goal. If the mission of the previous year had been largely to make a reconnaissance of the mountain, the objective on this occasion was brutally simple: an all-out assault on the summit. The expedition was led by General Charles Bruce, the man who had first proposed a conquest of the mountain. Bruce was an army man through and through, but where other old generals were all bluff and bluster, Bruce was a jovial patrician, whose mischievous sense of humour revealed a deep affection for the men in his charge.

Responsibility for leading the climbers on this occasion fell to another army man, Lieutenant Colonel Edward Strutt. With his prodigious talent, George Mallory was credited with many things, but being a leader of men wasn't one of them. Before departing, the expedition's climbing capability enjoyed a significant boost thanks to the restoration to health of the maverick Australian climber George Ingle Finch. A climber of similarly mercurial talents to Mallory's, Finch was likely to prove useful when battle with the mountain began in earnest. The two Georges were joined in turn by Howard Somervell, a surgeon by profession but also a powerful climber, and by Colonel Edward Norton, the grandson of Alfred Wills, whose pioneering ascent of the Wetterhorn had ushered in the Golden Age of mountaineering sixty-eight years earlier.

Things started well, the expedition sailing for Bombay at the beginning of March and arriving at Base Camp late the following month. The plan was to repeat Mallory's route of the previous year, establishing three camps in the Rongbuk valley and a fourth at the North Col, from where they would launch their bid for the summit. Under Strutt's direction, it was decided that Mallory's talent would best be realized if allied to the strength of Somervell, and so, climbing without the aid of oxygen, the honour of having first crack at the summit fell to them. If they failed, Finch and Norton would follow, this time using supplementary air.

It was the first time that oxygen had been taken to the mountain and, after some preliminary testing, the Mount Everest Committee had agreed a price of £400 for the supply of ten sets of apparatus. Based on the crude equipment used by pilots of the Royal Flying Corps in the First World War, the primitive cylinders leaked badly, and many were half empty when the equipment arrived at Base Camp. The mouthpieces through which the climbers were meant to breathe were so inefficient as to be useless. Finch, a staunch advocate of oxygen use, spent several days making alterations, but in the event a stomach bug forced him to withdraw. Somewhat inexplicably, both Mallory and Somervell found themselves in a new, enlarged, summit team that included not only Edward Norton but also another climber, Henry Morshead. If Mallory's bid were to fail and a second attempt was needed, the only climber left to accompany Finch – assuming he recovered – would be a man called Geoffrey Bruce, nephew of the expedition's leader. Bruce was game enough, but he had only limited experience.

Undeterred, Mallory wrote to Ruth as he contemplated the task at hand, 'I write to you on the eve of our departure for the highest we can reach, just because I shall feel happier, in case of difficulties, to think that I have sent you a message of love.' He closed with a reminder that he meant to conquer the mountain in her honour. 'Dearest one,' he wrote, 'you must know that the spur to do my best is you and you again ... I want more than anything to prove worthy of you.'

Having established Camp IV at the North Col by 17 May, as he prepared to climb higher Mallory felt optimistic about the challenge ahead. In a dispatch written for *The Times*, he declared, 'Prospects seemed extraordinarily promising ... Everything has been arranged so happily and satisfactorily that one could hardly doubt [the porters] would be able to establish our camp a great deal higher up the mountain next day.' It was about as good as things would get.

By the following morning, four of their nine Sherpas had gone down with mountain sickness but the climbers set out nevertheless, establishing their next station, Camp V, at 25,000 ft. The effort to reach it was considerable, and the next morning, 21 May, Morshead complained of feeling unwell and declared his decision to withdraw. On the morning of 22 May, what remained of the climbers and Sherpas set out to establish their highest camp thus far, Camp VI. The going was even more arduous than before, and fresh snowfall concealed sloping ledges and loose rocks. They planned to climb until two in the afternoon but by 2.15 p.m. they were still as much as 600 or 700 ft short of cresting the North-East Ridge. Mallory, bold as ever, was convinced they had the capacity to reach it, but the wind was bitingly cold. Exercising sound mountaineering judgement, he took the sensible decision to retreat. Their aneroid barometer, which calculated altitude by measuring the decrease in atmospheric pressure, showed an elevation of 26,800 ft. Norton would later query whether the calculation had been correct, but to Mallory it made little difference: it wasn't the summit, and his disappointment was as bitter as the wind that had driven them back.

Three days later, on 25 May, Geoffrey Bruce and George Finch took their turn, this time using the oxygen apparatus. They climbed well, reaching an estimated height of 27,200 ft, before substandard equipment got the better of them and mechanical failure forced them to retire.

The efforts of that week left most of the expedition party nursing some ailment or other. Mallory was diagnosed with a heart murmur and had frostbite in several fingers. Of those who had taken part in the summit bids, only Howard Somervell, the surgeon, was fit enough to continue, miraculously showing no ill effects of the hammering the climbing team had taken. Charles Bruce, however, had more than just his health to worry about. The considerable expense incurred by two expeditions, combined with the weight of public expectation, now meant he was coming under increasing pressure from London to deliver a successful summit bid. The regular letters he was receiving from Arthur Hinks and Sir Francis Younghusband, the respective secretary and chairman of the Mount Everest Committee, left him in no doubt that failure was not an option. With the committee keen to recoup some of the significant outlay of the past two years, they simply had to make the top that season, and would have to climb into the monsoon if need be.

Casting an eye over his battle-scarred troops, it was with some reluctance that Bruce named a third summit party: Howard Somervell, the inimitable George Finch and, of course, George Mallory. Sending up another party was a decision that Bruce made against his better judgement, and it was one he soon came to regret. 'No doubt you will have mixed feelings about another venture,' Mallory had written to Ruth, aware that, in light of their experience thus far, she would be anxious. 'But you will feel chiefly as I do that it would have been unbearable for me to be left out ... The finger is far from well and I risk getting frostbite by going up again, but the game is worth a finger.' He knew the demands he had put on her and the children by leaving for the mountain a second time; reaching the summit was surely a fitting way to repay her faith. 'Dear love,' Mallory wrote, 'believe that I will never forget the beautiful way you have behaved about this adventure.'

As they prepared to drive themselves up the mountain one last time, privately the climbers were aware of their depleted condition, realizing that in going up again they were papering over the cracks. 'It's an infernal mountain,' Mallory wrote to his good friend David Pye, 'cold and treacherous. Frankly the game is not good enough: the risks of getting caught are too great; the margin of strength when men are at great heights is too small.' But if a summit party was to go, there was a chance it would succeed – and for it to do so without Mallory was inconceivable. 'Perhaps it's mere folly to go up again,' he wrote to Pye, 'but how can I be out of the hunt?'

With a team of porters, the party left Base Camp on 3 June. It didn't take long for things to fall apart. Utterly exhausted, Finch was forced to pull out almost immediately. In the days that followed, heavy snowfall hampered the others further, and by the time they reached Camp III on 5 June, at just 21,000 ft, they were already using supplementary oxygen. It was when they decided to leave for Camp IV, on the North Col, that the fate of the expedition was sealed. Their chosen route to the col, directly up a steep snow wall, was fraught with risk. The size and steep gradient of the slope made it dangerously unstable, and following the falls of recent days it was thick with fresh snow. Mallory pressed on regardless, doing his best to pack down the powder, but it was so deep it proved hard going. They were about 600 ft beneath the col when Mallory heard 'a noise not unlike an explosion of untamped gunpowder'.

It was his first experience of an avalanche, but he knew what it was at once. 'I knew the meaning of that noise as though I were accustomed to hear it every day . . .' he wrote to Ruth. 'And then I was moving downward. Somehow I managed to turn out from the slope so as to avoid being pushed headlong and backwards down it.'

When he came to a stop, Mallory found himself and Somervell unscathed. Not so the porters. When the avalanche abated, all nine were missing, swept over a ledge and buried somewhere in the freezing debris some 200 ft below. Mallory and Somervell's struggle to reach their companions was desperate, and when they eventually found them the scene was one of horror. Digging frantically in the direction of the rope as it disappeared into the snow, by the time they reached the trapped men they found they were too late. All but two had been killed, some lying as they had fallen, with spare oxygen cylinders still strapped to their backs. Acceding to the wishes of the survivors, the dead men were left where they fell.

The tragedy hit Mallory hard. 'I'm quite knocked out by this accident,' he wrote to Geoffrey Young in the aftermath. 'Seven of these men killed, and they were ignorant of mountain dangers, like children in our care. And I'm to blame.' They had little choice but to wind up the expedition. Mallory knew that, back in England, a public outcry now awaited them. 'Do you know that sickening feeling', he wrote to Young, 'that one can't go back and have it undone and that nothing will make good?' Young, as ever, counselled in his friend's favour, advising Mallory that he had doubtless done the best he could. 'I don't much care what the world says,' Mallory replied gratefully, 'but I care very much what you ... think.' What the world thought, as evidenced by the exchanges of letters between the Mount Everest Committee and his fellow climbers, was that Mallory had been reckless.

He arrived home early in August, and spent the next month and a half with Ruth and the children. For all the furore surrounding the death of their porters, the pull of the mountain refused to lie dormant for long. Writing his chapters for the official account had forced him to reflect, and, as he played the images of the expedition through his mind, the loss of the porters wasn't the only thing he saw. Like a general surveying his encampment before a coming battle, he was struck by the nobility of the endeavour, the months of planning and preparation all coming together in one unified purpose:

> Now as I look back and see all those wonderful preparations [he wrote], the gay little tents with crimson flies or yellow ... the ferocious crampons and other devices, steel pointed and terrible for boots' armament, the business-like coils of rope, the little army of steel cylinders containing oxygen under high pressure ... the warlike sets of apparatus for using the life-giving gas ...

when I call to mind the whole begoggled crowd moving with slow determination over the snow and up the mountain slopes ... how can I help rejoicing in the yet undimmed splendour, the undiminished glory, the unconquered supremacy of Mount Everest?

Given what, by late 1922, Mallory knew about that unconquered supremacy, he was confident that a third expedition might finally deliver the prize he so desired. In a bid to maintain public interest, it was decided that he and the other climbers would embark on a series of lecture tours of Britain, the United States and Canada. But who best to speak? In the offices of the Mount Everest Committee, the general thinking was that the more of the 1922 expedition team that appeared on the speaker's rostrum, the more engaged the audiences would be. The agent contracted to arrange the speaking dates in Britain, a man named Gerald Christy, saw things differently. Rather than dilute the impact of the lectures with what he saw as peripheral talent, it was Christy's idea that efforts should instead focus on those who had 'starred' in the expedition of 1922. That, of course, meant George Finch. And, more than that, it meant George Mallory. The latter had experience of this kind of thing already. In the three months he had been in the UK between the expeditions of 1921 and 1922, Mallory had given a number of lectures around the country that had proved highly popular, as Christy well knew.

Christy was to be proved right, and in a programme of lectures running from October to December 1922 the British public came in droves to hear the two climbers speak. On the back of this success, in January, 1923 George Mallory sailed for New York en route to Washington and the first of a number of engagements designed to stir up the lucrative American market. Before his departure, it had been the Mount Everest Committee's express wish that the tour be conducted with such dignity as befitted their noble enterprise, and, on the advice of Christy, they had entrusted arrangements to an agent by the name of Lee Keedick, a man whom they deemed of sufficient integrity to carry out their wishes.

From Washington, Mallory travelled on to Boston, where things initially went well, the handsome Englishman so engaging audiences with tales of high-altitude adventure that he later wrote to David Pye that he felt as if he were 'casting a spell'. By the time he returned to New York, however, the picture had somewhat changed. To Mallory's mind, engagements were thin on the ground, and he held Keedick personally responsible for this. On several occasions, technical hitches spoiled his presentations, and one lecture in Canada was cancelled entirely. Though the press had initially found his characteristic English modesty appealing, any ambitions he had harboured to take continental North America by storm were soon stood down. The press, he discovered, had agendas of their own.

During one lecture, he happened to mention how brandy had helped fortify him and his comrades on Everest the previous year. He later found that this was the sole item reported from a long and elaborate speech. This was the era of Prohibition, but even so Mallory was entitled to feel aggrieved given the hardships the mountain had dispensed.

It was during one engagement on his American tour that he made what would prove his most enduring remark. Asked by a journalist what motivated him to attempt, for a third time, to be the first to summit the highest mountain in the world, he is alleged to have replied, 'Because it is there.' The quote first appeared in the *New York Times* on Sunday 18 March 1923, but, in the years that followed, its provenance was called into question. Whether or not Mallory uttered it directly or, as some believe, it was a confection penned by a quote-hungry scribe, it was a statement that would come to serve as Mallory's epitaph. Whether approximate fact or utter fiction, it came to act as a riposte to those who questioned the wisdom of climbing Everest. Mallory's relationship with the mountain had long since developed into a complex love affair, and it was also a statement made to a reporter that demonstrated the extent of his infatuation: 'If you cannot understand that there is something in man which responds to the challenge of this mountain and goes out to meet it, that the struggle is the struggle of life itself, upward and forever upward, then you won't see why we go.'

It was Mallory's sincere wish that the US tour might help provide some financial stability for Ruth and the children, but the early returns suggested otherwise. He travelled home despondent. A year previously he had caught a glimpse of what he hoped might be a future career when the Mount Everest Committee had given him a £400 share of the profits of that first lecture tour – more than he could earn in a year as a teacher at Charterhouse. It was somewhat ironic that it would be a return to teaching that would put his place on a third Everest expedition in jeopardy.

Around the time Mallory was heading home from the US, Arthur Hinks, the secretary of the Mount Everest Committee, had shared a train ride with a Dr David Cranage, an old friend who now ran extramural courses for working-class students on behalf of Cambridge University. Cranage was looking for a tutor for what was a well-paid job, and Hinks recommended Mallory on the spot. When Mallory was then offered the job, he promptly accepted. So when, in late 1923, the Mount Everest Committee began to assemble an expedition team for another assault on the mountain, Mallory's commitments to Cambridge meant that, for the first time, he found himself in a novel position: he was no longer an automatic choice. Preparing to take up his new position that autumn, George moved the Mallory family to Cambridge, taking over Herschel House, a large property in the city's Herschel Road. When the shortlist was drawn up for the expedition party for the following year, George Mallory's name, as before, was the first one on it. This time, however, alongside it sat a large question mark.

The only climber to rival Mallory's talent, George Finch, didn't have the luxury of ambiguity. His relationship with the Mount Everest Committee had been damaged beyond repair by a simmering contractual dispute which had boiled over during the lecture tours of 1923. There were plenty of candidates ready to take his place. Noel Odell had mountaineering merits that complimented his background as a geologist. Appointed as the expedition's oxygen officer, Odell was destined for one of the more poignant roles in the Everest story of 1924. In the summer of 1923 he had led an expedition to explore the mountains of eastern Spitsbergen in the Arctic Circle. It was a region Odell knew well (leading an expedition there in 1921 had prevented his participation in the first mission to Everest), and among the party that year were a number of undergraduates from Oxford University. One of them was a young chemistry student called Andrew Comyn Irvine. With his blond hair and fair complexion, he was known to almost everyone as 'Sandy'. Born in Birkenhead on 8 April 1902 and educated at Shrewsbury School, he was the son of affluent middle-class parents. 'If Andrew Comyn Irvine was not born with a silver spoon in his mouth,' wrote his younger brother Alec in a foreword to the publication of Irvine's diary in 1979, 'then at least it was of the very best Sheffield plate.' Odell and Irvine had first encountered one another when the younger man was still at school. Out walking in Wales with his wife one day, Odell had come across a young boy valiantly attempting to coax a chuntering old motorcycle over the high mountain pass of Foel Grach. It was Irvine.

From Shrewsbury, in 1922 he went up to Oxford, where he enrolled at Merton College. An accomplished athlete, Irvine was able to turn his hand to most sports, and when he did he would invariably display skills well above those of the average novice. First and foremost, however, he was a rower, an oarsman. Irvine had rowed for Oxford in the Boat Race of 1922, being selected for the university's first eight in only his first term at Merton. In a boat usually filled with more physically developed third-year students, he had rowed at number two. But the Cambridge crew had been far superior, each man a half stone heavier in a sport in which weight means power. When Oxford duly lost, Irvine was crestfallen. The pain of defeat would be brief. He set his sights on making the crew for the following year. A fine physical

specimen, he coped well with the gruelling punishment his training demanded, pushing his body beyond the point where lesser
athletes might consider themselves spent. An important attribute
in many sports, in top-level rowers this is crucial – something
modern sports scientists describe as the ability to sustain effort
above the 'lactic threshold'. Rowers know it simply as the ability
to row through pain. Twelve months later, in the Boat Race of
1923, it was Irvine's strength that helped Oxford gain revenge,
the first time they had beaten Cambridge since 1913.

It was a success not lost on George Mallory and his fellow members of the Mount Everest selection committee. In Spitsbergen,
Odell had been impressed by Irvine's endurance, but it was his
eternal enthusiasm and good humour which had most endeared
him to his fellows. Odell felt sure that, with his industrious
spirit, Irvine had what it took to cope with the rigours of
Everest. Mallory concurred. 'Irvine represents our attempt to
get one superman,' he wrote to Geoffrey Young, 'though lack
of experience is against him.' While Irvine's limited climbing
experience had impressed more seasoned exponents of the art,
both in Spitsbergen and on climbs in North Wales, it was true
that when it came to high altitude he had no experience whatsoever. Indeed, the highest he had been by 1923 was 6,000 ft – an
elevation he would have to better by almost 400 per cent if he was
to entertain any notions of reaching the summit of Everest.

Few who had seen Irvine in action had failed to be impressed
by his athleticism. And his physical prowess gave him a certain
aura, a confidence that extended well beyond the arena of sporting competition. These were the Roaring Twenties, and Irvine
was a student at one of the greatest seats of privilege in Britain.
He loved the theatre, he loved cars – and he loved women. In the
spring of 1923 he had embarked on a passionate affair with the
stepmother of a good friend, Dick Summers. Marjory Summers
was the wife of Harry Summers, a wealthy steel magnate significantly older than her. When they had married, in 1917, he had
been 52 and she just 19. Unsurprisingly, Marjory's affair with a

thrusting young buck, and a friend of her stepson to boot, caused something of a scandal in polite society and was a source of great embarrassment to the Irvine family. Sandy, young and impetuous, was either defiant or blind to his parents' discomfort as he and Marjory gallivanted around the social scene. They were sufficiently brazen to put in an appearance at the 1923 Henley Regatta. It was an event likely to be packed with friends and acquaintances of his parents, and they were even photographed together publicly. For Irvine, it was all part of the great adventure, and one that confirmed his burgeoning sense of manhood. Indeed, he was so taken with his own potency that on one occasion he had written in his diary how he and Marjory had made love four times before breakfast. On another, Irvine was rumbled sneaking out of his lover's bedroom at the Summers family home. It was the indiscretion that finally precipitated divorce proceedings.

If Irvine's physical strength made participation in the 1924 expedition to Everest likely, it was another of his qualities that all but secured it – and would ultimately seal his fate. If the Mount Everest Committee had disliked the gauche style of George Finch, they weren't so myopic as to fail to recognize the benefits of including in the expedition party someone with a natural aptitude for mechanics. Irvine's knack of getting the best from machinery and equipment, a skill the now-absent Finch had possessed in spades, bordered on genius; there was almost nothing he couldn't fix, and he excelled as both an engineer and a draughtsman. While still at Shrewsbury, he had sent plans for a number of inventions to the War Office, including designs for an interrupter gear that would allow pilots to fire through the propellers of their aircraft.

The letter from the Mount Everest Committee confirming his place on the expedition arrived at Merton College in October 1923. Irvine, beside himself with excitement, wrote to Noel Odell almost immediately: 'I am walking on metaphorical air,' he said.

At 21 years of age, Irvine had been too young to witness for himself the brutality of trench warfare. However, the Irvine family, like almost every other family in northern Europe, had not come through the war unscathed: Irvine's cousin Edward had been killed in Arras, in France, aged just 20; Irvine's brother Hugh had been gassed, an experience which left him with a lesion on his spine for the rest of his life. But such trauma must have seemed remote to Sandy, who was still young enough for it to be hard to believe that life was anything other than one grand adventure after another. And what a year 1923 had turned out to be. He had avenged his Boat Race defeat of the previous year and was bedding a sophisticated older woman, who was clearly besotted with him. And here he was being invited to join an expedition to the highest mountain in the world, and one that might well include no less a light than George Mallory, the greatest climber of his generation. For Sandy Irvine, high on the oxygen of possibilities to come, it must have felt as though he was indestructible.

As a sportsman, he felt the fire of competition burn brightly within him. It was what had got him into the Oxford boat crew – prematurely in the eyes of the more seasoned campaigners who might have expected his seat. Now chosen to join an expedition to Everest, he determined from the outset that he would do his utmost to deserve his place. To bolster his skiing ability, in the winter of 1923 he travelled to Murren in Switzerland, to taken lessons from Arnold Lunn, one of the founding fathers of downhill skiing. And from an early stage there seemed to be a suggestion that he was destined to climb with George Mallory. In their home town of Birkenhead, the local newspaper had already paired them off: 'Mount Everest', pronounced the headline: 'Two Birkenhead men in the party.'

In early 1924 Irvine was visiting some friends of the family when he a took a stroll with his hosts' youngest son. As they walked, the two companions discussed Everest, their tones becoming increasingly more excited as Irvine imagined himself closing in on the summit. 'If we get within 200 yards of the top, we'll go for it,' he is alleged to have told his young acquaintance. 'And if it's one way-traffic, so be it.' The look of determination etched into Irvine's face was something the boy would remember well into old age. If his inexperience worried others, it was clearly no burden to Irvine himself.

In the end, it was George Mallory's new employers, Cambridge University, that decided his place alongside Irvine in a third expedition to Everest. When they agreed to give one of the most experienced mountaineers in Britain six months' leave at half pay, he could hardly refuse. However bold Irvine's ambition, Mallory knew that he himself was the man most likely to get to the top. He also knew how hard parting from Ruth again would be. He had asked much of her in going a second time, and the tragedy of the seven Sherpas lost to the avalanche when he did had proved hard to shake and off. In the days following the accident he had written to Ruth, 'It was a wonderful escape for me, and we may indeed be thankful for that together. Dear love, when I think what your grief would have been I humbly thank God.' But how could he not go? 'It would look rather grim to see others, without me,' he wrote to his father, 'engaged in conquering the summit; and now that the prospect revives, I want to have a part in the finish ... I have to look at it from the point of view of loyalty to the expedition and of carrying through a task begun.'

Ruth had plenty of reasons for wanting him to stay. With his career as a writer or lecturer yet to yield any fruit, a teacher's wages meant their financial circumstances remained straitened, and they were overdrawn at the bank. A successful summit attempt would certainly help to alleviate that situation, but such an outcome was far from guaranteed. And heading off to face the epic challenge of Mount Everest meant he would be unable to tackle more mundane obstacles, such as work needing to be done on their new home. But, after much discussion, Ruth finally agreed that Mallory should join the expedition. How could she not? Whatever financial troubles the Mallorys were experiencing, Ruth knew only too well both the physical effort and the emotion that her husband had invested in the enterprise. So great was his determination to be the first to reach the top of the mountain that to deny him the opportunity to finish a job he had started three years previously would be unfair. 'I'm to go again,' Mallory wrote to his father. 'I only hope this is the right decision. It has been a fearful tug.'

The expedition was to be led once again by General Charles Bruce, with Edward Norton in overall charge of the climbing duties. If Mallory had been deemed less than leadership material before setting out in 1922, the deaths of the Sherpas that had brought the expedition to an end seemed only to confirm it. 'Mallory', the expedition's medical officer, Tom Longstaff, had written to another expedition member, Alexander Wollaston, in the wake of the Sherpa tragedy, 'is a good stout hearted baby but quite unfit to be placed in charge of anything, including himself.'

Mallory made his way to Everest for a third time by a route that was now familiar. After a farewell dinner the previous evening, on 29 February Mallory, Irvine and those other climbers not already in India set sail from Liverpool on the steamer SS *California*, bound for Bombay.

Ruth sent her husband on his way with her blessings – reluctant ones perhaps, but she was keen that the sun not go down on any wrath that Mallory might have detected on her part. 'I have rather often been cross and not nice, and I'm very sorry,' she wrote. 'The bottom reason has nearly always been because I was unhappy at getting so little of you. I know it's pretty stupid to spoil the times I do have you for those when I don't ... I do miss you a lot.'

Once on board ship, Mallory kept himself busy, running laps of the deck and getting to grips with the oxygen systems, which he regarded with some distrust. He even began to learn Hindi. Irvine, now officially installed as the expedition's equipment officer, spent much of the voyage exhibiting the technical prowess that had won him his spot in the first place and soon proved, as Mallory wrote in a letter to his sister Mary, 'a great dab at things mechanical', even if he was a touch parsimonious with conversation. Before their departure, Mallory had suggested to the Mount Everest Committee that, as both he and Irvine were Birkenhead men, it would be rather fitting if they shared a cabin. He was promptly invited to make his own arrangements and, administration being less than his forte, nothing more was done about it, although the two men often shared a table in the dining cabin.

As with Mallory's previous two expeditions to the great mountain, the team travelled on from Bombay by train to Darjeeling, where the other members of the expedition were coming together from various parts of the British Empire. Photographs from the time frequently show Mallory and Irvine together; whether as an act of clinical networking on Irvine's part or through the organic development of their friendship, the bonds of a relationship were clearly strengthening. It was in Darjeeling that they mustered their supply train, a vast contingent of 70 porters, including a number that had been with them on previous expeditions, and 300 mules. On 26 March, loaded with supplies that included pâté de foie gras and 16 cases of Montebello champagne, the 1924 Everest expedition set out on a route that, for many of its members, must have felt like an old friend.

The march to Base Camp would carry them over more than 350 miles, a journey of six weeks across some of the most barren terrain on earth. The early stages, however, were pleasant enough, through the wooded hills of Sikkim, rich in hibiscus and rhododendron dells, and photographs taken along the way show that they clearly travelled in hope. At Pedong, in Sikkim, Mallory, who had never needed a second invitation to shed his clothes, was snapped indulging in his much-loved habit of skinny-dipping, a pastime that had once left him naked and dripping wet on the grounds of Cambridge University when he returned from an evening dip to find the doors locked. On the road to Everest, he even persuaded his fellow team members to join him in hiking naked, wearing little more than hats, backpacks and smiles. Irvine enjoyed this part of the trek immensely, taking in these strange and wonderful lands and often joining Mallory on pony rides up into the hills.

On 9 April, less than two weeks after setting out from Darjeeling, the expedition suffered its first casualty. Charles Bruce, the expedition leader, had been experiencing heart trouble before leaving London. Now aged 58 (he had celebrated his fifty-eighth birthday in Phari, the point at which the expedition entered Tibet), as the climbers began to wind their way ever higher on to the Tibetan plateau, the highest land plateau on earth, at an average height of 14,000 ft, the increasing elevation began to cause him problems. Bruce had already taken a significant detour, travelling the first part of the route by way of a lower passage, but when he was struck down by a chronic bout of malaria he was faced with little choice. He would have to withdraw. It was a bitter blow. It was Charles Bruce who had suggested the first expedition to Everest more than twenty years previously; Bruce who had been forced to hand over the leadership of the 1921 expedition, again through ill health; and Bruce who had had the unenviable task of organizing compensation payments to the families of the Sherpas killed below the North Col in 1922. When Colonel Edward Norton assumed overall charge of the expedition in his place, his promotion meant that the role of climbing leader was now vacant. There was only one candidate. On this, his third visit to the mountain, George Mallory was the climbing leader at last.

Irvine continued to marvel at his surroundings, noting the wildlife he saw en route and entranced by the vast swathes of ornately coloured sand that ran in great folds between the mountains of the plateau. And when he wasn't marching, or writing in his journal, he was invariably engaged in only one pursuit

– tinkering. Irvine positively hunted for work, mending everything from beds, tables and stools to crampons and flashlights. He made improvements to his own clothing, adding pockets to the front of his 'Shackelton' smock, and also created tin shades for the expedition lanterns, replacing the highly ineffective (and highly flammable) cardboard ones. He even imparted his expertise to the porters, teaching them how to fire up the stoves and how to put up the tents quickly, even in strong winds. If his fellow expedition members were circumspect about his lack of climbing experience, they had to admire his ingenuity.

And nowhere did he display this to greater effect than in his work with the expedition's primitive oxygen equipment. If Noel Odell had been appointed the expedition's official oxygen officer, it was largely a management exercise. In common with other experienced Everest hands, Odell was less than convinced of the efficacy of what became known as 'English air'. The same went for George Mallory. Socially progressive though he was, Mallory could be quite reactionary when it came to climbing. A staunch advocate of the philosophy of using only 'fair means' to make an ascent, he shared the prevailing ethos of British climbers of the period that artificial aids should not be allowed to compensate for lack of technique or a climber's physical limitations – to compromise the Corinthian values of pitting man against mountain. The use of technical aids such as pitons – spikes driven into the rock for use in securing rope – had been common on the crags of continental Europe for many years; for British climbers, this merely fuelled their distaste. But though Mallory had once condemned the use of oxygen as a 'damnable heresy', the lacerating experience of climbing at high altitude meant he was rapidly leaning towards an acceptance of the benefits it could offer. His initial prejudice had lain in the fact that the early oxygen systems were weighty, ungainly affairs. Equally, some students of physiology argued that it was simply impossible for human beings to ascend above 26,000 ft with or without supplementary air – though the success of pioneering climbers such as George Finch, whose record altitude of 27,200 ft on the 1922 expedition could hardly have escaped Mallory's attention, suggested otherwise.

In the months leading up the expedition's departure, Noel Odell's professional obligations had required his presence in the oilfields of Persia. In his absence, he had asked Irvine to cast his eye over the equipment, and it was a task the ever-eager oarsman had taken to with aplomb. One day in the autumn of 1923 Irvine's neighbours at Merton College had been somewhat alarmed by regular clouds of smoke billowing forth from his rooms. It was nothing compared with the atmosphere inside as Sandy Irvine wrestled with the set of oxygen apparatus recently sent to him by the Mount Everest Committee. When the equipment had arrived, complete with a set of drawings, Irvine had been baffled by what he found. Developed for the Royal Flying Corps, the apparatus was heavy and, though cumbersome, the pipework that ran around it was fragile.

He set to work, spending long hours refining the equipment to make it more durable. As he worked, he used his skill as a draughtsman to produce an elegant set of drawings that he hoped would be useful to the company that manufactured the original apparatus. When he sent them to the supplier concerned, a company called Siebe Gorman, they duly threw them in the dustbin. What did a 21-year-old student from Oxford know about such high-tech gadgetry?

When Irvine reached India, towards the end of March 1924, the oxygen sets that greeted him carried none of the improvements he had worked so hard to make. He was furious, firing off angry letters to friends and family at home, complaining that what had been sent was practically unusable. 'The ox. ap. has already been boggled,' he wrote to a friend. 'They haven't taken my design, but what they have sent is hopeless, breaks if you touch it ... I broke one today taking it out of its packing case.' He set to work again, and in the course of the six-week march across Tibet his tent became an unofficial workshop. With limited equipment, he began restoring the changes he had made at

Oxford. First he removed much unnecessary pipework, significantly reducing the overall weight. Next he turned the oxygen cylinders upside down, making it easier for a climber to reach behind his back and alter the rate or 'flow' at which the air was supplied. Lastly he added a quick-release strap, enabling empty cylinders to be discarded.

By the time they reached the village of Shekar Dzong, on 24 April, Irvine had arrived at what he called his 'Mark Five' version of the apparatus – something he was now convinced would be serviceable on the mountain. They took the opportunity to test it by hiking to the town's spectacular medieval hill fort. When they subsequently weighed the cumbersome equipment, it was discovered that Irvine had managed to reduce its weight by as much as 3 lb.

With the four-day march to the Rongbuk valley still ahead of them, they gathered more porters, securing the help of a belligerent local headman only after they had brandished the seal of the Dalai Lama, the spiritual leader of Tibet. It was something that carried serious influence among their Buddhist hosts, and they had acquired the document that bore it specifically for the purpose.

It was while they were in Shekar Dzong that Norton called a meeting to disclose the identities of the two teams he had chosen to make bids for the summit. As an Everest veteran and the expedition's leader, Norton would make up half of one summit team, accompanied by Howard Somervell. They would climb without the aid of oxygen, whereas a second team would climb with it. One half of this second team would be George Mallory; the other would be Sandy Irvine. 'So Irvine will come with me,' Mallory wrote to Ruth to inform her of the news. 'He will be an extraordinarily stout companion, very capable with the gas ... The only doubt is to what extent his lack of mountaineering experience will be a handicap. I hope the ground will be sufficiently easy.'

If the composition of the teams was Norton's, the climbing plan was Mallory's. Starting from two camps, one at 26,500 ft, the other at 27,000 ft, each pair would climb independently of the other, and all being well they would meet on the top. The theory was that the party climbing with oxygen would be well placed to assist that without, and Mallory was thrilled: the strategy that might put the first man on the summit of Everest was his. 'The telegram announcing our success, if we succeed,' he wrote to Ruth, 'will precede this letter ... But it will mention no names. How you will hope that I was one of the conquerors! And I don't think you'll be disappointed.'

On 26 April they reached the Pang La, the last of the great mountain passes that separated them from Everest. At 16,400 ft, Pang La translates as 'Meadow Pass'; bleak and windswept, there is little there to warrant such a bucolic title. What it did offer, however, was an unparalleled view of Everest and its neighbouring Himalayan behemoths. Of the fourteen peaks in the world that stand above 8,000 m, five now revealed themselves: Makalu, Cho Oyu, Shishapangma, Kanchenjunga and, standing sentinel in the centre of them all, Everest itself.

It was from the Pang La, 35 miles from Everest, that the expedition now mentally 'climbed' the mountain, using binoculars and telescopes to plot their course. As they did, all eyes turned to what was clearly going to prove the greatest challenge: the long, sloping shoulder of the North-East Ridge. As Edward Norton would later write in *The Fight for Everest*, the official account of the expedition, 'We took the climb to the North-East shoulder – over 27,000 ft – as done, and every eye was turned on the last 2,000 ft.' They were looking at a part of the mountain in which no life is sustained, an arid, frozen desert, in which no further acclimatization to the thin air is possible. The use of oxygen here might mean the difference between living and dying. The area would come to be known by the climbers who followed by a suitably ominous nickname – the Death Zone.

Before setting out for Everest for a third time, Mallory had confided in a conversation with his good friend Geoffrey Keynes 'that what he would have to face would be more like war than adventure, and that he did not believe he would return alive'. Whether Mallory was expressing genuine fear or whether his comments were tinged with a shade of the melodrama that even the most sober climbers were occasionally susceptible to, his anxiety seemed real enough to Keynes. Later, Keynes wrote that Mallory had his 'literary counterpart in Melville's Captain Ahab and his pursuit of the White Whale, Moby Dick'. On 27 April the vast fleet of the 1924 expedition to Mount Everest entered the Rongbuk valley. From a sea of cloud, the great white whale rose up before them.

7

Finding the Way

THE RISE AND fall of the lama's looping monotone was mes-
meric as Conrad Anker and Leo Houlding sat cross-legged
at the base of Mount Everest. Before the large stone cairn, a
'chorten', the younger of the two men was doing his best to
focus, to look suitably spiritual. Directly above them, 'wind
horses' galloped across strings of prayer flags, mystical symbols
soliciting favours from the gods. When the holy man paused for
breath – a natural break in an incantation refined over centuries
– Houlding was sure he could hear it again, that familiar, faint
trill. The lama pressed on, nodding sagely as he made offerings
– rice for the gods, native barley or *tsampa* for the team of climbers assembled now behind Anker and Houlding. The lama had
come up that morning, 9 May 2007, from the monastery in the
Rongbuk valley to conduct the 'puja' ceremony, a traditional
blessing intended to bring climbers luck on the mountain. Anker
didn't know what the lama was saying, but he guessed the prayers
were asking Everest, Chomolungma, Mother Goddess of the
World, to show compassion, to keep the climbers safe on her
shoulders. What he did know was that without such a blessing
the Sherpas that had signed on to escort him to the mountain's
summit wouldn't even leave Base Camp.

One by one, the members of the Anker's expedition had
stepped forward, placing items on the chorten: bits of climbing
gear; candy bars; even cans of beer. The lama had blessed them
all. But as the chanting continued, Houlding heard the sound
again; this time it was unmistakable. The monk broke off and,

reaching beneath his saffron robes, pulled out a mobile phone. The climbers stared at the ground, waiting until the impatient caller was satisfied, whereupon the lama took up his mantra once more.

When it had come to his turn to lay personal effects on the stone pile, Houlding had included a number of photographs. One was of himself and his wife, Jessica; another of his late father-in-law, William Corrie, who had died on the eve of the expedition. The timing of the bereavement had, understandably, put Houlding's participation in doubt, and having to leave his wife at such a difficult time was something that had forced him to reconsider at the eleventh hour. In the end, however, he left with his wife's blessing. Climbing was what he did, and doing so in the footsteps of two of the most iconic climbers in history wasn't an opportunity that came along very often.

His first glimpse of the mountain had come two days previously, when, on the drive to Base Camp, the expedition had reached the high pass of the Pang La. Houlding's first sighting of Everest had included something very important to him – a clear view of the summit. Wherever he climbed in the world, he took being able to see the top of a planned conquest as a good omen – 'auspicious', as his Buddhist hosts might put it. 'When your working day could start with the burning red sunrise of a Yosemite morning,' Houlding would say, 'or end bedding down on a glacier, at the point where a 5,000 ft tooth of granite punctures the earth's crust, it made you want to believe in something.' For Houlding, religion and superstition were chapters from the same volume of fairy tales, but on Everest he would take all the help he could get.

That the lama was well connected telephonically as well as spiritually was only the latest in a string of surprises since their arrival. On the north side of Everest, Houlding discovered, reaching Base Camp meant passing through a small but thriving tourist hub clustered about a wooden sentry gate raised for vehicles on their way to and from the main plateau of the glacier a kilometre or so above. Around this notional checkpoint, a drab strip of tented 'guesthouses' ran up against the sides of the dirt road. Crudely painted signs advertised the 'Panorama Hotel', or 'Snow Crest Guesthouse'. Basic though the accommodation was, the establishments boasted views to shame any hostelry on earth, and the Tibetan traders running them offered an increasingly expanding range of services to the growing stream of tourists entering their lairs. Outside, local hawkers sold jewellery and yak skin clothing, while, inside, dark airless 'rooms' were scented with cheap Chinese beer and, in some cases, occupied by local prostitutes. During the day, pony carts ferried day-trippers to the main camp, beasts of burden roped by the tongue as they jig-jogged their way round the dusty switchbacks that climbed on to the Rongbuk Glacier, streams of meltwater burbling beneath as they joined the Brahmaputra River at the start of its journey to the sea.

Anker's team arrived on 7 May, their vehicles easing past a tented garrison of Chinese soldiers before rocking across the flat moraine into camp. Houlding could hardly fail to notice the sleeping leviathan that loomed above everything: you didn't need a climber's eye to appreciate that you were in the presence of a monster. To say that Everest dominates the Base Camp sky-line barely begins to tell the story. A mountain with just 3,000 ft of visible elevation gain, Anker was fond of saying, can seem mightily impressive to most people. The foot of Everest is located at 17,000 ft, the summit at more than 29,000 ft – a rise in eleva-tion of a staggering 12,000 ft. The next thing that registered was the number of people milling around. It was like arriving in a refugee camp.

In 1924 Geoffrey Bruce had described the industry of his uncle's expedition after its arrival at Base Camp as 'ant-like'. Eighty-three years on, the mountain once again looked down upon a hive of industry, only now the colony had grown. Row upon row of tents in 'expedition' red and yellow were centred on a large geodesic dome. Inside was a small bar and what was to all intents and purposes an improvised cinema, offering a widescreen TV and an assortment of the latest DVD releases. The entire outfit was powered by a large generator which also supplied an editing suite for visiting film crews, known as 'the Shack', which offered the chance to recharge any electrical device you cared to mention. To a climber like Houlding, raised on base camps as rudimentary as they were remote, it was a little disconcerting.

The season was in full swing. A veritable army of international climbing teams was on its way to posting an impressive number of summits. By the season's close, some reports would claim 300, others nearly twice that, a discrepancy caused by the increasing number of climbers either acting without an accredited guide or not sponsored by one of the numerous national mountaineering associations. To support them all, additional platoons of Sherpas, yak-herders, cooks and dishwashers contributed to the throng, a community running to several hundred people. If such traffic at a base camp was a new experience, Houlding had 'been to enough music festivals to know the toilets were likely to present a challenge'.

The evening following the puja ceremony, Anker's team gathered to discuss their assault on the mountain. It had been three years since Anker had got that first call from Anthony Geffen, thirty-six months of what now seemed endless conversations, and changes in climbing teams and possible departure dates. The intervening period had seen the establishment of a new company by a group of private investors enthralled by the Mallory story. They called their new venture, appropriately, Altitude Films, and backed Geffen's vision not only for a theatrical release film, but also for a television documentary following the behind-the-scenes story of the expedition and a major interactive website, UEverest.com. This would allow a global audience to follow the progress of the Altitude Everest Expedition 2007 moment by moment as the team climbed the mountain. The expedition was now destined to be part of a major multi-platform event bringing the story of George Mallory and Sandy Irvine to a twenty-first century audience.

Of the original idea, little had changed. In the coming weeks, the Altitude Everest Expedition 2007 would attempt to scale the North-East Ridge of Everest, following the same route as that pioneered by George Mallory and Sandy Irvine. Wearing detailed reconstructions of period clothing at key points in the ascent, they would climb in much the same manner as their illustrious forebears, with plans to use the gear as high as the 23,000 ft of the North Col if frostbite, or rather the lack of it, allowed. From the North Col they would climb on, to attempt a free climb of the obstacle that held the key to Mallory and Irvine's route, the 90-ft rock cliff known as the Second Step. It was near there, on 8 June 1924, that the two men had disappeared into history. The team now assembled around the dinner table in the expedition's large mess tent included some of the finest climbing talent in the world. They had last met in January in Salt Lake City, at one of the vast retail shows at which professional climbers make appearances on behalf of their sponsors.

The number of international visitors makes Base Camp something of a Western fiefdom in the heart of Tibet. The man to whom the Altitude team were now listening, the man with the task of getting them into position for their summit bid, was its feudal baron. Russell Brice was a bluff New Zealander who had spent every spring season for the past thirty years guiding parties on Everest, and the corresponding autumns on the nearby peak of Cho Oyu. A celebrated mountaineer, in 1988 he had been part of a team that was the first to make a treacherous traverse of a route on Everest known as the Pinnacles, a climb that had previously defeated some outstanding mountaineers. He set up a small guiding company, Himalayan Experience, designed to cater for the ever increasing number of amateur climbers with the ambition, and more importantly the hard currency (Brice's standard Everest package cost upward of £30,000), to climb the summits of the world's highest mountain range. 'Himex' had established itself as the leading operator on the north side of Everest.

At Base Camp, Brice oversaw everything from summit schedules to what expedition teams ate for breakfast. Anker called him the 'mayor of Rongbuk'; most referred to him simply as 'Big Boss'. With weather-beaten features and sun-bleached eyebrows and lashes, he could, on occasion, show a frosty exterior to mirror the environment. He could be blunt to the point of rudeness, as if discussing anything other than climbing the great mountain was a waste of valuable breath in such rarefied air. He knew the mountain better than anyone, from long and painful experience of the extreme dangers that climbers faced. That he ran his operations with an efficiency that sometimes seemed to border on ruthlessness was borne of nothing other than necessity.

Spending three decades fighting the fickle moods of Mount Everest would test the resolve of any man, and there was something of the Wild West sheriff in Brice's prolonged stand, founding his small but lucrative empire on the greatest wilderness frontier on the planet. He and his loyal team of Sherpas had played a leading role in numerous rescues, and had saved almost as many lives as they had put climbers on the roof of the world. If anyone could get the Altitude team in position for an assault on the Second Step it was him.

High altitude is defined, rather arbitrarily, as anywhere above 9,800 ft. The higher you climb, the greater the reduction in atmospheric pressure. As air becomes less dense, it contains less oxygen. On the summit of Mount Everest, at 29,035 ft, the air contains as little as 30 per cent of the amount of oxygen found at sea level, and human performance can be seriously affected as a result. The problem for climbers is that, at the same time as the level of available oxygen is declining, so the degree of physical effort increases. Living in the space this creates can be seriously unpleasant. Above 7,000 m, or 23,000 ft, the body's capacity to operate effectively is less than 40 per cent of that at sea level. Above 8,000 m, or 26,246 ft, things get even worse. Here, in the so-called Death Zone, the body is unable to adjust to the altitude any further, and the lack of oxygenated blood causes tissue to die, a process known as 'necrosis'.

Even an ascent to an altitude well below the Death Zone can leave a climber feeling unwell, but the symptoms, such as a headache, or the need to lie down, usually disappear within a few days. The higher the altitude, of course, the graver the potential consequences. High Altitude Pulmonary Edema (HAPE) is a condition that effectively causes a climber to suffocate in his or her own bodily fluid. Crudely put, a constriction of the pulmonary blood vessels leads to an increase in blood pressure, which in turn forces liquid to leak out and accumulate in the lungs. Following a distinct and unpleasant crackling in their breathing, victims then deteriorate before eventually 'drowning'. HAPE's sister condition engenders an even greater fear among mountaineers, operating as it does by stealth. Early symptoms of High Altitude Cerebral Edema (HACE) are dangerous precisely because they resemble those experienced in less life-threatening reactions to altitude. In this instance, fluid leakage results in a swelling of the brain, a condition that can accelerate into coma and then death before it is even diagnosed.

The villain of the piece is something known as 'hypoxia', a condition in which, as a climber's brain is slowly starved of oxygen, everything from vision to cognitive function and muscle response becomes ever more compromised. For those suffering from acute oxygen debt, the irony is that, instead of feeling pain, a hypoxic person can feel quite the opposite. In her book *Life at the Extremes: The Science of Survival* Frances Ashcroft recounts the experience of a French scientist by the name of Gaston Tissandier. In 1875 Tissandier ascended to more than 8,000 m in a balloon to study the effects of altitude. As hypoxia took hold, he described a feeling of 'inner joy, as if filled with a radiant flood of light' – a sensation that goes some way to explaining the response of those climbers who, when struggling at the highest altitudes, simply sat down in the snow to embrace their fate.

It was the threat of acute mountain sickness, or AMS, that meant the Altitude Expedition's ascent of Everest would be less than straightforward. Crucial to success at altitude is allowing the body sufficient time to adapt, to 'acclimatize'. The longer you take, the better your chance of adapting. Rather than making an all-out assault the moment they arrived, the Altitude team would ascend by a process of incremental gains, a series of 'rotations' each one taking the climbers higher up the mountain, followed by time lower down to recuperate.

From Base Camp, the Altitude team would head for an advanced base camp at around 21,000 ft, from where their rotations would begin. For Mallory, this ABC was his Camp III. Unlike their modern counterparts, the early expeditions chose to begin the numbering of camps on the flat moraine of the Rongbuk Glacier, establishing three previous camps in the valley, including Base Camp. So what modern climbers know as Camp I, the North Col, was Mallory's Camp IV. Only when the Altitude team had acclimatized fully would they begin a four-day push for their own Camp IV, located at around 27,000 ft. Here they would be forced to endure a night inside the much-feared Death Zone, before waking early the following morning to go for the summit. Before they reached it, they would have to tackle the Second Step. And it was now that things got even more complicated.

Whereas Mallory had taken a month and a half to reach Base Camp, acclimatizing gradually on the 350-mile march across the Tibetan plateau, the Altitude team had covered a similar distance in just four days. In order to replicate the conditions under which Mallory and Irvine might have climbed the Second Step, they would need to remove the metal ladder bolted to it more than thirty years earlier. Before they could do that, they had to wait until every other team had cleared the mountain. In the modern era, an acclimatisation schedule from Base Camp onwards can keep expedition teams busy for up to eight weeks. In Salt Lake City in January, Conrad Anker and Russell Brice had planned the schedule in detail for the expedition in consultation with the other team members. Given the experience in the team, comprised predominantly of professional climbers and athletes, many with impeccable Everest credentials, they judged that five weeks would be a sufficient acclimatization period before attempting the summit. As well as capturing key sequences for the film and behind-the-scenes documentary, the team would be sending daily updates to UEverest.com, including video feeds, photos and blogs. Meanwhile, their bodies would be adjusting to cope with the numerous unpleasant side effects of life at high altitude. These included a loss of appetite, as the body diverted its energies to priorities other than digesting food, and insomnia, the reduced oxygen content sometimes causing a climber to wake repeatedly. It was undoubtedly going to be a demanding schedule, but Brice – who has guided numerous film crews up Everest's slopes – was confident that it was realistic.

As Brice and Anker talked through the plan, other members of the team offered the benefit of their own experience. 'I've known plenty of guys that have gone up too fast,' said one. 'They got shredded.' The voice belonged to Jimmy Chin. Hired as the expedition's stills photographer, Chin was an adventurer with a heavyweight CV. When he spoke, people tended to listen. His physical confidence was almost palpable, and his charismatic presence and good looks made him a regular in various celebrity magazines. Of Taiwanese ancestry, he wore his glossy black hair long, falling on to deeply tanned skin. With a compact frame, not to mention a low centre of gravity, he would have looked as at home surfing the vast breaks off Maui as on the end of a climbing rope. At 34, he was already an old Everest hand. His first summit bid, in 2003, had ended in failure after an ambitious 'alpine-style' ascent of the mountain's North Face. He eventually made the summit a year later, and in 2006 he made the top again, this time with two 'ski-mountaineers', the husband-and-wife team of Rob and Kit DesLauriers, neighbours from Chin's home town of Jackson Hole, in Wyoming. The trio had reached the summit with Dave Hahn, who had been with Conrad Anker on his 1999 expedition to the mountain.

At the summit, Hahn watched as Chin and the DesLauriers took the express route home – by skiing down the mountain. Wearing oxygen apparatus in addition to skis, they carved steep arcs down the Lhotse Face, a treacherous descent on the south side of the mountain. Covering almost 16,500 ft, much of it at an incline above 45 degrees, it was the sort of 'fall-and-you-die' run from which Anker had excused himself on Shishapangma; just one wrong move would pitch a skier off the mountain to almost certain death. Unsurprisingly, Chin's descent was an eventful one: he ran out of oxygen, and on several occasions fragments of old climbing rope threatened to send him tumbling into the void. But he made it nevertheless – a success which owed much to the fact that he and his partners had skied as a team. For Jimmy Chin was nothing if not a team man. He possessed, in the words of *Outside* magazine, 'an ego that was post-Copernican – out there orbiting around with everyone else's, not at the centre of anything'. For all his quiet reserve, however, Chin wasn't afraid to speak up if he thought something needed to be said.

Anthony Geffen listened as intently as anyone. During his career, he had filmed in some pretty inhospitable locations, including war zones and underground tombs that threatened to collapse at any time. But the challenges that Everest presented would be his toughest assignment yet, and he knew that he would be reliant on the expert advice of Brice and Anker to get the film completed successfully. Brice's advice would be particularly important in judging the weather. As every Everest climber knew, this was an obstacle that could stand in the way of the best planned expeditions and the most experienced climbers. By the time the Altitude team would be arriving at Base Camp, the annual monsoon would already have gathered itself in the Bay of Bengal and would be making its way north, preparing to vent its anger on the mountain. Brice and Anker had factored extra time into the schedule as contingency for delays caused by bad weather, but the window for summiting Everest is short, and if the Altitude team ran into any serious problems, there was every chance they would be overtaken by the monsoon's heavy snows before they got so much as a sniff of the summit.

To track that weather system's progress, Russell Brice relied on highly specific data supplied by MeteoTest, a private meteorological service based in Basle in Switzerland. At a cost of thousands of dollars a year, the information didn't come cheap, but it was precise enough to predict everything from the volume of anticipated snowfall to the speed of the wind, and even the angle at which it would strike the mountain. So accurate were the figures the Kiwi had at his disposal that when he told his own teams to go for the top, a good many others usually followed. This year's snows were some way off yet, Brice reassured Altitude, but they were coming.

Anker had chosen climbers he could trust. He had climbed with Kevin Thaw many times before. It was while climbing with Thaw in the Yosemite valley that Anker had first met Leo Houlding. At 42, Thaw sported a full head of greying hair and, with his fiercely bright eyes, had the air of a wise old owl. His home was now the US climbing heartland of Joshua Tree in California, but Thaw had been born and raised in the Chew valley, in Yorkshire. He was steeped in the climbing traditions of his native north of England and, something of a blue-collar philosopher, he harboured a decidedly fatalistic approach to life.

Thaw had started his climbing education in experimental fashion. When still at school, he suspended a length of washing line above a rock face at his local quarry, and during the next few months he and his friends began testing themselves by scrambling up the rock face alongside it. If they fell, or thought they were going to, they had precisely the time it took to grab the line before they plunged to earth. As his climbing began to improve, to reach the crags that lay further afield he had bought himself a motorbike he could scarcely afford in a fire sale. When, to his horror, he discovered the insurance cost twice as much as the bike, his solution was as ingenious as it was resourceful. In his college workshop, he supercharged the engine until it was just marginally quicker than the local constabulary's high-speed patrol car, a souped-up Ford Capri that prowled the lanes above the Chew valley in search of uninsured teenage bikers. It was Thaw's presence on the trip that helped to convince Leo Houlding to sign up.

The friendships and alliances of those who lived their lives 'on expedition' were easy associations, ones that could survive being put down at a moment's notice, only to be picked up again at some indeterminate point in the future. As one 'job' rolled on to the next, they were relationships that burnt intermittently but brightly in the rarefied air of high altitude. Now, as they discussed the coming ascent in the tent at Base Camp, Leo Houlding sat quietly, listening intently whenever Anker spoke, restricting his comments only to the subject he knew plenty about – climbing. Whenever they had discussed the particulars of high altitude, Geffen noticed how Houlding would listen to Anker, willing, for all his rock climbing brilliance, to defer to his partner's greater experience.

If Houlding felt like a fish out of water, it was nothing compared with how the least experienced member of the team was feeling. Gerry Moffatt was another expatriate Briton, a Scot, and had made a name for himself not on the great mountains of the world, but directly beneath them. One of the leading exponents of 'expedition kayaking', he had built a career by throwing himself into the boiling waters of some of the world's most lethal white water. Like most of those now gathered at Base Camp, he had begun his career in the days when expeditions were undertaken as much for love as for money, cutting his teeth guiding overland trips across Asia. It had been an itinerant life, where the main skills were rebuilding truck chassis from scratch and negotiating your way past truculent border guards. His talent on water meant he was well known in the Himalayas; he even found the time to act as a 'river adviser' to the government of Bhutan.

The high point of his paddling career had come in 1995, when he had become the first European to paddle down a section of river known as the Grand Canyon of the Stikine, a perilous descent in California comprised of some truly monstrous rapids. Falling as it did between the peaks of El Capitan and the neighbouring Half Dome, it was known to kayakers, somewhat ironically given his current situation, as the Everest of rivers. The obstacles it presented were what kayakers called 'must-run' rapids. With no alternative route, 'When you paddle the Stikine,' Moffatt would say, 'you're not really testing your skills, you're simply rolling the dice.' He was an engaging personality, and highly experienced in filming expeditions. It was for this reason that he had been invited along, not by Conrad Anker, but by Anthony Geffen, being hired to help make the behind-the-scenes documentary of the expedition. Though climbing was by no means his first language, he did have considerable experience as an expedition leader in his own right and Geffen knew that if the team ran into any difficulties, Moffatt would be a good man to have in a tight spot.

As the first days in Base Camp ticked over into a week, the Altitude team settled into what seemed, on the face of it, to be an obvious hierarchy: Brice the field marshal, drawing up plans, Conrad Anker the general, effecting them in the field, shored up by his trusted lieutenants. Even by its usual frenetic standards, the Base Camp of spring 2007 was a busy one. In addition to the Altitude team, Brice was accommodating another film crew and with the season not due to finish until early June, a host of other teams had their sights trained on the summit. For all this activity, however, it wasn't a bottleneck of other teams that caused Altitude their first delay.

In fifteen months' time the curtain would go up on the 29th Olympiad, in Beijing. In a show of superpower swagger, the Chinese authorities were keen that the relay bringing the Olympic torch to the country's capital should showcase the full extent of their dominions – including the summit of Mount Everest. In the 1920s, the Mount Everest Committee had hoped that a British first summit of the mountain might allow them the opportunity for some imperial showboating of their own, and it seemed that little had changed.

Sharing tent space with the Altitude team on the Rongbuk Glacier was a group of Chinese climbers preparing for a 'dummy run', a rehearsal of the climb that would see the Olympic torch on Everest's summit. In the week the Altitude team had spent travelling to Base Camp from Kathmandu, a group of demonstrators had succeeded in unfurling banners at Base Camp in protest at the Chinese occupation of Tibet. The press coverage they generated was massive, provoking a predictably heavy-handed response from an already paranoid administration. To ensure the team taking the 'flame' to the summit suffered no impediment to their progress, the Chinese Mountaineering Association now enacted a curfew. Until the mock flame reached the summit, the other teams were going nowhere.

Not that the enforced wait meant that the Altitude team was short of things to do. There was background material to film for a start, and lots of it. Anker, Houlding and Geffen spent the days scouting the area, often rising as early as 4 a.m. to head far out of Base Camp to locations that had a strong symbolic significance for Mallory and Irvine. Back in camp, meanwhile, Gerry Moffatt would pass the time interviewing fellow team members, consulting with Russell Brice on the state of the weather or quizzing Kevin Thaw on the various pieces of electrical equipment he was 'repurposing' for use higher up the mountain. Combining serious climbing expertise with his role as a satellite communication specialist, organising data transmissions, live web dispatches and video streaming, Thaw would be responsible for gathering the behind-the-scenes footage with Moffatt. This would then be relayed around the world on the expedition's official website, to give an intimate view of expedition life – everything from what the climbers ate for supper to how they slept on a given evening. With a worldwide online audience likely to run into millions, if anything went wrong on the climb it would be a very public failure. This was the first time they had met, but Moffatt and Thaw soon began to form a strong bond, a sort of natural pairing. Both were British expatriates; both knew what it meant to lead the itinerant life of the 'adventure athlete'. And, unlike Conrad Anker and Jimmy Chin, neither felt the burden of expectation that came with having summitted the mountain previously.

A climber who did was Ken Sauls. A highly experienced cameraman from Silverton in Colorado, Sauls was a specialist at high altitude and had summitted Everest not once, but twice before. It was Sauls who would be responsible for capturing the crucial action on the Second Step. He wore a thick beard and, with wire-rimmed spectacles, had a bookish air. It didn't take his fellow team members long to fashion him a nickname. 'Spielberg' was a more apposite moniker than perhaps they realized. 'Commercial jobs', such as working on Mount Everest, allowed Sauls to spend the rest of his time on other endeavours, including what he referred to as 'concept movies' – films that sought to portray the art as well as the adrenalin of climbing.

While his burly physique suggested an outdoorsman of the classic variety – he had the look of a late-nineteenth-century logger – when he spoke, he did so in a flat drawl peppered with popular surf idioms. He invariably described conditions on the mountain as 'gnarly' or 'radical', and to Geffen's mind he could often come across as pretty 'out there'. On Everest, he was back on familiar territory.

It was thanks to his two previous summits that he knew what lay in store. Climbing the mountain was likely to prove tough enough, but filming at the most extreme altitudes would bring additional pressures. Just getting the cameras to the top would involve significant risks for the dedicated camera Sherpas tasked with the job. Moving around with them thereafter, setting up or reshooting scenes, would be slow, incredibly dangerous and exhausting in the thin air.

Meetings conducted around the dinner table soon became a regular feature of camp life, the ideal opportunity to talk through the day's events or to vent frustrations. A mess tent at the base of Everest is a curious place; if the weather is good, you could be camping in the South of France; if it is against you, it can sound like the Devil himself is throwing a tantrum outside. It wasn't long before the Himalayas gave a warning of some of the pitfalls that lay in store for the unsuspecting climber. On 12 May, in their second week at Base Camp, the team awakened to the sound of heavy snow falling on their tents. It was a prelude to bad news. As the Altitude team gathered for breakfast in the mess tent that morning, they heard that a Sherpa directly connected to the Altitude team had perished the previous day. The brother of one of their lead Sherpas, Gombu, had been guiding two clients at the base of a nearby peak when all three had been killed crossing a crevasse field.

Altitude's Sherpa party was overcome with what Anker called 'a small wave of grief'. Gombu was one of the most experienced in their support team, and he knew the daily risks run by the Sherpas all too well. But it didn't make it any easier. He retreated into his shell, asking not to go up high on the mountain or carry any heavy loads. His comrades respected his request, shouldering his burden for what, at least publicly, would be a very brief period of mourning.

The word 'Sherpa' is a Nepali twist on an old Tibetan term, *sharpa*. Roughly translated it means 'inhabitant of the east'. These days the term is used to cover all the indigenous groups that make their living as high-altitude porters, but it is the hardiness and endurance of the ethnic Sherpa that enjoy the loftiest reputation. In supporting those climbers whom Anker referred to as 'Westies', the Sherpas invariably got the thin end of an already narrow wedge. The porters whose deaths had brought the 1922 Everest expedition to a close were the first reported to have died on Everest, but they would certainly not be the last. Carrying heavy loads to one of the most dangerous places on earth meant that, every season, it wasn't just climbers who died on the mountain. For every three climbers who had died on the mountain between 1980 and 2002, around two Sherpas had perished with them.

The peak on which Gombu's brother had met his end – Shishapangma – was one that Conrad Anker knew only too well. In 1999 the expedition's Sherpas had built a memorial cairn at the foot of the mountain as a tribute in honour of his great friend Alex Lowe. In 2000 Anker himself had helped found the Khumbu Climbing School (KCS), a training centre in Nepal dedicated to improving the skills of aspiring Sherpa guides. Whereas once the 'interview process' for Sherpas had been rudimentary (if the camp cook had the same size feet as an available pair of boots he might find himself high on the mountain all too quickly), when KCS graduates went out to work, they did so carrying crucial pieces of kit and knowledge of the subtle changes in mountain conditions that were harbingers of danger. The school couldn't offer such complex training as that provided by the Union Internationale des Associations de Guides de Montagne (UIAGM), the internationally renowned guiding association that sends expert guides to work in mountains around the world. But tuition at the KCS was specific to the Himalayas, and the many thousands of dollars it took to train one UIAGM guide went a long way in such an impoverished region.

After becoming the first man to reach the summit of Mount Everest, in 1953, Sir Edmund Hillary devoted much of the rest of his life to improving conditions for the people of the region, aided on occasion by one Russell Brice. Many in the climbing community considered 'putting something back' a moral duty, and their time and investment paid dividends. Accompanying the Altitude team was Phurba Tashe, a head Sherpa or sirdar who, since their arrival at Base Camp, had impressed Anker with his quiet, competent authority and was a powerful climber in his own right. Anker knew he hadn't become one of Brice's head guides by chance.

News of the death on Shishapangma only made Leo Houlding more determined that, when they got higher up the mountain, if any of their party were to get into trouble, he wouldn't be among them. For all his swagger, he knew that most fatalities happen when people push themselves beyond their ability, when their body is unwilling to guarantee the cheques that their ambition is writing. He was well practised in listening to his body, but, even so, in the letters he was now writing home he chose not to mention the deaths of other climbers. He hoped the letters to his own wife, Jessica, might give him a better understanding of how Mallory and Ruth felt, so far apart and with correspondence taking months to arrive. In their day, letters that left Base Camp did so by postal runner, taking days to reach India, to be loaded aboard ship for the voyage to England of several weeks. Conrad Anker took a more pragmatic approach to staying in touch and he had called home every day since the team's arrival at Base Camp. With a fourteen-hour time difference between Tibet and Montana, 9.30 in the evening was 7.30 a.m. back home, when his wife, Jenni, was making breakfast as their three boys got ready for school. If the satellite phone was down, he used his cellphone. It was an expensive way of staying in touch, but it was one he budgeted for accordingly. News of another death on Shishapangma could hardly fail to register.

One afternoon while he had been gathering footage, Gerry Moffatt had been talking with a visiting journalist when he happened to remark that, as a professional kayaker, there was no way he could afford to lose a finger to frostbite. A toe, on the other hand, might be a fair trade for standing on the roof of the world. Leo Houlding didn't have the luxury of playing so fast and loose with his digits. Climbing Everest was, he knew, a great opportunity, and he quite fancied the idea of himself as a film star. But his fingers and toes were how a professional climber made his living, the tools of his trade. Successful though he was,

Houlding simply didn't have the money to insure his hands and feet independently. Insuring the climbing team against frostbite had been taken care of by the expedition, but for Houlding the policy couldn't begin to compensate if he returned with less than the full complement of his extremities.

Climbing friends of his had paid dearly on some of their adventures in extreme cold. One, after a particularly epic winter climb, had returned minus one of his big toes. He got back in the game, even did OK, but losing 'one of your main forms of leverage' could only ever reduce your future career options: had Geoffrey Winthrop Young not lost a leg in the trenches during the First World War, he might well have been advising Mallory on the slopes of Everest rather than counselling him remotely.

For Houlding there was something else at stake – pride. Houlding was first and last a climber; an ascent of the North-East Ridge under 'modern' conditions therefore represented a dilemma. On the one hand, here he was on a commercial undertaking, an artistic one even, a climb being made, in some sense, in the name of entertainment. There was no way he was prepared to risk his future livelihood on what was, as Kevin Thaw never failed to remind him, a 'punter's peak'. On the other hand, his reputation was based on daredevil heroics. Specialist technical climbers such as himself regularly dismissed peaks such as Everest as 'high-altitude walking'. If he failed to get to the top, with a team of Sherpas to carry his bags and with the fixed ropes that now lined much of Mallory's route to pull on, it wouldn't look good.

To truly understand what life must have been like for the early Everest pioneers, Conrad Anker and Leo Houlding planned to do more than just climb in the footsteps of their forebears. To get a better sense of the conditions on which Mallory and Irvine climbed on Everest, they were fitted out with a full set of replica 1924 clothing. The seemingly rudimentary nature of the clothing and equipment used on those first forays to the world's highest peak had, over the years, been one of the central planks in the arguments of the Mallory and Irvine doubters. On seeing the first photographs taken at Everest Base Camp, weather-beaten faces beneath wind-tossed hair, the writer George Bernard Shaw had famously remarked to Noel Odell that the climbers' 'country formal' attire appeared that of a 'picnic in Connemara surprised by a snow storm'. For many years, what started life as a pithy one-liner morphed into a kind of received wisdom. Kitted out in little more than hobnail boots and tweeds, Mallory and Irvine had taken on the might of Everest in garb that Conrad Anker described as 'clothes for walking in the forest'. That they had paid for this act of colonial-era hubris with their lives was only to be expected.

Recent research hinted at a different reality. By the 1920s, climbers and mountaineers were already used to working with specialist manufacturers to produce clothing and equipment that took full advantage of the latest technology. The Australian climber George Finch, for example, had pioneered an early version of the down jacket now ubiquitous in cold climate expeditions, as well as a lightweight sleeping bag made from parachute silk, a design well ahead of its time. Those who have taken a more scientific approach to 1920s clothing than Bernard Shaw, re-creating apparel after extensive research and with technical precision, have found tightly woven gabardine jackets manufactured by Burberry of London, such as those worn on Everest, to be extremely windproof. When Anker had discovered George Mallory's body, it still bore remnants of the numerous layers of wool, silk and cotton which, after their two previous visits to the mountain, the Everest pioneers had come to trust as reliable means of insulation.

In *The Fight for Everest,* team leader Edward Norton described an outfit consisting of 'thick woollen vest and drawers, a thick flannel shirt and two sweaters under a lightish knickerbocker suit of windproof gabardine, the knickers of which were lined with light flannel'. To this he added 'a very light pyjama suit of

Messrs. Burberry's "Shackleton" windproof gabardine', along with numerous pairs of gloves, a 'fur-lined motorcycle helmet' and a pair of goggles 'sewn into a leather mask that came well over the nose'. From the Altitude offices in London, the expedition's backroom staff had sourced a wide variety of period equipment: tents, food, even replica sets of oxygen apparatus, a detailed reconstruction of the finest equipment available to climbers of the period. With the help of some of the original manufacturers – companies such as Burberry and John Smedley – two full period outfits had been tailored with care, not to mention a certain pride, to ensure they met the standards expected by a 1920s climber. Woven in autumnal shades, they were a far cry from the garish reds and yellows of the down suits designed to make modern mountaineers as visible as possible. As they made their way up the mountain, Anker and Houlding planned to switch from modern mountaineering dress into period costume, testing it as high as the 23,000 ft of the North Col.

Inside a squat canvas tent on the outskirts of Base Camp, Leo Houdling pulled a silk base layer over his head, followed by an undershirt made from fine Shetland wool. The cuff buttons were fiddly, particularly beneath cold fingers, and he was glad when, having added a sizeable woollen sweater, he plunged his arms into a heavy gabardine overcoat. Outside the tent, the net effect surprised him: he felt warm. When Anker had duly taken his turn in the dressing room, the two climbers could hardly resist an exchange in cod period English. Having not been worn on a long march across Tibet, such as much Mallory and Irvine had made, the outfits looked crisp and fresh. How they would perform at higher elevations was hard to say, but there was only one way to find out.

On the morning of 13 May, the Altitude team rose early once again as they set out to re-create the epiphany that George Mallory must have experienced when he at last found a route on to Mount Everest. At 23,000 ft, Ring Ri was one of a number of satellite peaks clustered around Everest in an interlocking network of valleys, glaciers and their tributaries. While it has little of the grandeur of some of its neighbours, it was one of the peaks climbed by Mallory on his first visit to Everest, in 1921, as he sought the elusive route to the summit. It would therefore offer Anker and the Altitude team the opportunity to experience for themselves the problems that Mallory might have encountered. Dressed once more in their period outfits, Anker and Houlding had risen at 3 a.m. and started out on the short march from Base Camp to the foot of the peak.

In the dark, picking their way across the slew of glacial detritus, it wasn't long before the climbers came to a small river, across which the most obvious route appeared to be a narrow bridge of ice. Not everyone agreed. As Anker, Houlding, Geffen and the team eased their way across the frozen span, at least one of the production crew chose to wade through the icy water. Tripping on some loose material on the river bed, he took a freezing soaking for his troubles.

The ascent of Ring Ri, their first major elevation gain since their arrival, proved trickier than expected. It was steep, and the ground was loose beneath their feet, so Anker chose a line that took them over larger rocks – those less likely to move as the gradient increased. Following the curve of the slope, they set a course for an identifiable ridge line.

At this stage in their acclimatization schedule, attempting the summit would be a step too far, certainly one beyond common sense. As the altitude increased, they found the going harder and harder. At 18,500 ft they took a break. The unfortunate cameraman who had taken an early soaking now stopped dead in his tracks, felled by the sudden onset of a severe and splitting headache known to climbers as 'the tomahawk'. The rest of the team pressed on and, as the sun began to rise, Houlding and Anker buried their hands in their fur-lined period gloves, preferring the pricking jabs of heat rash to the burning glare of the sun. On Everest, Anker was fond of reminding Houlding, you could only ever be too hot or too cold. Geffen, too, climbed well, making up with sheer determination what he lacked in climbing experience.

They made another 1,500 ft before the effect of the altitude forced them to stop again, at an elevation of 20,000 ft above sea level. When they came to a halt, Anker and Leo Houlding cast their gaze back toward Everest. In 1921, Mallory had climbed Ring Ri as he and Guy Bullock, his Winchester school friend, had tried to unlock a route to the North Col. As Anker and Houlding looked across the interlocking spurs of the lesser summits, somewhere down among them was the East Rongbuk Glacier and the small drainage hole that served as the gateway to the mountain. Anker sensed the frustration Mallory must have felt, how dispiriting it must have been to have been thwarted time and again. Then again, it must surely have been worth the epiphany.

Kevin Thaw was deprived of the chance to take in the view. He had been dispatched to guide the stricken cameraman back to Base Camp.

That evening, having returned to Base Camp, other members of the expedition team felt the effects of the jump in elevation too. Leo Houlding slept badly, and the next morning he felt awful. It was a new experience, but he was far from alone. Ken Sauls, a senior climber as well as the chief cameraman, was struggling, suffering from a bad case of dehydration. In addition to the considerable demands of climbing Ring Ri, he had needed to film Anker and Houlding as they had wound their way up the slope. The effort he had expended to get ahead or to one side of them meant he had needed to cover more ground than anyone else. For all his experience, he had neglected to drink the additional fluid his body required, and now he was beginning to regret it.

Jimmy Chin had come through relatively unscathed. Shortly after the climb, he checked through the photographs from Ring Ri. As he watched one shot fade into the next on the screen of his digital camera, there was one image that stood out from all the others. The period clothing that Anker and Houlding had worn on Ring Ri had done more than simply make them look the part. The cut of their jackets and trousers had been so unfamiliar, restrictive even, that it had forced them to alter the way they walked. Chin's image captured just that: Anker and Houlding gingerly traversing a ridge in clothing not seen in these parts for the best part of a century. With nothing but the immense wall of the North Face of Mount Everest behind them, they were just two climbers 'finding the way' once more.

Since 1980, there have been an average of just over five fatal climbing accidents on Everest every year. The spring season of 2007 had seen just one recorded death. Word now came from Brice's guides higher up that, in the last forty-eight hours, three climbers had been killed in a single night. The first was a Japanese climber, Ishi San, who had made the summit on the north side of the mountain only to collapse and die on his descent. Aged 62, he had passed away despite the efforts of a Sherpa guide to revive him.

He had been climbing with a team from his native Japan, the Adventure Guides Company, and his tent, to which he would now never return, lay just yards from the Altitude camp. That same night, two Korean climbers, Ho Hee-Joon and Lee Hyun-Jo, both young men in their thirties, had been climbing on the mountain's southern slopes when, at around 26,200 ft, they had been caught in a rock fall. Both were killed instantly. Though the Sherpas believe that to leave a climber where he or she fell allows them to retain their dignity, plans would eventually be made to retrieve the bodies of the two Koreans. However, Everest invariably presents a dilemma when it comes to the retrieval of corpses, for any rescue is laden with exactly the same risks as those which resulted in the original fatality.

Given the grim news from higher up, coupled with how rough some of the team were feeling, in the days that followed the ascent of Ring Ri it was perhaps inevitable that the matter of the future schedule would be raised. When the team mustered in the mess tent now, everyone had the chance to say their piece. Anker referred to these gatherings as 'Come to Jesus' meetings. Acclimatizing in time would be a close run thing – they had always known that – but the exertions of the previous weeks had gradually seen some of the team begin to grumble about the workload, complaining that the early starts were proving a drain on their energy reserves.

Anker, for his part, was beginning to worry. The toll taken by the demands of the expedition thus far had been greater than he'd been expecting. For him the 'real story', climbing the Second Step in Mallory's honour, was higher up. If they spent too much time lower down the mountain, there was a chance they would be overtaken by exhaustion or the approaching monsoon, possibly both. In the two weeks since they had left Kathmandu, the team had been kept pretty busy. Geffen did his best to allay Anker's concerns; he knew the workload was proving more taxing than Anker had anticipated. Anker had been filmed on expeditions before, but on those occasions the cameramen had simply followed him as he climbed. Geffen had a much more demanding brief which included filming dramatic reconstructions of Mallory and Irvine, as well as the documentary elements of walking in Mallory and Irvine's footsteps and taking on the Second Step. But Geffen also knew that he had to take Anker's concerns seriously – the Second Step would be the climax of the film.

News of the travails of another team that Brice was assisting merely emphasized the scale of the challenge. Two climbers had recently returned from Advanced Base Camp after ascending too quickly. One had been temporarily blinded, a victim of snow blindness or solar keratitis, a painful burning of the cornea that occurs due to the significantly increased amount of light that reflects into the eye from a snow-covered mountain. The other, suffering from acute mountain sickness, had been evacuated in a 'Gammoff' bag, a device not unlike a mortuary body bag which could be inflated with oxygen to simulate the more oxygen-rich atmosphere that exists at lower elevations.

It was Brice who now suggested they delay their departure from Base Camp. The Chinese 'torch relay' practice had at last come to an end, and the Altitude team were due to leave for Advanced Base Camp, at 21,000 ft, in the next few days. Given how they were feeling, Brice was mildly concerned that, if they didn't take some extra time to recuperate from the Ring Ri climb, they might be forced to turn back before they got there. And the Kiwi had good reason to be cautious. For one thing, he was already making concessions for some members of the team. Before he would let his commercial clients sign on for Everest, Brice asked that they scale at least one of the world's thirteen other peaks above 8,000 m. Neither Leo Houlding nor Gerry Moffatt had done that, and, while Brice trusted Anker's judgement, it was still trust that had secured their places. A delay was something the team could ill afford, but Brice's experience was second to none. If he said they should stay, they should stay.

Leo Houlding, meanwhile, used the time to continue packing, endeavouring to streamline the vast array of modern mountaineering gear he'd been issued with to wear when not in period clothing. It proved the chore he'd always thought it might be. Miles of ropes he was used to, even the occasional tent and stove, but this was paraphernalia beyond the call of duty: numerous different types of sock, custom insoles, heated foot warmers, crampons (a choice of step-in and strap-on) – and that was just for his feet. There were also the goggles, helmets and ice axes, all with their own seemingly endless variables. Back in his home town of Bozeman, Anker prepared for expeditions by laying his gear in his basement weeks ahead of departure. Paying it regular visits, he would then pare it down one item at a time. It was fastidiousness bordering on obsession, but it worked. As Anker had reminded Houlding constantly on the road, the higher they climbed, the more important it would be to pay attention to 'the margins'. For the modern adventurer, packing is a precise science, being just ten minutes behind everyone else on summit day could leave you with a lot of ground to make up in the slow-motion atmosphere of high altitude. Polar explorers routinely drilled holes in their toothbrushes to reduce the weight of their sleds; for climbers with a finite summit window, the main enemy was time.

On 8 June 1924, Mallory and Irvine had set out from their high camp at somewhere between seven and eight o'clock in the morning. Compared with modern mountaineers, who, thanks to the invention of the humble head torch, begin their final summit pushes in the early hours of the morning, Mallory and Irvine had started late. Their delay had often been attributed to a possible final round of adjustments to the oxygen equipment by Sandy Irvine. At close to 27,000 ft, however, it can take a tired climber hours just to get his boots on. Having everything ready the night before, Anker had warned Houlding – knowing where your water was, or your headlamp – was crucial.

Jimmy Chin had more important things to worry about than his gear. In a US hospital, his mother lay seriously ill battling a pernicious form of cancer. Just a few days earlier he had received a call from the United States to say her condition was deteriorating. It had been an anxious time as he ruminated on whether he should withdraw from the trip and it was a relief when at last he received word that she had stabilized.

Though the expedition had already received a blessing from a lama who had come up to Base Camp from the Rongbuk valley, Conrad Anker took the opportunity to re-create another small piece of history. When the expedition of 1924 arrived at the small monastery at the entrance to the valley, the members of the expedition stepped inside to receive their puja, the traditional blessing that would bring them luck on the mountain. The welcome was less than auspicious. The senior lama they hoped might conduct the ceremony had been taken ill, and, to make matters worse, one of the monastery's walls was adorned with an alarming mural. It depicted a terrifying scene of white climbers (from the previous expedition, of 1922) being cast from the mountain by demons and into hell. The message from the monks could hardly have been more stark. This was no ordinary mountain, no plaything to feed the ambitions of white men from far-off lands. This was Chomolungma, Mother Goddess of the World, a revered deity with the power of life and death. It had driven them back before, and it would drive them back again.

Precisely eighty-three years later, Conrad Anker led Leo Houlding under the monastery's portico and into the same small courtyard. In an adjacent quadrangle, a group of nuns were performing a traditional dance, in preparation for the festival of Sagadawa, which celebrates the enlightenment of the Buddha. There was no ominous mural to greet them, just a small group of French visitors. Houlding thought the Rongbuk monastery was a tourist trap. The monks barely acknowledged them, and on the wall a handwritten sign instructed visitors that the taking of photographs was permitted only in exchange for cash. Anker was more pragmatic, aware of the damage inflicted on this holiest of places by Mao's Red Guard. He also knew how little some of it had changed in the eight decades since Mallory had stepped through that its doors. He only hoped that when he and Houlding at last reached the Second Step, Mallory's 'demons' wouldn't be waiting for them.

8

A Desperate Adventure

O N 29 APRIL 1924 the members of the third British expedition
to Mount Everest celebrated their arrival at Base Camp
with a sumptuous meal. Grandly indulgent, the five courses
included quails' eggs and foie gras, washed down with a glass or
two of the Montebello champagne they had carried all the way
from Darjeeling. They had earlier woken to a 'bloody morning',
Sandy Irvine noted in his diary – one of driving snow which had
left him 'very cold' and '[feeling] rather rotten'. Sitting down to
such a spread could only have lifted his spirits. As the rattle of
cutlery and the chinking of glasses drifted across the moraine of
the Rongbuk Glacier, the light from their lanterns spilled from
the door of their mess tent. High above them, the summit of the
mountain pierced the night sky. The ultimate prize, it still lay
more than 12 miles away.

Buoyed by his promotion to climbing leader, George Mallory
was in optimistic mood. Gone were the doubts, voiced to his
good friend Geoffrey Keynes, that he might not return alive,
and now his sentiments seemed to chime more with a letter
written to another friend, Tom Longstaff. In 1922 Longstaff, the
expedition's doctor that year, had been among Mallory's most
vociferous critics when the death of seven Sherpas brought the
expedition to an end. Their friendship now restored, Mallory
had written the previous March of his confidence in engaging
Everest once more. 'We're going to sail to the top this time,'
he wrote, 'and God with us – or stamp to the top with our
teeth in the wind.' When they did, the expedition's official

cinematographer, John Noel, would be there to capture it, and his thrilling record would help secure Mallory's new career as an eminent public figure, an explorer to stand alongside the likes of the great Ernest Shackleton.

Of all the deals struck to finance the early teams to Everest, the one engineered by Noel proved crucial. The former army captain had travelled to the region in a range of guises: in 1913 he had made a covert sortie to Tibet; in 1922 he was back, hired as the expedition's official photographer. His intervention in Mallory's final expedition to Everest was timely. The Mount Everest Committee had struggled to fund a third expedition in four years, and so when Noel approached the committee with two business proposals they were only too glad to listen. Offered £8,000 for full rights to both still and film images, or £6,000 for film rights alone, it didn't take the cash-strapped committee long to plump for the larger sum. The deal secured the bulk of the funding they needed, but Noel was taking a punt. For one thing, he didn't have the money. To get it, he set up an investment vehicle, Explorer Films Ltd. Convinced there was still sufficient public interest in a third expedition for a film to prove popular at cinemas, he offered shares in return for a share of the profits. He had the good sense to invite Sir Francis Younghusband to become chairman of the company, for with him came an extensive network of contacts, and the Aga Khan was just one of those to take a stake in Noel's venture.

Having arrived at the mountain, the team planned, as in previous years, to set up three camps in the Rongbuk valley, before establishing a fourth, on the North Col, at 23,000 ft, from where they would launch their bid for the top. The six-week march to the foot of the mountain gave them time to acclimatize gradually. Once they reached Base Camp, the expedition leader, Edward Norton, was keen they get moving. On his previous visit to the mountain, in 1922, the monsoon had arrived on 1 June. To ensure that they summitted well before inclement weather hit them, Norton devised a schedule that aimed to put a man on top of the mountain by 17 May. It was by no means an overly ambitious scheme, but it wouldn't be long before Mallory came to view the optimism with which he had written to Tom Longstaff as somewhat premature.

Preparations for establishing camps higher up the mountain began in earnest. All of them needed to be provisioned, and with a dizzying assortment of equipment: tents, oxygen apparatus, food, cooking stoves, to say nothing of ropes and climbing gear. Crucially, all of it needed to be carried up on foot. Irvine, in his official capacity as the expedition's transport officer, set about arranging the loads or 'carries' that each of the porters would bear. He had a natural way with the 'coolies', and took time to make their lives as easy as possible. On 4 May, for example, he noted in his diary the need to rethink the carries of the previous day, as the porters had found them too heavy. They were doubtless grateful for his trouble.

That morning, Mallory and Irvine, along with Noel Odell, the oxygen officer, and another climber, John de Vere Hazard, set out to establish Camps II and III. Irvine found it hard going. Having stopped to study a map, 'When we moved on,' Irvine wrote later, 'a devil must have got into Mallory, for he ran down all the little bits of downhill and paced all out up the moraine. It was as bad as a Boat Race trying to keep up with him, in spite of my colossal red corpuscles.' When they reached Camp II, Irvine did his best to make amends for his slowness, supervising the building of a 'sangar', a low stone wall designed to provide shelter for their tents. 'I worked for about 2½ hours shifting colossal boulders,' Irvine wrote, 'trying to set an example to the coolies … My nose began to bleed slightly in the middle of building operations so I went to sit down while Odell and Mallory went up the glacier.'

Since setting out for Everest, Irvine had done his best to match his more experienced colleague. If they were to reach the summit together, he wanted to ensure he was more than a passenger. For all his natural athleticism as a rower, to say nothing of the advantage he held over Mallory in years, he lacked the older man's natural aptitude for high altitude. Combined with Mallory's superior experience, this ensured that Irvine would only ever be playing catch-up. On the climb to Camp III, Irvine confessed to his diary that 'I have found it difficult to keep up with George and the rough ice shook my head terribly ... I became completely exhausted, panting about twice to every step and staggering badly at times. George trying a new route ... which made me still more exhausted.'

However, the friendship between Mallory and Irvine grew strong. They had shared meals together on the long voyage to India, and pony rides during the extended march that followed. Now they were working side by side as they sought to be the first to the summit, and the relationship was clearly good-natured. 'Mallory got up about 6.30 to supervise stores coming up,' wrote Irvine on one occasion. 'Energetic beggar.' From 7 May, entries in his diary refer simply to 'George', the only member of the party not represented by his surname. Mallory was equally enamoured. '[Irvine] has been wonderfully hard working and brilliantly skilful about the oxygen,' he wrote to Ruth. While he expressed concern about the Merton man's inexperience and questioned his ability to conserve energy on easier terrain – a crucial skill at high altitude – he remained glowing in his praise for his chosen climbing partner. He was, without question, 'the star of the new members'.

The first consignment of supplies reached Camp III on 5 May, a week after the expedition's arrival. It was just one camp short of the North Col, their gateway to the summit. But there was a problem.

In 1922 it was the pioneering Australian climber George Finch who had first introduced Mallory to the benefits of climbing with oxygen. By the time Mallory was making his third visit to the mountain, his conversion from a sceptic about 'English air' to one of its staunchest advocates was complete. Norton confirmed as much in naming the expedition's summit parties, as they made their way to the mountain at the end of April 1924. It would be Mallory, accompanied by Irvine, who would make up the party that would use supplementary air, while the other party, Norton and fellow climber Howard Somervell, would go for the summit without.

The responsibility for the delivery of supplies to Camp III fell to Mallory, and it was now that the shortcomings in his organizational skills – something that had led to him being overlooked for leadership of the expedition – were exposed. In his eagerness to ensure a plentiful supply of oxygen, Mallory chose to bring several loads of apparatus and spare canisters at the expense of food and sleeping bags for the Sherpas. It was Mallory's intention that a following group would bring enough to meet the deficit, but before this group could reach Camp III a blizzard moved in, forcing them to dump their supplies some way short of camp and head up without them. Mallory now found himself in charge of both his own porters and those who had followed, and with not nearly enough provisions and sleeping bags for either. To make matters worse, the temperatures plummeted, to an achingly bitter −22 °C, and the effect on the poorly provisioned porters was all too predictable. Many woke the next day in poor health, some showing signs of the early stages of frostbite.

And the weather got worse. The winds that accompanied the freezing temperatures proved so ferocious that Irvine spent one particularly bad night hanging on to the inside of his tent simply to stop it blowing away. 'Had a terrible night with wind and snow,' he noted in his diary on 10 May. 'I don't know how the tent stood it. Very little sleep and about 2 in of snow over everything in the tent. Had a lot of rheumatism in the night and an awful headache this morning.' Norton was left with little option: on 11 May he sounded a temporary retreat, ordering all members of the expedition to return to Base Camp.

The enforced lay-off in the week that followed was frustrating, and Mallory seemed to feel the delay more keenly than most. 'I had opportunities of observing his restless energy and ambition,' wrote John Noel. 'He seemed ill at ease; always scheming and planning. It was obvious to me that he felt this setback more acutely than any of us.'

Anxious though he was, Mallory did what he could to lighten the mood. Ever the tutor, he introduced some literary diversions, and by lantern light in the mess tent the climbers would read from an anthology of popular poetry, *The Spirit of Man*. When the weather finally relented, the challenge that had so far defeated them, the establishing of a camp at the North Col, would still need to be addressed. Yet, amid the naked, untamed anger of the storms that now fell upon the mountain, the poetry readings were a civilizing influence, and must have come as a welcome relief. 'We all agreed that "Kubla Khan" was a good sort of poem,' Mallory wrote to Ruth. He thought Irvine, the chemistry undergraduate, a little 'poetry-shy', although he 'seemed to be favourably impressed by the Epitaph to Gray's "Elegy"'. This begins:

> Here rests his head upon the lap of Earth
>   A Youth to Fortune and to Fame unknown ...

The week they spent at Base Camp meant that the original summit date of 17 May was no longer an option, and Norton began to grow concerned. The minor fiasco that took place at Camp III was deemed to have been largely of Mallory's making. It got worse. Of the porters that had endured nights with little more than a blanket, and, with only meagre rations of barley, two proceeded to die from their injuries. One had succumbed to extensive frostbite in his legs, while the other suffered a cerebral oedema. Herbert Carr, who edited Irvine's diary for publication, would later attribute the atrocious weather to heavy winds 'blowing in from Afghanistan with hurricane force'. It was these, coupled with brutally cold conditions – the worst recorded by any of the expeditions – that meant that, after nearly three weeks on the mountain, the vital camp at the North Col had yet to be occupied. Even Camp III had not yet been held for any length of

onrad Anker and Leo Houlding test out their replica 1924 climbing gear at 23,000 ft

oubling as Mallory and Irvine, Conrad Anker and Leo Houlding being filmed at 24,000 ft
he highest costume drama filming ever undertaken

Leo Houlding desperately tries to warm up after a day's filming at North Col – the risk of losing his toes to frostbite was a big concern for Leo

ing in the Death Zone – the climbers and crew rested at this high-altitude camp on the
ht before their summit attempt

ark Woodward and Dean Staples – the two mountain guides who joined the expedition
m to help film Conrad Anker and Leo Houlding's free climb of the Second Step

Conrad Anker at Mushroom Rock, just below the Second Step, as the sun rises on summit (

High-altitude filming – a member of the crew sets up one of several cameras used to film tl
free climb of the Second Step. Conrad Anker and Leo Houlding can be seen below

Conrad Anker and Leo Houlding using supplemental oxygen in the Death Zone – the available oxygen at this altitude is a third less than at sea level

Conrad Anker approaches the Second Step along the North-East Ridge as the Sherpas above him remove the ladder from the Second Step

Conrad Anker during his historic free climb of the Second Step – this was the key moment in the 2007 expedition which sought to determine if George Mallory and Sandy Irvine could have reached the summit in 1924

Conrad Anker and Leo Houlding triumphant on the summit of Everest, 14 June 2007

Conrad Anker and Leo Houlding heading towards the top of the summit pyramid of Evere

time, and the porters were already wrung out. Only the resolute efforts of Norton and the other climbers, Carr concluded, prevented a complete rout. Mallory endeavoured to keep his chin up. 'It is an effort to pull oneself together and do what is required high up,' he wrote to Ruth, 'but it is the power to keep the show going when you don't feel energetic that will enable us to win through if anything does.'

To ease the pressure, on 15 May Norton gathered the expedition's entire company and marched them back down the valley to the Rongbuk monastery. It was here that the expedition at last received the traditional Buddhist blessing which was deemed to bring luck on the mountain. When they had first visited the monastery on their way in to Base Camp and the lama they had hoped might conduct the ceremony had been ill, being forced to continue on towards Everest without his official approval was in itself enough to convince the porters that the mountain was against them. Upon now receiving the lama's blessing, the porters were suitably fortified. Two days later, on 17 May – the date on which they had originally planned to be at the top – the weather was glorious. 'Not a cloud on the mountain till 11.00 am,' noted Irvine. 'Perfect climbing day ... What a pity.'

Three days later, on 20 May, a party including Mallory, Norton and Noel Odell reached the North Col and were at last able to provision a camp there. For Mallory, this small but crucial success must have provoked a mix of emotions. In 1921, it was on reaching the North Col that he had successfully 'found the way', locating a possible summit route for the first time as the three great ridges that rose from the col to the top of the mountain revealed themselves. Just twelve months later, however, it was during an attempt to reach the col via the great snow wall that formed the approach that seven Sherpas died in an avalanche, an accident for which he was roundly condemned. When he led the assault on the col this time, Mallory was determined to avoid even a whiff of controversy. In consultation with Norton, he guided the party up a new route, which required him to negotiate a particularly challenging ice cliff that rose close to 200 ft high, followed by a narrow 'ice chimney'. Such ascents were Mallory's natural metier. When he reached the foot of the wall, casting his eye back and forth as he sought a line of ascent, Norton recalled seeing his 'nerves tighten up like fiddle strings' before he scaled it with aplomb, if considerable effort.

Where George Mallory was concerned, for every small success Everest granted, the mountain asked for something in return. Reaching Camp III had come at the expense of two porters, and for attaining Camp IV some payment would be exacted once again. In 1922 the slopes below the col had claimed seven lives on the way up; now they saved their bill for the descent.

The return to the more hospitable environment of Camp III that same day was treacherous, a descent marked with patches of slick ice that caused both Norton and a number of the porters to fall. Leading the way, Mallory was making his descent unroped when suddenly the ground gave way beneath him and he fell into a crevasse. Hidden by the undulation of the slope, he was out of sight of his teammates, and none of his fellow climbers saw or heard a thing. 'I went in with snow tumbling all around me,' he wrote to Ruth, 'down luckily only about ten feet before I fetched up half blind and breathless to find myself most precariously supported only by my ice axe somehow caught across the crevasse and still held in my right hand.' The axe – the only thing that now separated him from a headlong plunge into the yawning black chasm that fell away beneath him – had saved his life. He began to shout, hollering for his teammates. 'I had some nasty moments before I got comfortably wedged and began to yell for help up through the round hole I had come through,' he wrote. But all were otherwise engaged, negotiating the difficult terrain for themselves. It would be rum justice indeed if Mallory's dream were to end there, more that 6,000 ft shy of the summit. It soon began to occur to him that no help was coming; if he wanted to rejoin the expedition, he would have to get himself out.

It was now that the mountain decided to give him a small

break. Unlike many of the crevasses, which disappeared straight down into the bowels of the glacier, this one ran almost parallel to the surface of the incline enabling Mallory to dig his way out. Easing his body into a secure position, he began to scrape away at the snow, a little at a time, until he made a hole sufficiently large to climb through towards daylight. Even then, it was only by cutting steps for himself across a smaller but no less treacherous ice slope that he made his escape. The incident bolstered Irvine's respect for his new friend. 'They had a pretty exciting time coming down', he wrote later, 'Norton glissading out of control and George going down a crevasse unseen and unheard by the rest.'

The establishing of a camp at the North Col now gave the expedition the platform they needed to launch their assaults on the summit. But if Camp III had given Norton one headache, Camp IV – seriously behind schedule – gave him another. The need to provision the camp at the North Col was urgent. The day after Mallory had led the first team there, Irvine, Somervell and Hazard returned, with a band of twelve porters to deposit supplies. While Irvine couldn't match Mallory's physical prowess at high altitude, his resourcefulness – by now universally acknowledged among his teammates – would prove just as useful. The route to the North Col included a narrow ice chimney, and it was here that Irvine installed a makeshift ladder which he fashioned from rope and pieces of bamboo. It was a crude construction, but, the porters were glad of it, and it increased Irvine's reputation among them yet further.

With their loads deposited, Irvine and Somervell headed back to Camp III once more, leaving Hazard to oversee the camp. It was now the weather turned on them again. Hazard and the twelve porters found themselves trapped. For two days the small company endured a freezing blizzard, until on 23 May a slight break in the weather gave Hazard his chance, and he made ready to lead his bedraggled flock back down the mountain. But when he arrived back at Camp III early that evening, he did so with a contingent of just eight. Hazard now explained that, while the porters had shown courage in attempting to return, when they had reached a treacherous traverse, four had turned back. With the weather threatening again, the men in question had preferred to try to return to Camp IV rather than risk being caught in a blizzard halfway. Now they were marooned and in dire trouble: they had very little food, and two were suffering from serious frostbite.

Once again, Norton faced a serious situation. Keen as the expedition was to achieve a first summit, the loss of their porters, both in 1922 and in recent weeks, instilled in him a fierce desire to ensure that no further fatalities took place. The condition of those stranded at the North Col, however, combined with the scarcity of food, meant they wouldn't last long. If they were to have any chance of survival, a rescue they would have to be attempted the next day, regardless of the weather. It was Mallory who led the charge. Norton, in a demonstration of great leadership went with him, and chose, wisely as it turned out, to take Howard Somervell too.

Mallory wasn't alone in thinking the chances of finding everyone alive were slim. Snow had fallen throughout the night and, as they climbed up towards Camp IV, in places it was now waist deep. They found the trapped porters on an ice shelf, not far from where Hazard had left them; all had survived the night. It was Howard Somervell who went after them. Climbing out on a long rope, he reached the group and helped two back up the line before returning for the other pair. Suddenly the remaining men slipped and began to slide down the mountain, coming to a halt only thanks to the snow that gathered beneath their feet. When Somervell manoeuvred again to reach them, he found the 200-ft rope which secured him to his colleagues fell a few feet short. In an act of extraordinary bravery, he untied it from his waist. Wrapping the rope around his arm, he then pushed his ice axe into the snow and hooked the length joining him to his colleagues around it for what little extra security it might provide. Using the span of his arms to bridge the final few feet, he grabbed each man in turn. When the last of the porters was saved, the party returned to Camp III in the dark, being met on the walk in by Noel Odell and John Noel carrying flasks of hot soup. Both the rescuers and rescued were clearly spent from the effort. 'They had seen the welcoming twinkle of our lanterns,' Noel later wrote. 'When we met, the whole lot of them sank down in the snow. They were absolutely done! The porters were like drunken men, not knowing what was happening. Norton, Somervell and Mallory hardly spoke.'

The mountain gave them little time to recuperate. Blizzards continued to rip across the glacier, strafing their tents. It grew colder still, and while the climbers themselves were setting no records, they were now experiencing temperatures as low as −24 °C, the coldest yet recorded on Everest. When the extreme cold wasn't making life miserable, the sun proved just as punishing. On his first visit to Everest, as he had sought a route to the North Col, Mallory had written to Ruth of conditions 'more burning than bright sunshine', and of how 'one seemed literally at times to be walking in a white furnace.' With his fair hair and pale complexion, Irvine now began to suffer from chronic sunburn. By the end of May he was regularly noting his ever-increasing discomfort in his journal. 'Good night,' he signed off on 24 May, 'but face very sore indeed.' His discomfort was to be made all the harder to bear by what happened next.

In 1922 the monsoon arrived on 1 June. That date was roughly a week away, and so the expedition now found itself facing a crisis. They had reached the North Col, although it remained poorly provisioned, and yet for all their gruelling weeks on the mountain, they still found themselves more than 6,000 ft short of the summit. On the march to Base Camp, Mallory had written to Ruth brimful of optimism: 'It is almost unthinkable I shan't get to the top; I can't see myself coming down defeated.' Now, the realization of how little they had achieved left them in despondent mood. 'Dear Girl,' Mallory confessed to Ruth, 'this has been a bad time altogether. I look back on tremendous efforts and exhaustion and dismal looking out of a tent door onto a world of snow and vanishing hopes.' To his friend David Pye he summed up the cumulative effect of three wearying visits to the mountain: 'The adventure appears more desperate than ever.' John Noel thought Mallory seemed tired, his body wracked by a harsh, dry cough. 'It has been the devil...' Mallory wrote to Ruth, 'I couldn't sleep, but was distressed with bursts of coughing fit to tear one's guts.' He spent increasing amounts of time in his tent, and such energy as he did display, Noel observed, seemed to be of a fitful and nervous nature.

Norton called a meeting and laid bare their situation: as things stood, they were going backwards. They had little choice but to change their approach. The consensus, quite rightly, was that it had been the porters who had borne the brunt of the punishment so far. It had been the porters who had suffered the greatest hardships in reaching Camp III, the porters who had endured the most hellish of conditions at Camp IV. From the contingent of fifty-five who had arrived with them at Base Camp, only fifteen were now fit enough to continue. There had, thankfully, been no more fatalities, and Norton was adamant it stay that way. If they were to have any chance of reaching the summit before the monsoon arrived, they would have to reduce their reliance on the porters dramatically. It had been the job of the porters to carry the heavy canisters, and getting them into position was arduous work. Norton therefore now named two new summit teams, both of whom would climb without the aid of oxygen apparatus, and both of whom would be made up of those with previous Everest experience. One party was to include Norton himself, along with Howard Somervell – just as they had planned en route to the mountain. The other would be led, reasonably enough, by the expedition's climbing leader, George Mallory. Chosen to climb with him, however, was Geoffrey Bruce. Irvine would have to sit this one out.

'Feel very fit tonight,' Irvine wrote in his diary on 28 May, unable to mask his dismay. 'I wish I was in the first party instead of a bloody reserve.' Mallory could hardly fail to be aware of his friend's disappointment, and the problem of keeping everyone happy was something he had long acknowledged. 'The whole difficulty of fitting people in so they take a part in the assault according to their desire or ambition', he had written to Ruth, 'is so great that I can't feel distressed about the part that falls to me.'

Nevertheless, Mallory remained sceptical about the new strategy, and the decision to climb without oxygen in particular. 'All sound plans are now abandoned for two consecutive dashes without gas ...' he wrote to David Pye. 'If the monsoon lets us start from Camp IV, it will almost certainly catch us on one of the three days from there.' His cynicism lay partly in the fact that the original summit plan had been his. Now it had changed, his destiny might ultimately be decided by someone else. He took consolation, however, from the fact that, by altering their plans, they might yet force a conclusion to the expedition. 'The issue will shortly be decided,' he wrote in a dispatch for *The Times*. 'The third time we walk up the Rongbuk Glacier will be the last, for better or for worse. We have counted our wounded and know, roughly, how much to strike off the strength of our little army as we plan the next act of battle.'

Bruce and Mallory reached the North Col on 31 May, in preparation for a summit bid the following day. It was to prove a brief chapter in the story of the expedition. They set out the following morning, 1 June, without oxygen, and, much to Mallory's chagrin, were greeted by a vile wind that knocked them sideways as they battled their way towards a viable site for Camp V. The porters struggled once again, and they were forced to make camp at 25,300 ft. Bruce and one of the porters carried several loads a further 200 ft, establishing Camp V at 25,500 ft, before returning to their impromptu camp for the night. Their strategy for the following morning would be to establish Camp VI at around 27,000 ft and, from there, make a dash for the top. When the sun rose, however, the porters could not be stirred, and Bruce too felt unwell. There was little option but to abandon the attempt. Bruce's condition would later be diagnosed as some sort of heart strain.

Mallory who had slept little during what was an horrendously windy night was dejected. 'Show's crashed,' he wrote, in a note fired off quickly to Norton. 'Wind took the heart out of our porters yesterday and none will face going higher today.' In a show of tremendous team spirit, however, Mallory and Bruce spent the remainder of the morning of 2 June improving Camp V, during what must have been a period of crushing disappointment. With Norton and Somervell already on their way up from the North Col, at the back of Mallory's mind must have lurked the sneaking suspicion that his last chance was gone, snuffed out through no fault of his own.

Sandy Irvine, meanwhile, had awoken early on the North Col that morning. He had set going the Primus stove, for it was left to him – the 'bloody reserve' – to prepare breakfast for Norton and Somervell before they set off on what might prove to be a conclusive summit effort. His sunburn was by now proving more than a mere inconvenience. 'My face was badly cut by the sun and wind on the col,' he wrote in his diary that evening, having made his way back to Camp III, 'and my lips are cracked to bits, which makes eating very unpleasant.' The next day proved worse, and he was forced to endure 'a most unpleasant night when everything on earth seemed to rub against my face, and each time it was touched bits of burnt and dry skin came off, which made me nearly scream with pain.'

As Mallory made his way back down the mountain, however, he brought with him the ideal balm. His bid with Bruce had ended in failure, but the disappointment that followed was brief. Now it gave way to a strange sense of liberation. The hammering they had taken earlier in the expedition had drained the climbers both physically and emotionally, but they had survived to take on the upper mountain at last. For the moment, at least, the opportunity to be the first to the top lay with others, and in the days ahead Norton or Somervell might seize their chance. Should they fail to grasp it, however, Mallory had come to a decision. He was going to go again. This time he would take oxygen – and this time he would take Andrew Irvine.

On the morning of 4 June, having established Camp VI at 26,800 ft, Edward Norton and Howard Somervell began their push for the summit. The terrain was treacherous – Norton later described it as 'like the sloping tiles of a roof'. Climbing now diagonally along the Yellow Band, the limestone cliffs visible from Base Camp, their pace was slow. They had reached Camp V the previous day only after 6½ hours of effort. For the first time in his two visits, it was the hitherto unstoppable Somervell who found the going toughest, battling so severely with the extreme altitude that he was forced to stop for breath after almost every step.

When Somervell could go no higher, Norton pressed on alone. He climbed for another hour, struggling against the onset of double vision. He tended not to wear his protective goggles, and so harsh was the glare that reflected from the snow that now it began seriously to affect his sight. Despite this, Norton climbed on, over great slabs of rock that teetered at dizzying angles. From the point at which he left Somervell he made a further 128 ft before he too succumbed to the elevation and was forced to make his way back down the mountain.

The two men began their descent unroped – common practice at the time, as Mallory showed on his near-fatal descent from the North Col – with Norton leading the way. When they reached 25,000 ft, Somervell was forced to stop once again. 'When darkness was gathering,' Somervell later wrote, 'I had one of my fits of coughing and dislodged something in my throat which stuck so that I could breathe neither in nor out ... Finally, I pressed my chest with both hands, gave one last almighty push and the obstruction came up. What a relief!' In the harsh, dry air, what Somervell had brought up from his airway was a part of his own larynx. Though in time he would make a full recovery, he was forced to endure a painful descent.

Mallory and Irvine had spent the morning of 4 June at Camp III, preparing for an attempt on the summit they might not get to make. For all they knew, somewhere above them Norton and Somervell might well have pipped them to the post. Their creeping anxiety was heightened when a porter arrived with the news of Norton and Somervell's success at establishing their high camp at 26,800 ft. 'George believes he has seen their downward tracks some 700 ft below the summit,' Irvine wrote in his diary that day. 'I hope they've got to the top, but by God, I'd like to have a whack myself.'

With no sign of their colleagues, Mallory and Irvine set off for Camp IV, planning to meet them on their descent. 'George and I put the worst aspect on things ...' wrote Irvine: 'we decided to go up the North Col and be ready to fetch sick men down, or make an oxygen attempt ourselves a day later.' They spent that afternoon scanning Everest's upper slopes for signs of the returning climbers. At eight in the evening Norton and Somervell duly appeared, picking their way over the snow. It was Mallory and Noel Odell, already at the North Col to assist the bid, who went up to guide them down the final stretch. The party walked in an hour and a half later, to where the ever-reliable Irvine was brewing tea and soup. It was now that he discovered what Mallory already knew: Norton and Somervell had failed.

When Mallory and Bruce had passed their colleagues after aborting their bid on 2 June, Mallory had chosen to say nothing of the stirrings of his plan for a final push of his own. The buffeting wind had rendered meaningful conversation all but impossible, and it was as much as both parties could manage to exchange nods of acknowledgement. It was now that Mallory chose to lay his scheme bare, announcing to Norton that he was going for the summit again, and that he was taking Irvine.

Norton, physically spent though he must have been, tried to persuade him otherwise. Why Irvine? By far the most obvious choice of those climbers not yet used in the summit attempts was Noel Odell. A highly experienced mountaineer, Odell had acclimatized slowly, but having done so he had climbed strongly throughout the expedition. In fact he had adjusted so well to life in thin air that he spent his time on the mountain climbing without the need for any supplementary oxygen. But Mallory would not be swayed. He had decided on Irvine, and that was how it would remain. If Irvine's growing friendship with Mallory had won him a nomination for this final summit bid, it was his intimate knowledge of the oxygen systems that finally secured his place. As the expedition's oxygen officer, Odell was hardly a stranger to the apparatus, but he showed nothing like the natural aptitude which, to a technophobe such as Mallory, gave Irvine the air of an alchemist.

Beyond that, Mallory and Irvine complemented one another. While Mallory and Odell got on well enough, the latter was slow and methodical by nature. Mallory, on the other hand, existed on the sort of 'restless energy' that John Noel had observed during the week-long delay at Base Camp. It was the same near-hyperactive enthusiasm that Norton had witnessed, causing Mallory's nerves to 'tighten up like fiddle strings' when faced with a stiff challenge ahead. It was also quite likely that Mallory felt an obligation to his young partner, perhaps to assuage his disappointment at having been the 'bloody reserve'. Irvine had increasingly come to view Mallory as a mentor, and for that reason Mallory could be certain of his willingness to take instruction. As a rower, being asked to push himself to his physical limit, or beyond, was second nature to Irvine. Utterly in awe of George Mallory, the star climber, he was the perfect blend of stoicism and compliance. Odell, a more seasoned climber, would be far more likely to argue the toss if things got difficult. Whatever the reason for Mallory's choice, the die was now cast.

At Camp IV, on the evening of 5 June, Irvine made what would prove his final entry in his diary. 'My face is perfect agony,' he wrote. 'Have prepared two oxygen apparatus for our start tomorrow morning.'

He and Mallory woke the next day to begin their assault on the summit. It was a brilliant, sunny morning, if a little cold. Amid the general air of optimism, however, the condition of their two colleagues offered a chastening foretaste of what to expect if they themselves gained the highest reaches of the mountain. Howard Somervell looked a shell of the imposing climber that had so impressed on two Everest expeditions. As he prepared to head back to Camp III, Somervell handed Irvine something that might prove useful. It was a Kodak 'vest-pocket' camera, which he had used to photograph Norton during the hour, high on the mountain, that his friend had climbed on alone. Summoning his last shred of energy, Somervell then began his descent. Norton was in no position to join him: the expedition leader was suffering badly from snow blindness. His colleagues did what they could to make him comfortable, covering his tent with sleeping bags to make it as dark as possible.

Mallory and Irvine began their march from the North Col at around 8.40 am. Before they left Noel Odell snapped a final photograph of them, goggles pulled down, shouldering their oxygen cylinders – for Mallory, the equipment that would make the essential difference from the failed previous bids – as they prepared for the off. Any photographs of the two men higher up – or, indeed, on the summit – would have to be taken by Mallory and Irvine themselves, using Somervell's loaned camera.

As Mallory took his first strides from the safety of the North Col, he must have realized it was the last roll of the dice. He was 38 years old, and unlikely to get another chance at the mountain. His employers at Cambridge University would take a dim view of a second request for such an extended leave of absence. And after all he had asked of Ruth – a sacrifice measured in years, as time and again he had left their home and children – he simply couldn't afford to fail now. 'Darling, I wish you the best I can,' he had written to her in one of his final letters home, 'that your anxiety will be at an end before you get this, with the best news, which will also be the quickest. It is fifty to one against us but we'll have a whack yet and do ourselves proud. Great love to you.'

From the North Col they climbed quickly, making such good time that when they arrived at Camp V, at 25,500 ft, they were able to send down four of their eight porters the same evening.

The following day, 7 June, Mallory and Irvine at last reached the 26,800 ft of Camp VI, where they released the last of the porters, sending them on their descent with two notes for their teammates below. One was for Noel Odell, the man overlooked by Mallory for the final summit bid. Climbing a day behind his two colleagues, in support, Odell had spent 7 June making his way to Camp V. 'Dear Odell,' Mallory had written, 'We're awfully sorry to have left things in such a mess – our Unna Cooker rolled down the slope at the last moment. Be sure of getting back to [Camp] IV tomorrow in time to evacuate before dark, as I hope to. In the tent I must have left a compass – for the Lord's sake rescue it: we are here without.'

The state of the tent and Mallory's having sent a cooker tumbling down the mountain would have come as little surprise to Odell. Elegant as he was on rock, Mallory could be spectacularly ham-fisted. And absent-minded by nature, as the request for the compass confirmed, he was always leaving his teammates to clear up after him. 'He's a great dear,' Charles Bruce, the leader of the 1922 expedition, once remarked, 'but forgets his boots on all occasions.'

Mallory concluded his note to Odell with a report on the performance of the oxygen apparatus on which Irvine had worked so tirelessly. 'To here on [i.e. using] 90 atmospheres for the two days,' he wrote of the forty-eight hours since they had left the North Col. 'So we'll probably go on two cylinders – but it's a bloody load for climbing.' In 1924 a full cylinder of air had a pressure of 120 atmospheres. This means that Mallory and Irvine had used three-quarters of their air between Camps IV and VI.

The other note was for John Noel, the cinematographer now waiting patiently to capture the action from the North Col. In it were lines destined to become among the most haunting in the history of exploration: 'It won't be too early to start looking for us either crossing the rock band under the pyramid, or going up skyline at 8.0 pm.' Mallory had most probably meant to write 8 a.m., but was nevertheless well aware of his obligation to Noel. And it was in Mallory's own interest to ensure that they got the best pictures possible. If he and Irvine were to manage a successful summit bid, it wouldn't be just Noel's future livelihood that might depend on them.

The morning of 8 June broke clear and sharp, and sometime after breakfast Mallory and Irvine set off on the third and final summit attempt of the 1924 expedition to Mount Everest. When, from the high pass of the Pang La, the members of the expedition had traced a line of ascent along Everest's North-East Ridge, they had noted the pronounced notch in the skyline they came to know as the Second Step. Opinion on the best way to deal with it varied, as shown by the differing approaches the final two summit teams took to it. Norton and Somervell chose to traverse along the thick limestone of the Yellow Band in order to avoid the Second Step entirely. It was a route that took them into the vast ice gully later known as the Great Couloir instead of along the shoulder of the North-East Ridge. Mallory saw things differently. As a 'ridge climber', he would always prefer the quickest line to the crest that offered suitably good holds for climbing. When he and Irvine set out that morning, he selected a route that would take them directly up through the cliffs of the Yellow Band, bringing them to the base of the Second Step.

Noel Odell received his message from Mallory after arriving at Camp V on 7 June, and the following day he set out for Camp VI alone. As morning turned to afternoon, the clouds began to roll in, a characteristic typical of the pre-monsoon conditions. A geologist by profession, Odell was carrying with him samples of rocks that he believed might represent the first fossils found on Everest. In a state of high excitement about what his samples might contain, at 12.50 p.m. he looked into the sky and saw the clouds part. His gaze was drawn to two small specks moving along the summit ridge. 'My eyes became fixed', he wrote later, 'on one tiny black spot silhouetted on a small snow-crest beneath a rock step in the ridge; the black spot moved. Another black spot became apparent and moved up to join the other on the crest.' Odell was convinced he had seen Mallory and Irvine making good progress on the Second Step, 'going strong for the top'. He thought them a little late in starting – perhaps Irvine had delayed them, unable to resist one final tinker with the oxygen apparatus. Still, they seemed to be going well enough and, excited by what news they might ultimately bring, Odell continued on toward Camp VI. By the time he arrived at the high, exposed location, at 26,800 ft, the weather had deteriorated and it had begun to snow.

The inside of the tent was, just as Mallory had written, a jumble of gear. Concerned that his two friends might be forced to turn back, to beat a hasty retreat in the worsening conditions, Odell headed out into the storm, shouting and yodelling in a bid to guide them down. When his cries received no answer, he returned to camp to wait out the blizzard. When it stopped sometime later, there was still no sign of the two climbers. It was now that Odell made his way back to Camp IV, on the North Col. Mallory's note suggested that he too meant to reach it by nightfall, but when Odell got there he found, not surprisingly, only the teammates he had left the previous day.

That night, the vast North Face of the mountain sat cold and impassive as, beneath a bright moon, Odell looked for signs of descending mountaineers. At Camp VI earlier in the day he had found, amid the chaos of the tent, one of a number of magnesium flares that Mallory intended to take with him to the summit. Even so he still had several other flares, as well as a lantern and a torch. As Odell scanned the mountain in the darkness, there was nothing.

The next morning he headed back to Camp V, accompanied by a small team of porters. With no sign of Mallory and Irvine at 25,500 ft, he sent back the porters and carried on to Camp VI alone. It was here that his worst fears began to crystallize.

He spent the next two hours climbing higher still, following the route that his knowledge of Mallory told him the two men might have taken. All he found was the mountain. In a state of rising despair, Noel Odell bowed to the inevitable: George Leigh Mallory and Andrew Comyn Irvine were lost.

Whatever had happened to them, only Mallory and Irvine knew the outcome of their summit bid. If they had failed, it would represent the final blow in what had proved a protracted and gruelling battle against the mountain. Yet perhaps they had perished bringing word of a different outcome. Perhaps, having devoted the best part of four years of his life to the mountain, George Mallory had, after all, been the first man to reach the summit of Everest. If so, it was news they never got to dispatch. At some point below the Second Step, one of them fell. Whether it was Mallory or Irvine, the result was the same, roped together as they were. Tired and dehydrated, the very method by which one climber might arrest the fall of his partner now worked against them. Mallory would have recognized their predicament instantly. With a drop of some 8,000 ft to the Rongbuk Glacier below, he would have sought to drive his ice axe into the snow and arrest their fall. Instead, they gathered speed, both men falling until, perhaps snagging on a piece of rock, the rope pulled tight.

Mallory had been in similar situations before. In 1909, when he climbed in the Alps with his great friend and mentor Geoffrey Winthrop Young, he had found himself similarly strung, suspended above a glacier on the 12,545-ft peak of the Nesthorn. On that occasion the rope held, saving Mallory's life. Not so now.

The two men had finally tackled Everest together, but, when the rope binding Mallory to Irvine broke, each was consigned to his own course down the mountain. Mallory's ultimately took him to a snow terrace at around 27,000 ft – roughly the altitude from which he had set out that morning. After the chastening which had greeted their arrival on the mountain, Everest reserved the bloodiest battle for last. During Mallory's sliding descent, his right leg broke, just above the ankle, both tibia and fibula, at the point where they entered his boot. And, unlike his encounter with the crevasse on his descent from the North Col, this time when he fell Mallory's ice axe was wrenched from his grasp. It was a misfortune which left him with nothing more than his hands to try and halt his progress.

Despite the strength in his fingers, what must have been frantic clawing at the slope caused his right arm to break. At some point thereafter he suffered the last of his injuries, a heavy puncture wound to the forehead. And then he stopped. In a desperate attempt to provide his right leg with some sort of protection, he placed the left leg over it.

As the sun disappeared beneath the clouds, in the world far below lay every single living creature on God's earth. Night plunged the mountainside into impossible cold, while far away, in England, Ruth remained blissfully unaware of her husband's plight.

If, in his final moments, Mallory had lapsed in and out of consciousness, what might he have imagined? Noel Odell, reliable as ever, coming to his aid. If he did, the apparition would have been fleeting, insubstantial like the fronds of cloud floating below. Perhaps he had called to Irvine. Drained as he was, the shock fast consuming his body, he would have struggled to make himself heard against the roar of wind – neither cruel nor triumphant: just a blast of air high on the slopes of the mountain known to the native Tibetans not as Everest but as Chomolungma, Goddess Mother of the World.

A week later, on 16 June, *The Times* carried a report of the failed summit bid of Edward Norton and Howard Somervell. Alongside it ran an account of the rescue of the four porters from the North Col that had been successful thanks largely to Somervell's efforts. The article was written by George Mallory.

9

The Leader Must Not Fall

S WINGING WITH MEASURED force, Conrad Anker brought the point of his axe down hard, watching as it glanced off the hard-packed ice. Behind him, Leo Houlding followed closely. The two men inched their way upward, two tiny figures on the frozen expanse of the great snow wall which led to the North Col of Everest. When they had set out that morning, 21 May 2007, dressed once more in period climbing gear, Anker had been glad of the feel of the glacier beneath his hobnailed boots. It was a part of the mountain where, for the first time, the terrain steepened sufficiently for climbers to need to wear crampons, and for that reason was known to modern climbers as Crampon Point. Their climb of Ring Ri, a week previously, had taken them over mostly rocky terrain; today they would discover what the snow-laden slopes of Everest itself had felt like to the pioneers of eight decades ago. It was on these very slopes that the deaths of seven porters had brought the 1922 Everest expedition to a close. Two years later, they had been the scene of Howard Somervell's daring rescue of four porters trapped by bad weather.

Anker and Houlding were on a trial run, climbing just enough of the great wall to test the gear on suitably demanding terrain. As history lessons went, however, it was proving a rude introduction. Anker's ice axe rose and fell with an expert rhythm, but it was exhausting work as the American laboured to chop a series of small steps into the ice. Of all the changes to mountaineering technique in the twentieth century, the cutting of steps, or rather the need not to, had been one of the most significant. It had not just transformed how mountains were climbed, but had brought terrain once regarded as impossible within the modern climber's compass.

As he toiled away, the American was forced to pause repeatedly for breath. Quite apart from the draining cocktail of effort and elevation, Anker was at a distinct disadvantage to his illustrious forebears. To the alpinists of the 1920s, step-cutting would have been only too familiar. Indeed, the Swiss guides employed by the early mountaineers viewed it as a positive art form, even holding competitions on Alpine glaciers to see which local man could carve the most elegant staircase. George Mallory, who had considerable Alpine experience of his own, had been a renowned step-cutter. He had even written to *The Times* on the subject, explaining that, not being natural mountaineers, the Sherpa porters were thankful for the steps cut by the ice axe of the 'sahib'.

Since the discovery of 'Irvine's axe', in 1933, the nature of the tool had changed markedly. The earliest models, such as those used by Jacques Balmat and Michel-Gabriel Paccard in their pioneering 1786 ascent of Mont Blanc, were little more than sticks with metal hooks attached. It was a design that remained largely unchanged until the inter-war period, when tools sporting shorter handles began to offer considerably improved performance. Then, in the late 1960s, a Yosemite climbing legend named Yvon Chouinard created something truly innovative: an axe with a short, curved handle and a curved or 'radiused' pick. Designed to follow the arc of the arm as it struck the mountain, the modern ice axe had been born. When this combined with developments in another specialist ice tool – the crampon – the death knell for the elegant art of step-cutting, at which at George Mallory had been so proficient, was finally sounded.

Despite being one of the oldest aids to be used by climbers, crampons were one of the last to gain widespread acceptance. References to 'spiked shoes' being used on treacherous terrain can be traced back as far as the sixteenth century, when Italian woodcutters wore *grapettes*, a system of spikes designed to prevent slipping on logs. George Mallory, like other British mountain-eers of his era, believed in climbing by 'fair means', free of any 'artificial' aid that might compensate for lack of technique. Most British mountaineers considered crampons to be cheating, until the intervention of a number of pioneering individuals began to persuade them otherwise.

In 1909 a brilliant young British alpinist by the name of Oscar Eckenstein – an occasional house guest of Geoffrey Young's in those days at Pen y Pass – was just one of a number of writers in climbing publications who began reporting the incredible feats possible on glaciated terrain when wearing these 'spiked shoes'. However, it would be many more decades before his fellow countrymen accepted their legitimacy. Part of the problem lay in the boots worn by the early Everest climbers. Cut from soft leather, they meant that, when a climber had bound crampons tightly enough to be effective, the straps attaching the spikes had a tendency to restrict circulation. The higher the elevation, the greater the consequent risk of frostbite was deemed to be. But, just as Mallory had come to appreciate the benefits of oxygen by 1924, so climbers came to realize the advantage that crampons could offer. Even so, Edward Norton dismissed them as 'useless' anywhere above 23,000 ft, and for this reason the climbers under his command wore them no further than the North Col.

The boots that Anker and Houlding wore as they edged their way toward the North Col offered an alternative. Instead of using crampon spikes, Mallory and his teammates gained trac-tion on snow and ice by means of hobnails, driven through a leather sole with the points downward. A layer of felt was then added to reduce 'conductivity', metal nails having the unfortu-nate effect of drawing heat away from the foot and down into the ground. For increased purchase, V-shaped cleats, commonly used by lumberjacks and known as 'tricouni' nails, were then added to the outside of the sole.

Being not nearly as sniffy as their British counterparts, Continental climbers had happily continued to push the boundaries of crampon technique and design until, in 1932, a blacksmith named Laurent Grivel, from Courmayeur in Italy, came up with a small but ingenious innovation. With the addition of two front spikes or 'points' to the spikes traditionally located on the sole of the foot, a technique would soon be born that would change the sport of mountaineering for ever. Known as 'front pointing', where step-cutting had made it necessary for climbers to zigzag back and forth across a slope, front points allowed a climber to tackle a face directly. Climbing like cats, mountaineers could now take on not just vertical but overhanging terrain, thanks to four points of contact with the ice: an axe in each hand, and formidable armoured claws on each foot.

Conrad Anker would have been grateful for either as he laboured up the slope. The blue ice that covered it was stubborn and unyielding, and it wasn't long before the soft metal head of his period axe buckled completely. Below him, Houlding scanned for another hazard common on this part of Everest – one George Mallory had known only too well – crevasses. However, it wasn't the ones you could see that you needed to worry about, but those hidden by a 'snow bridge'. If the bridge concealing one of these lurking monsters gave way, a climber might find himself plunged hundreds of feet into the earth. Climbing unroped, as Mallory had been at the time, had been unwise, yet it was hardly uncommon on such a descent. Without the protective aids enjoyed by modern climbers, which Houlding and Anker used as a matter of instinct, the only way for the early climbers to harness themselves to a rock face was by means of a piton hammered into a crack, or by winding their rope around a spike of rock. In keeping with their philosophy of climbing by 'fair means', many British climbers of the period considered such protection unsporting. Climbing when roped together offered some protection, but only the 'second' – the climber following up the face, with the leader secure above him – could afford a mishap. If a lead climber missed his footing when roped to his colleagues, there was a reasonable chance he would take them down with him. Houlding and Anker discussed this as they worked their way up the slope. In Mallory's era, Houlding observed, climbers lived, and all too often died, by a simple maxim: 'The leader must not fall.'

Following the advice of Russell Brice, the Altitude team had delayed leaving Base Camp by several days in a bid to better prepare themselves for the challenges ahead. They had departed on 17 May, ten days after arriving at the foot of Everest. After posing for the requisite photographs, they set off on the 14-mile march to the 21,000 ft of Advanced Base Camp. The ascent was a gradual one, taking the climbers for the first time on to the glaciated slopes of the main Rongbuk Glacier, and they broke their journey at an interim camp that evening. In the 1920s, this interim camp had been used as a supply depot, one of the chain of provisioning stations en route to the North Col christened the 'via dolorosa', after the route along which Jesus carried his cross on his way to be crucified. Leo Houlding took the opportunity to break his communications embargo and call his wife, Jessica. It was her birthday.

Compared with the ascent from the south, from Nepal, the early approaches on the northern side of Everest are relatively undramatic. The great snow wall that leads to the North Col is certainly treacherous, yet it in no way rivals the ever-changing maze of crevasses on the southern side that appear as great fractures in the mountain, part of an infamous obstacle known as the Khumbu Icefall, a constantly moving river of ice that can shift by as much as a metre a day. Rightly regarded as one of the most dangerous stretches of that entire summit route, it is a challenge that must be met not long after leaving Base Camp. Chief among its myriad dangers are blocks of ice or 'seracs' the size of small houses which can, when weakened by the sun, come crashing down without warning. Woe betide any climbing team standing below. The start of the northern approach was tame by comparison – a series of incremental climbs and descents. On the Tibetan side, the principal danger existed far higher up, in the extended period of time that climbers must spend above 27,000 ft, on the long, sloping shoulder of the North-East Ridge.

To a man, the Altitude team had been pleased to get going. Conrad Anker and Jimmy Chin were glad at last to be 'moving up', and both Leo Houlding and Gerry Moffatt were just thankful to be free of the hustle and hassle of Base Camp. As they resumed their climb to ABC the next morning, vast towers of glacial ice reared into the air, some as much as 100 ft high. And they completed the march through the heaviest snowfall since their arrival – a storm that started at two in the afternoon and blew until well after nightfall. When Houlding finally reached camp, however, he wondered if they hadn't just gone round in a big circle. Climbers on satellite phones or cruising wireless internet connections were a common sight wherever you climbed in the world these days, but he hadn't expected so many of them here. ABC seemed to be just a smaller version of the tented metropolis they had left behind the previous day. During the pre-monsoon season, the permanent encampment of red and yellow mess tents was stationed on shale platforms and serviced by numerous yak trains. Climbers returning from battle higher up the mountain understandably came to see it as something of a sanctuary.

Members of the early Everest expeditions viewed it with mixed emotions. In 1924, Mallory's haste to get oxygen to their 'Camp III' had ended in disaster. On the other hand, the shale base it provided for tents was far preferable to sleeping on snow: when body heat warmed the ground sufficiently to melt the snow, sleeping climbers would wake the next morning wet and grumpy.

Tent technology, such it was, was evolving slowly in the 1920s, but while polar explorers were experimenting with gabardine, a fabric that was both wind- and snow-proof, the climbing parties sent out by the Mount Everest Committee stuck rigidly, quite literally after a wet, freezing night, with canvas. Tents were of a rudimentary triangular design, supported by a ridge pole, and doors were laced shut. Any flurry of driving snow would soon discover the eyelet holes. One of the more curious features common in the early tents taken to Everest was a vent incorporated into the roof. It was an age when diseases were thought to be caused by stale air, and so sleeping in draughty houses, with windows left open, was common. Even so, given the extreme conditions on the mountain, such emphasis on hardiness bordered on masochism. Not until 1975 did the tents now taken for granted by modern adventurers begin to appear. That was the year an American equipment company called The North Face introduced a tent designed around an octahedron, whose dome-like shape dissipated the load of a blizzard or snowstorm across numerous plane faces. If it did collapse, it would simply spring back into shape when it was cleared of snow.

By the time the Altitude team pitched up, ABC had bid farewell to a multitude of climbing teams. All that remained of them now was their waste. When the sun climbed high in the sky, strafing the camp with UV rays, the stench from the refuse and toilets could be intense. And the conditions could be painfully hot. For every elevation gain of 1,000 ft, UV radiation increases by about 3 per cent. Each morning, the Altitude team woke to find a layer of frost melting on the inside of their tents. But minimum daily highs of 35 °C, amplified by the glare reflecting from the snow, made life seriously uncomfortable later in the day. 'On Everest', Anker often reminded Houlding, 'you're either too damned hot or too damned cold.' In 1924 Irvine had suffered terribly from the sun. And, after months spent worrying about how he would deal with the cold, Leo Houlding now felt as if he was getting cooked. Others were feeling the heat too: Anthony Geffen, for one, found himself with a severe case of sunburn, his face deeply reddened and blistered.

The heat and poor sanitation of ABC meant bugs and viruses were an ever-present danger. For this reason, Anker emphasized constantly the importance of what he referred to as 'self-care' – the need always to boil drinking water and to wash your hands in sterile cleaning solution. Even if Houlding thought it occasionally verged on the obsessive, it was good advice: the damage a virus could do to an expedition team could sink its summit plans overnight.

In the days following their arrival at ABC, word arrived of another fatality high on the mountain. Libor Kozak, from the Czech Republic, was 47 years old, and had been making for the summit early on the morning of 17 May. When he began to feel unwell, he had taken the sensible decision to turn round, making for his team's high camp at 27,000 ft. Wise though this action had been, it proved to be too late. His condition had deteriorated rapidly, until the effort of moving proved overwhelming and he succumbed to the altitude – what Leo Houlding referred to as 'the silent menace'. That the mountain had brought such an abrupt end to the summit ambitions of a man widely regarded as a strong climber was something not lost on the Altitude team.

On the morning of 27 May, in the pale, nylon light of a large dome tent, Leo Houlding and Conrad Anker once again ran through the now familiar ritual of dressing like 1920s climbers as they prepared to step out on to the narrow plateau of the North Col. They were there on the team's first rotation, the first of two climbs to higher elevations designed to prepare them for their final summit push. High above them, the top of the mountain was being lashed by ferocious winds. The jet stream had covered it with a thick veil of cloud that now rendered it all but invisible. The Altitude team had come up from ABC the previous day, Anker leading the line, Kevin Thaw and Leo Houlding moving strongly behind him, as they negotiated the last hazard of the ascent, a ladder spanning a deep crevasse.

Gerry Moffatt, the least experienced member of the team, had opted for a softly-softly approach to this, waiting for one of his colleagues to arrive before making his crossing. He knew that an ill-timed trip might prove his final contribution to the expedition, being only too aware of the misplaced footstep that had once left George Mallory hacking his way out of a potentially fatal dilemma. On the plateau itself, the col's soaring ice cliffs and tumbling precipices were as dramatic as they were beautiful – nature both wild and pristine.

The latter could not be said for the camp. Established in advance by a team of Russell Brice's Sherpas, it had stood in the sheltered recess of an ice wall. So strong were the winds that battered that part of the mountain, however, that the team had arrived to find it buried under several feet of snow. The effort required to dig it out, and so soon after the 2,000 ft ascent separating the col from ABC, was exhausting. Only Conrad Anker seemed energized by the experience. Since leaving Base Camp he had relished the fact that the team had joined battle with the mountain proper at last, and, when he had finished freeing the last of the tents, he had spent the remainder of the afternoon levelling the platforms on which they stood.

The North Col was a camp he particularly enjoyed. The large dome tent in which he and Houlding now dressed offered one of the few opportunities to to spend any time socializing with their Sherpa escorts. Once they climbed above the North Col, they would be forced into small, two-man tents all the way to the 27,000 ft of their high camp, the narrow, icy ledges of their Camp IV, where the mountain was as miserly with tent space as it was with oxygen. Their pulling on their replica gear at 23,000 ft would also prove a significant professional landmark for Anthony Geffen: filming a reconstruction of Mallory and Irvine at the North Col would constitute nothing less than the highest period-costume drama in history.

As both men applied the finishing touches to their apparel, making fast their leather motorcycling helmets and adjusting their goggles, Ken Sauls, the expedition's cameraman preparing to film them, warned them to take no chances. Even 6,000 ft below the summit, a harsh wind was now approaching speeds of 60 mph. With the wind chill sending temperatures to −20 °C and below, it would be crucial to leave no skin exposed. Houlding didn't need reminding. On the evening of their arrival, he had been making minor adjustments to his replica pack and boots in the foot well of his own tent. Despite the relative shelter, the ambient temperature had been so cold that he had only been able to work for a few minutes at a time before needing to plunge his hands back into his gloves.

When Houlding and Anker at last emerged, the contrast with the protection offered by the tent was brutal. Directly in front of them the wind scoured the ground, stirring up great flurries of snow before diving off the mountain and into the void beneath. As they moved from the lee of the tent into the teeth of the wind, it bit hard. The close weave of their jackets seemed to keep the worst of it at bay – to begin with at least – but as they made their way across the plateau they were left with little option but to lean fully 45 degrees into the oncoming gale just to stay on their feet. And all the while an icy blast snatched up shards of snow and ice and flung them into their faces.

George Mallory had described it as a wind in which no man could survive for more than an hour. Leo Houlding needed just half that time to accept Mallory's judgement: just thirty minutes after stepping on to the col, he and Anker were forced to retreat back to the safety of their tent. This was the point at which their experiment with period clothing would come to an end. It was only as he was getting changed that Houlding realized he could no longer feel his toes. He was also shivering uncontrollably. Ming Ma, one of the Sherpa contingent, now set about massaging his feet, just as George Mallory had done for his colleague the geographer Edward Wheeler on that first visit to the North Col in 1921. After ten minutes of vigorous rubbing, Ming Ma's efforts seemed to be having little effect, and the concern that Houlding read on the Sherpa's face was all too evident. Houlding had every right to be concerned too, knowing that, at extreme altitude, the body's way of coping is to save what supply there is of poorly oxygenated blood for the brain and core organs. Hands and feet are useful tools for a climber, but are not essential for the survival of the mother ship. This time, however, he had been lucky, and eventually, the familiar pinpricks of returning circulation began to percolate into his toes. Even so, it was another hour before he was warm again.

As Houlding lay staring at the ceiling of the tent, he wondered out loud what it must have been like for the early explorers, seeking refuge from the blast of the elements under nothing more than canvas. Wherever he climbed, he regarded his tent as something of a sanctuary, what he called his 'zone of salvation'. What must it have been like to battle the most extreme elements and then not have a warm, dry shelter to return to? The replica clothing lay in a heap next to him. It worked, up to point, but the lack of feeling in his toes had given him a scare. His accident on Cerro Torre, and the excruciating descent that followed, jarring his injured foot repeatedly while being carried by Kevin Thaw, had given him as much of an insight as he needed into what life might been like with an irreparable injury. George Mallory might have thought 'the game was worth a finger', but he didn't.

Two days later, when they arrived back at Advanced Base Camp from their filming trip to the North Col, everyone was tired. A number of the team were nursing viruses, Jimmy Chin, Kevin Thaw and Ken Sauls among them. In his online diary, Houlding noted that even Conrad Anker, a man 'with the thermostat of a polar bear', had been visibly shaken by the experience. Draining though the effort had been, the team didn't get long to recover. On 1 June they were back at the North Col again, on their second rotation on the mountain. Spending two nights on the wind-blasted eyrie, from here they would climb higher still, to their Camp II, at 24,600 ft. It was a part of their acclimatization training that came with a kicker. After three decades on the mountain, Russell Brice had developed ways of assessing how a climber was coping with the unique challenges of Everest. The ascent to Camp II was in effect a test of how well the Altitude team had adapted to life in thin air. If any member of the team failed to cover the climb – 1,500 vertical feet – in the six-hour time frame Brice was now giving them, his part in the expedition would be over. It was as simple as that.

When the climbers emerged for breakfast on the North Col the following morning, the subdued atmosphere made it immediately apparent that something was wrong. Jimmy Chin had received a phone call from his sister in the United States the previous evening to say that their mother had taken a turn for the worse in her battle with cancer. Conrad Anker was one of the first people he consulted. The two men had a long discussion about what Chin's next course of action should be. Brice's Sherpas aside, Chin had more experience of the mountain's upper reaches than anybody. In addition to being the expedition's stills photographer, he was also competent with the team's high-definition video camera. Should anything happen to Ken Sauls before they reached the crucial free climb of the Second Step, Chin's expertise and eye for a shot would make him a crucial reserve.

The numerous trips that Chin and Anker had made together meant that the two of them were extremely close, and on this expedition they had confided in one another regularly. Whenever Anker had a problem, it was invariably Chin's opinion he sought first, and his fellow American almost always backed him up. He was also a mine of useful information for the less-experienced members of the team, an ever-reliable source of advice and reassurance to both Leo Houlding and Gerry Moffatt. Leaving with a job half-finished was something he had never done before, and it was a record he was keen to keep unblemished. As someone who made a living from expeditions, Chin was only too aware of his professional obligations. More than that, he also considered his teammates to be his friends. In the days before mobile and satellite phones covered the planet in a web of 'connectivity', Chin would have had no decision to make. News, good or bad, simply took so long to reach a climber perched high above the earth, or a polar explorer trudging alone across the Arctic Circle, that situations such as the one that now faced him invariably resolved themselves.

The next morning, 3 June, as the team prepared to make the climb to the 24,600 ft of Camp II, it was without Jimmy Chin. In the end it had been Anker, in consultation with Geffen, who helped him make a difficult, if unavoidable, decision. As Chin had made his way back to Base Camp the previous morning, he had done so with the understanding of his teammates. But his departure represented something of a dent in the team's resources, and compelled Ken Sauls to offer an assessment of their status. Down a good man before their summit push had even begun, the higher they climbed, Sauls pointed out, the more likely things were to get 'fucking radical'. On mountains of lesser stature than Everest, an ascent such as the one to Camp II would constitute a modest climb. Climbing from 23,000 to 24,600 ft, on the tallest mountain on earth, however, was a different matter. If the body of one of the Altitude team chose not to co-operate, if this was the day the legs, lungs or heart said no, they would soon find themselves following in Jimmy Chin's boot tracks. But the six-hour window Brice had given them two days previously was now the only thing that mattered, and at 8 a.m., they headed out.

The unremitting winds that scoured the North Col were renowned and reviled by climbers in equal measure, and the part of the summit route immediately above it hardly had a reputation for being welcoming. On the slopes that led to Camp II, climbers often had to endure violent, gusting crosswinds which ripped from west to east, regularly knocking them off their feet. Clipping to the fixed lines one after another, the Altitude team wound their way up through snow and ice, grateful for what were, relatively speaking, calm conditions. Though bumped by the occasional gust, they climbed well, and after five hours of effort Leo Houlding marched into Camp II not far behind Conrad Anker, and closely followed by Kevin Thaw. When Gerry Moffatt materialized over the crest to join them half an hour later it meant that, crucially, each and every member of the summit team had made the cut-off point – they were ready to make their push for the top.

But it wasn't just the climbers who made the ascent to Camp II. Anthony Geffen reached it, utterly spent, after 10½ gruelling hours. It was a personal target he had set himself before leaving for Everest, but was as high as he would be going. Houlding's reward for making the climb to Camp II in the allotted time was a restless night. The increase in elevation meant, once again, a drop in temperature, and he had clambered into his sleeping bag still dressed in his down suit. Despite being one of the slighter members of the group, which meant he had more room than most, the experience was as uncomfortable as it was unfamiliar, sharing what space there was with water bottles and socks crammed alongside him to prevent them freezing.

Over the course of the next few days, the remaining teams on the mountain began to conclude their business. Advanced Base Camp began to empty, the trickle of teams turning into a steady stream, some utterly elated at their success, others stony-faced, completely exhausted from their efforts. Inevitably, a number remarked on what awaited the Altitude team. Going up so late in the season, didn't they mind climbing in the snows that would soon arrive with the monsoon? Leo Houlding was glad to see the back of them – and not just because of the questions. The presence of so many 'non-climbers' unsettled him. Accustomed to mountains with far fewer climbing teams, during the peak-hour traffic of the previous weeks he had come to regard ABC as a circus – one whose rings were occupied by 'garbage, frostbite, egos and attitude'. 'I'd rather take my chance with the monsoon than this bunch of psychos,' he wrote scathingly in one web dispatch.

By 6 June, plans for the Altitude team's summit attempt were at last falling into place. High above Advanced Base Camp, a team of twenty-nine of Russell Brice's Sherpas were putting oxygen supplies and provisions in place. The day was one of crucial significance. In 1924, it was on 6 June that George Mallory and Sandy Irvine had set out from the North Col on the last climb they would ever make. Before departing, Noel Odell had photographed them for what proved to be the very last time. Irvine had his back to the camera as he prepared to go. Mallory, meanwhile, fiddled with something in his chest pocket. Could it have been the goggles that Conrad Anker found there seventy-five years later? Among Irvine's equipment was another camera, the Kodak vest-pocket model loaned to him by Howard Somervell. 'Irvine's camera', as it came to be known, remains one of the great missing pieces in the jigsaw of Mallory's and Irvine's disappearance. The film within it might well contain images confirming that the two men reached the top, and which might be as spectacular as they would be conclusive. When climbing from the north, certain views on the southern side of Everest, such as the neighbouring peak of Lhotse, are visible only from the summit. Preserved by the frozen air, perhaps the camera records Mallory or Irvine posing triumphantly with such views in the background. Until the camera is found – perhaps even on the body of Sandy Irvine himself – the mystery will remain.

The following evening, 7 June, Monica Piris, the expedition team's doctor, arrived to check up on Ken Sauls. The virus the cameraman had picked up earlier in the expedition had been reluctant to leave, and during the past week an unpleasant cough had grown more serious. It was so bad that he was now confined to his tent. It didn't take Piris long to diagnose that Sauls's condition wasn't improving.

In 1924 it was a hacking cough that had caused Howard Somervell to bring up part of his own larynx as he made for the summit on 4 June. Somervell's cough had begun as a respiratory infection, and Piris thought she detected something similar in Sauls – the early signs of the onset of bronchitis. Mallory himself had spoken of a cough 'fit to tear one's guts', and Sauls was now coughing so hard that if he attempted to go any higher his condition was all but guaranteed to get worse. If it did, climbers in similar situations had been known to crack ribs. At sea level such an injury was relatively minor, if painful. At high altitude, however, it was likely to compromise everything from Sauls's decision-making to the already complicated business of breathing. The Altitude team's tilt at the summit was due to begin in a little over three days' time. But it was obvious to anyone within earshot of the cough that now wracked Ken Sauls's body that he wasn't going any higher.

The collateral damage induced by life at high altitude had been a feature of Everest expeditions ever since the first team arrived on the mountain. The early punishment meted out in 1924 had left Mallory contemplating how many they would need to 'strike off' from their dwindling army of climbers. Now the strength of Anker's own battalion, or rather the lack of it, was something that concerned the American deeply. If Jimmy Chin's departure had dented his confidence, losing Sauls was to prove a hammer blow. Both Kevin Thaw and Leo Houlding were experienced climbers, but within the space of just five days the expedition had lost its two most experienced Everest hands – a third of the summit team. Two members of the production crew had also returned to Base Camp, victims of the ever-pernicious altitude sickness. As far as Anker was concerned, things could hardly be worse. With the exception of the Sherpas, among whose number he could at least still count on the talents of the indomitable Phurba Tashe, he now found himself the only member of the team with direct experience of what it took to stand on the summit.

In their early rounds of discussions, Conrad Anker and Anthony Geffen had pulled together a back-up plan detailing who might step into which role in the event of one of the team falling by the wayside. Yet even their most pessimistic scenario had never accounted for two of their most experienced team members having to retire. That these were the main cameraman for their attempt on the Second Step and their dedicated stills photographer, both good friends to boot, only made the pill more bitter to swallow. As Anker now saw it, his was an army shorn of its principal front-line officers. He had spent most of his adult life on expeditions of one kind of another; he knew the sound of wheels falling off when he heard them.

The 'Come to Jesus' meeting held on the night of 8 June came at a tense moment. Here they were, Anker said, entering the second week of June, and the monsoon was about to 'bite them in the ass'. His family back home would be monitoring events closely via the internet, knowing only too well how the weather could catch out climbers in the Himalayas. Base Camp was deserted, he went on; all the other climbing teams had gone, and now their own was all but in pieces. Now, the American feared, the team wouldn't have the strength for the battle to come. Whereas George Mallory had only a vague idea of what awaited him on the Second Step, Anker knew precisely what to expect. The situation they now found themselves in seemed impossible; with so little summit experience between them, could they go on? Anthony Geffen respected Anker's concerns and considerable experience but urged him to think positively. They had gone a long way, come so close to the top; he was keen not to give up until they had explored all the possibilities. When Anker walked out of the dinner tent on his own that night, everyone could see that something was wrong. Conrad Anker was feeling the pressure.

Anker spent much of the following day in his tent. It left the other team members feeling more than a little uncertain. Geffen made anxious satellite phone calls to London to see what, if anything, might be done to save the project if they couldn't go on. Recreating the climb elsewhere was an option, but it couldn't make up for the loss of the opportunity to take on the Second Step as they had planned. Leo Houlding was keen to keep going. Like everyone else, he had invested time, energy and not inconsiderable emotion to get himself to this point. For all his flippant remarks about 'high-altitude walking' he was first and last a climber. Having come this far, he was more than a little reluctant to head home without having even seen the legendary

Second Step. He recalled the motto that he and Anker had discussed when they had chopped steps on the great snow wall that led to the North Col more than two weeks previously: the leader must not fall.

Conrad Anker's sense of obligation to his team-mates was almost overwhelming. He was an honourable man, almost archaically so. At times this meant he could be pathologically earnest, but he felt his responsibilities deeply. Now they presented themselves as a checklist of priorities. In free climbing the Second Step, they had hoped in some small way to pay tribute to George Mallory's pioneering spirit. He felt an obligation to the team-mates with whom he now climbed and he also felt an obligation to Geffen. He had realised from their first meeting that Geffen was a driven man – it was one of the reasons they had clicked – but only once they had arrived on Everest had he come to realise just how driven he was. And only now could Anker appreciate just how demanding an undertaking this film and expedition was. Now, with time running out on the mountain, and the effect of living at high altitude taking its toll, Anker was questioning in his mind if his determination to carry out his obligation to the Altitude team was coming into direct conflict with the obligation he regarded as the most important of all: the need to return safely to his wife and family. For him, it had become an agonising choice.

In the environments in which he made his living, climbing in even the most innocuous conditions could have tragic results. Just as a relatively calm Denali had caught Mugs Stump off guard in 1992, so Shishapangma had tricked Alex Lowe just seven years later. Professional climbers liked to reassure themselves that commercial expeditions, such as a film project, were different, less laden with risk than those made in pursuit of notable firsts. The problem was that Mother Nature failed to see the distinction.

Anker raised his concerns in telephone calls home. Jenni Lowe-Anker had indeed been monitoring the team's progress online. Before Anker had left for Everest, both he and his wife had been keenly aware of the whisper of eerie portents that surrounded the trip. Here he was, going to make a film about a dead guy he had found five months before the shattering event that had changed both of their lives for ever. Was his obsession with understanding what had happened to George Mallory exactly eighty-three years earlier worth what he felt he was putting his family through? Jenni was, of course, concerned that Anker might be taking an enormous risk. As she studied the satellite imagery of the weather on her computer screen every day, she could see for herself how the weather window was closing and the monsoon was coming in all too quickly. 'You need to be confident that you can make it,' she recalls telling Anker on the satellite phone. 'But if you have a chance to climb the Second Step, I want you to do it. I want you to go for it.' Only now, with his wife's blessing, would Anker have the conviction to go on.

10

Psalm 103

IN APRIL 2007, just a few weeks before setting out for Everest, Conrad Anker modelled his period climbing clothing in the kitchen of his home in Montana. 'Would you climb Everest dressed like this?' he asked his wife, Jenni, and the children, as they sat around the table. The response was one of good-natured indulgence, save for one dissenting voice: 11-year-old Isaac, the youngest of the Lowe-Anker boys. 'I wouldn't climb Everest,' he said ruefully.

The sense of foreboding that Jenni Lowe-Anker experienced before her husband's departure was something the families of all climbers got used to. Jenni's anxiety was rooted in – the family's painful experience with the Himalayas and what took place in the months following Anker's previous visit to Everest. But rare was the wife of a climber untroubled by a nightmare of her loved one in peril. Before setting out in 1924, George Mallory had famously confided to his Cambridge friend Geoffrey Keynes that conditions on Everest were so ferocious that the expedition would be 'more like war than adventure'. He even doubted he would return alive. Anker regarded modern expeditions, particularly those that offered no prospect of a first ascent or other groundbreaking achievement, to be a variation on that theme. 'It's like volunteering for a risky foreign war,' he said, 'when everything is peaceful at home.'

The price that far-off peaks exact from those foolish enough to develop an infatuation with them can be a high one, but it is those left behind who must pick up the pieces when things go wrong. The pain of parting from his wife and family, the 'fearful tug' of which he had written to his father, was something that never got any easier for George Mallory, for, despite her reservations before his departure, he and Ruth were very much in love, as both the extent and the nature of their correspondence proved. In 1999, when Anker and his research team discovered Mallory's body, they found on it a number of documents. One thing they failed to find, however, was the photograph of Ruth which Mallory had promised to leave at the summit in her honour. Some suggested its absence was a sign that Mallory and Irvine had indeed made it to the top of the mountain – that, having summitted, Mallory must have weighted the photograph down before it was ripped from the mountain by the wind.

In her later years, her father's promise and the photograph's absence when Anker found him were to prove of great consolation to Clare, the eldest of Mallory's three children. Just eight years old when he left for Everest for the final time, she had the most vivid memories of the parent whom she and her siblings had barely known. Echoing the experience of climbers and their families down the decades, Clare Mallory (later Millikan) recalled a man who sometimes found it difficult to know his place when he returned to the family home after months away on expedition. On one occasion, she remembered, he was so unsettled by her protests at having her hair brushed that he simply downed tools and walked out on her.

Otherwise, she recalled a devoted and loving father who taught her French and who, on a family holiday to France in 1922, looked on as she made her own early climbs, scurrying around the grounds of the house in which the Mallorys were staying. One of Clare's last memories of her father was looking up into his face, his affection clearly visible before he said goodbye. According to Clare, Ruth had been visited by a similar sense of foreboding to that of Jenni Lowe-Anker. If George went to Everest again, things might not end well. She sent him on his way nevertheless.

When a climber falls in the field, their body suspended black-ened and frostbitten at the end of a rope, or found as a pile of limbs at incongruous angles at the foot of a precipitous drop, the bell that tolls for their passing echoes far beyond the mountains. Perhaps one of the best attempts to articulate the experiences of bereaved relatives is a book by the author Maria Coffey. *Where the Mountain Casts its Shadow* not only recounts the emotional turmoil of losing a loved one, but also challenges the much-cherished belief that to 'die what you love doing' is a fundamental right, rather than a failure to honour responsibilities to a family back home.

Coffey's book is based on bitter personal experience. In 1982 her then boyfriend, Joe Tasker, was climbing on the North-East Ridge of Everest with a fellow Briton, Peter Boardman. Both men were fast establishing themselves as among the brightest talents of their generation. Neither was ever seen alive again. More than a decade elapsed before any trace of them was found, when a party of climbers on the North-East Ridge came across a frozen and badly weathered body. It was not Tasker but Boardman. When Coffey eventually saw a photograph of his remains she was devastated. 'Desiccated skin,' she wrote, 'drawn tight over bones, hair bleached white, the head uncovered, the hand glove-less in the snow.' As shocking as the ravaged body, however, was 'the supreme bleakness of the place where it lay'.

Climbing mountains as challenging as Everest might 'elevate the human spirit', as Francis Younghusband once claimed, but the potential consequences also made it a singularly selfish act. Those whom Coffey interviewed in the climbing communities of both Europe and North America were a roll-call of the great and good of the sport – Alex Lowe among them. Climbers, she discovered, had much to recommend them. Just as Mallory felt as if he were 'casting a spell' over US audiences in 1923, and Anker could make a corporate boardroom 'smell the fear', Coffey recounts how Tasker held not audiences rapt as he spoke, 'brim-ming with hubris, spinning tales of daring and death', while she watched spellbound from the rear of the auditorium.

Living vicariously through one's partner can be very seductive, particularly if you are not of an adventurous bent yourself. Wives, girlfriends and partners left behind talk of a sense of renewal when their men return from expedition, their relationship not allowed to wither on the vine of humdrum daily life. So it was for Ruth Mallory; so it was for Jenni Lowe-Anker. The latter was only too aware of the effect that Alex Lowe had on other people, of how his charisma and talent drew people to him. His was 'a very magnetic personality', she remembered, 'kind of a pied piper. He was one of those guys who would light up a room. He had ... a following of people who thought he hung the moon.'

Though she lacked George's technical brilliance, Ruth Mallory accompanied her husband climbing on numerous occasions. She climbed with him on Great Gable, where Leo Houlding had tried some of the harder routes for himself, increasing his appreciation for George Mallory's climbing skills immeasurably. Conrad Anker often said that if he *were* a soldier, if his chosen vocation *was* war and not mountaineering, then the dangers he faced might be more abstract to his wife and thus reduce her worry. But to Jenni Lowe-Anker the risks were all too apparent. Like Ruth, she too was a climber, and she even had some notable first ascents to her name. In 1988, for example, she had been the first woman to lead a climb of a treacherous ice route known as the Rigid Designator, in Colorado.

But the similarities between the Lowes and the Mallorys didn't extend to the next generation. George Mallory's children also became climbers, following their late father to the Welsh town of Pen y Pass. It was here that Clare, along with her younger sister, Beridge, made a first ascent of a new route on Clogwyn d'ur Arddu – the same peak on which a 16-year-old Leo Houlding later made headlines. George Mallory's only son, John, emigrated to South Africa, where he had five children. In 1995, one of them, George Mallory II, travelled to Mount Everest to complete a climb of the North-East Ridge in his grandfather's stead.

The Lowe-Anker boys, on the other hand, Max, Sam and Isaac, hadn't taken to climbing with any real enthusiasm. For Anker and Lowe it was a compulsion, a habit they needed to feed every day, knowing from an early age that this was what they would spend the rest of their lives doing. But, for the boys, climbing was only a passing interest, in which they dabbled occasionally – though Anker was only too happy to offer them coaching if they wanted it.

Anker couldn't say for certain whether this was a reaction to losing their father, but it was hard not to associate the two. When he set off on an expedition, he knew their well-being depended upon his own, and there was no way he was prepared to put them through the grieving process again. The day he left for Everest, he woke the boys and made them breakfast, as he did every morning when he was at home. When the time came to 'zip the bag shut' and leave for the airport, it was, as always, 'a heavy moment'. Professional climbers were, he acknowledged, institutionalized: pack the gear; face danger; return home. It was a familiar drill, but it was also a habit. And, just as for Ruth Mallory before her, there was a certain inevitability to Jenni Lowe-Anker letting her husband leave. She understood his passion for the Mallory story, and even remembered the announcement of his finding Mallory's body. Alex had heard the news on the radio, and came rushing to tell about his friend's success. Since they had got married, Anker had, as a gesture, cut back on some of his more dangerous climbing – the sort that he and Alex loved to share. Alex's death had taught Jenni that, however much you planned, the idea that you could ever really control your life was an illusion, but she was grateful for Anker's gesture nonetheless.

A well-known American climber, the late Royal Robbins, believed that a mountain which had claimed the lives of others intrinsically held more value than one which had not. This was certainly part of Everest's enduring appeal, to both amateur climbers and professionals alike. Conrad Anker regarded losing friends in the mountains as an inevitable part of a climber's career: if you climbed for long enough it was unavoidable. Anker liked to quote Ernest Hemingway's maxim that climbing, along with bullfighting and motor racing, was one of only three genuine sports. Everything else was 'just games'.

Leo Houlding's relationship with risk was a complex one that had changed as he got older. He still loved the rush, the short, quickfix of adrenalin that climbing a dangerous route gave him. But he also felt something else – something serious, sublime, perhaps even spiritual. Unlike surfing, the art of which was rooted in fast reactions of thought and body, climbing a difficult route was a long-drawn-out process. The further you strayed from the protective equipment placed in the rock, the more realistic you had to be about whether you could get the job done safely. It became mathematical, a problem-solving exercise: the difficulty of the terrain set against a finite reserve of energy. If you failed to get a handle on the equation you could wind up dead. As a result, climbing was for Houlding a 'constant battle between your ambition and your sensibilities'. It was a challenge he relished. Taking it to its logical conclusion, his good friend Kevin Thaw articulated it well. To Thaw, climbers really performed at the limit of their powers only in those moments before they fell. It was keeping the right side of an invisible line, extending indefinitely the period of not falling, that separated merely very good climbers from great ones.

For all his skill, keeping just ahead of that line as it followed him up the mountain, Leo Houlding was under no illusions about the nature of what he did for a living. 'You're putting your loved ones and the people that care about you in a tight spot,' he said. 'They're not getting anything out of you dicing with your life. That's my greatest weakness – I'm inherently selfish.' Marriage made him more cautious, but he wondered whether it was ever really possible for professional climbers to be truly selfless when the rewards of what they did were so personal. Those that made a living climbing were, in the final reckoning, pretty self-obsessed.

When Houlding first announced his intention to go to Everest, his family expressed misgivings. On epic ascents of bare rock they trusted both his talent and his judgement entirely. Yet the extreme altitude of Everest, the 'silent menace' that lay in wait on the great cathedral of snow and ice, was a different matter. His battles with Patagonian rock behemoths or the weathered face of El Capitan were familiar territory, but when he announced his plans to travel to Tibet, the extent of his family's concern surprised him.

In those places where death was always lurking in the shadows, it was the sheer arbitrariness of some accidents that kept a climber's loved ones awake at night. So it had been for the Mallorys. 'We settled long ago that there's no reckoning with Death,' Mallory had written to Ruth during his time in the trenches of the Western Front during the First World War. 'Everyone out here who goes anywhere near the fighting line has narrow escapes,' he wrote. 'You may have a million or a dozen.' The same immutable law existed in the mountains.

Even for those who live to tell the tale, high altitude is a tough place to earn a crust. It causes otherwise rational people to lose perspective, and grown men to behave like petulant children. The stress of working in rarefied air worked in increments, wearing down the combatants in Anker's 'risky war' by a process of attrition. After weeks, even months, of poor sleep, poor diet and relentless physical exhaustion, stress could reach such levels that in some cases even a teammate chewing his food the 'wrong' way could bring climbers to blows. Such friction was evident in even the first expeditions to the mountain. After the Sherpa tragedy in 1922, in the same note to his colleague Alexander Wollaston in which Tom Longstaff, the expedition doctor, described Mallory as a 'stout hearted baby', he also condemned other members of the expedition. Howard Somervell he found to be 'the most urbanely conceited youth I have ever struck', while another climber, Arthur Wakefield, 'could not face the altitude at all ... and is ignorant of the arts of mountaineering'.

With Conrad Anker's commitment to completing the expedition reinforced by his wife's reassurances, the Altitude team could now address how to get to the summit, and film the rest of the expedition, with their depleted team. It was Russell Brice who first suggested that they enlist the help of two of his Kiwi countrymen. Mark Woodward and Dean Staples had both spent the season guiding commercial clients for Brice's Himex operation. Though neither offered the finely honed camera skills of Ken Sauls, both had great experience of high altitude and of Everest in particular. If they got a crash course in operating the cameras, Brice reasoned, they would be worth a punt. They also brought the distinct advantage of being as tough as nails. As Mallory and Irvine had proved, it was a quality that got you a long way on this mountain. The two men were far from an ideal solution, but it was better than heading back to Base Camp. Geffen and Anker agreed that it was their best course of action.

On 10 June, a little over a month after their arrival, the Altitude Everest Expedition of 2007 began their final push for the summit. With the mountain completely clear of other climbers, Leo Houlding was looking forward to the sort of wilderness experience he was more familiar with. As the team made for the North Col again, the rotations up and down the mountain seemed to have worked. With just shy of four days climbing ahead, that evening they bundled into the mess tent for their last opportunity to socialize and eat together. Higher up, they would make do with cramped two-man tents in which eating was entirely functional. But now seven 'Westies', as Anker called them, squeezed in alongside eight Sherpas. It was dinner for fifteen, and the American climber was being mother.

Wherever Anker climbed, he always carried some provisions from home, and this time was no different. Into a pot of water, he placed a sizeable amount of dried meat, several kilograms of bison jerky from Montana. He watched as it began to absorb the water, becoming 'more pliable'. He added an assortment of other ingredients, some cheap curry sauce and some noodles.

The Sherpas looked on through thinly veiled disgust. At lower elevations they were used to their own kitchen tent, and most regarded Western cuisine – or at least a climber's version of it – with deep suspicion.

As the rising steam gathered in narrow rivulets on the ceiling of the tent, Anker lowered a large aluminium ladle into the pot, doling out the dull mixture in generous measures. In a sudden change of heart, the Sherpas wolfed it down. In the convivial atmosphere of the mess tent, there was something about eating in company that fortified everyone's appetite, and the team went to sleep sated that night.

The next morning, as they repeated the march to Camp II, the weather did its best not to help. During the night, a thick veil of fog had moved in, reducing visibility to a matter of feet. Anker reminded himself that, back in the US, they hiked, even skied, in the fog. But this was fog was different. It was a denser vapour than usual, caused by a significant increase in the moisture content in the air. The monsoon was nearly with them. After all the discussion, the weeks spent monitoring its gradual approach, the urgent conversations Anker had held with his wife back home, Russell Brice's ever-reducing window now narrowed to just one day. If they didn't hit their summit date of 14 June, Brice informed them, they wouldn't be summitting at all.

The fog brought with it heavy snowfall, and so a small deputation of Sherpas went ahead to clear the fixed ropes for the rest of the team. One by one, the climbers clipped on to them before heading off. First Anker, then Houlding. The Sherpas and the two Kiwi guides came next, followed by Kevin Thaw. Everyone wanted to get on with the job.

Last to clip on to the lines was Gerry Moffatt. The Scotsman had woken that morning convinced he was taking no further part in the expedition. Of the various bugs and viruses that had done the rounds lower down the mountain, and that had ultimately accounted for Ken Sauls, one had finally caught up with Moffatt. The familiar march to the North Col was one that, since acclimatizing, he would have expected to complete in four hours. The previous day it had taken him more than twice that. Heaving himself up the great snow wall that led to the col, Moffatt felt weak and devoid of energy. In the tent he had shared that night with Kevin Thaw, he had drifted in and out of sleep, bathed in sweat, the familiar silhouette of his water bottle beside him. Staying hydrated was crucial in the harsh dry air, and all the more so if your system was depleted by fever. Yet as he lay there, motionless, he found himself unable to reach for the bottle. By the time the dim light of morning began to seep into the tent, he had resigned himself to the fact that his chances of summiting had all but evaporated. The higher they went, the harder it would be to recover his health. That, after all, was why Sauls was no longer with them.

With Moffatt mired in what the Scot would later describe as 'a bloody great wobble', Anker got on the radio to Geffen, who was monitoring events down at Advanced Base Camp. Geffen knew Moffatt well – well enough to know that he had a tendency to dramatize extreme situations in which he found himself. He sympathized with his friend's condition, but, with their summit options reduced to a one-day-only deal, they had lost enough of the team already. The tick-tock paranoia that besets climbers at high altitude is common, often manifesting itself in a series of ever more introspective questions: 'How am I feeling? What colour's my pee? Have I got an oedema?' The problem is how to ensure a climber is safe without allowing him to wander into self-indulgence. If he does, his physical condition is immaterial. If a climber's mind isn't committed to the sheer bloody slog of putting one foot in front of the other high on the mountain, it is a good bet his body won't be either. Geffen radioed back. Moffatt was going to be fine. He was strong, and had been in countless sticky situations before – just get him moving. Thaw, meanwhile, tried a different approach, insisting all his friend needed was a good feed. He ran through a brief menu: 'We've got raven soup,' he joked, 'or raven with rice. We even have raven stew.'

Leo Houlding sympathized. He knew Moffatt was nervous – he was mildly apprehensive himself, but he at least had the benefit of his exceptional climbing talent. When they left the North Col, he wished he was putting it to good use somewhere else. Climbing with a heavy pack was mind-numbing work. The Sherpas shouldered most of the burden, but they weren't yaks, and each member of the Altitude team still had to carry around 20 lb of his own supplies. In his down suit, Houlding felt like a well-insulated mule, and five hours and more than a few profanities later it was with some relief that he arrived back at the top of the snow ramp that delivered him to Camp II.

Anker, in contrast, spent that morning happily walking behind one of the Sherpas as he made his way up the ridge. Whenever he climbed in the high Himalayas, he made it a point of principle to always carry the same weight as the Sherpas who supported him. Rather than seeing it as an inconvenience, it was a show of solidarity, with men who were prepared to carry his gear across some of the most treacherous terrain in the world for just $10 a day. It was part of the attitude that had led him to establish the climbing school in Nepal's Khumbu valley, and that meant he didn't ask the Sherpas to take routes or make traverses he himself was not prepared to risk. Beyond the fog, snow-laden peaks reared up in all directions. For now, Anker settled for a view of his own feet and the rhythmic plod of his footsteps. Somewhere above them, the Second Step was waiting.

As Houlding climbed on towards Camp III the next day, he contemplated how, rather than if, he would tackle the Second Step. He began to think that he might have been a little hasty in dismissing an ascent of Everest as 'high-altitude walking', even if, in purely technical terms, the Second Step was no more complicated than climbs he made at home several times a week. He recalled a conversation he had had several months before departing with a good friend of his, a well-known British climber called Andy Cave. Cave warned how serious things could get on Everest if things turned against you, citing as evidence the experience of a mutual friend of theirs. Sean Hutson was a highly experienced alpinist who had been climbing on Everest the previous year. During a busy summit day, he found himself caught in a bottleneck at the base of the Second Step. With the ambient temperature around −40 °C, the wind chill sent it plunging further still, down to possibly twice that. When the bottleneck cleared, Hutson reached the summit. It was only when he returned down the mountain that he discovered his toes were badly frostbitten. So bad were they, in fact, that he had little alternative but to have several of them removed. With no other teams on the mountain now, there would be no similar logjam to worry about with, but, as the step drew ever closer, the conversation with Cave seemed ominous.

If George Mallory had succeeded in being the first to summit Everest and had returned to tell the tale, the obstacle that came to be known as the Second Step would probably be named in his honour. After all, the summit route on the south side of the mountain is home to a Hillary Step. Instead, it was Edward Norton's altitude record of 28,128 ft that entered the record books in 1924 – a feat that remained unsurpassed for another twenty-nine years. In 1952 a Swiss expedition climbing on the south of the mountain, Nepal's borders being open once more, reached 28,210 ft, trumping Norton by just 82 ft. Their record was to be broken by Edmund Hillary and Tenzing Norgay less than twelve months later. In 1959 China converted what was a genuinely autonomous Tibet into the Tibet Autonomous Region. The following year a massive Chinese expedition took on Everest's northern slopes, determined to make the great leap upward, a first confirmed northern summit, in honour of Chairman Mao. The account of their successful assault on the Second Step appeared in a propaganda magazine, *China Reconstructs*. It was this that led Anker to doubt the veracity of the Chinese claims.

To most who had seen the Second Step for themselves, the assertions that the Chinese made seemed dubious. The various attempts to climb the obstacle over a three-week period apparently included a team member who allegedly made four attempts in one outing before giving up to spend the night in a bivouac. In fact the night he allegedly spent – cold and exhausted – in the open would have killed even the hardiest of the far-better-equipped climbers who followed. Eventually, responsibility for climbing the Second Step fell to a young man named Chu Yin-hua. After removing his gloves and boots, Chu apparently stood on the shoulders of his comrades, levering himself upward and reaching the top of the step after three hours of effort. That the Chinese had succeeded using such 'combined tactics' seemed remote. As Anker put it in *The Lost Explorer*, his account of the 1999 expedition that first brought him into the orbit of Anthony Geffen, Chu's account 'read more like a homiletic Maoist tract than a mountaineering narrative'. The very idea that anyone could summon sufficient energy to battle the step for so long, even with the use of oxygen, seemed preposterous, and subsequent descriptions of the step by the Chinese contained a number of inconsistencies.

Having failed there himself in 1999, Anker had sought to rate the difficulty of the climb. Using the American numeric system of classification (which runs roughly from 4 to 5.12 and where figures after the decimal point are treated as a whole number), he awarded it a difficulty of 5.5. To put that into some sort of context, the hardest climbs being made by British climbers in the 1920s were around 5.7, possibly as high as 5.8. It meant, technically speaking, that Mallory and Irvine might have succeeded. But there was more to any climb than numbers. Much advice was offered to would-be suitors keen to wed their climbing to the Second Step's particular charms. Jochen Hemmleb, Anker's fellow expedition member in 1999, had written an explanation of how to climb the cliff face, and had even been public-spirited enough to post his theory on the internet. Hypothesizing of this kind irked Anker. He believed the only way to learn to climb the feature was to feel its face beneath your own fingers, to 'let the altitude kick your ass'.

Negotiating with the Chinese Mountaineering Association for permission to remove the metal ladder attached to the step had been a long and delicate process. Russell Brice had long-established contacts within the organization, and his promise to replace the ladder with a new one – 'a bit of housekeeping', as he put it – no doubt sweetened the deal. Specially trained Sherpas would go ahead to loosen the snow and ice around the ladder and, as this was the property of the Chinese government, the substitute would need to be in position as soon as Anker's climb was over. The ladder had been embedded in rock and ice for more than three decades, suggesting it would take a good deal of work to release it. The task was both challenging and dangerous. In the event of any mishap, an additional team of Sherpas would be garrisoned in reserve, at an elevation of around 26,000 ft.

When the Altitude team reached 25,600 ft, Camp III, there wasn't much to welcome them. At the height of the spring climbing season, a ragtag line of tents meandered for close to a thousand feet along the North-East Ridge of Everest. But now the ridge was deserted. Remnants of old camps lay everywhere: discarded oxygen bottles, tattered tent fragments – the detritus of high-altitude ambition. The views, on the other hand, were more appealing. In some places they dropped away as far as Advanced Base Camp. Elsewhere they stretched out across a sea of cloud dotted with island peaks before it crashed on to the arid brown mainland of the Tibetan plateau. But this particular sea view came at a price. Wherever they were sited on the ridge, most campsites had to bear the brunt of vicious winds from the north. It was wise to secure your tent well if you wanted the same view in the morning, just as it was to tune out to an iPod if you expected to get any sleep.

When he arrived on 12 June, it was all Leo Houlding could do to collapse in a heap in his tent. He was exhausted. Taking off his boots took what little energy he had left, and, like a rheumy-eyed dog, he lay on the floor of his tent just as Gerry Moffatt, who by now was feeling considerably better, had done at the North

Col. Now it was Houlding's turn to stare at his water bottle, and with the same lack of inclination to open it. That evening, it was Conrad Anker who came to his rescue. He moved briskly between the tents, handing out the supplementary-oxygen gear they would use for the first time and which would accompany them all the way to the summit. The 9-lb cylinders, each 4 litres in volume, were about to make life dramatically easier. Houlding pulled the mask over his face and turned the valve. It was the first time he had used the aid the early mountaineers called 'English air', and he was amazed at the difference it made.

Among the artefacts that Anker retrieved from Mallory's body eight years previously had been two letters: one for his brother, Trafford, the other addressed to the mysterious 'Stella'. The columns of numbers found on the 'Stella' envelope made up a detailed inventory of all the oxygen cylinders and the pressure each contained. The result of comprehensive tests to see which canisters were leaking and how badly, the information confirmed that the early oxygen cylinders were notoriously unreliable, but also indicated that the team of 1924 had a good deal more oxygen than originally thought. That being so, it may have significantly increased their capability on the upper reaches of Everest. In 1999 Conrad Anker had set out for his unexpected meeting with George Mallory without the aid of supplementary oxygen, keen to see how his body would cope. As he settled into his tent alongside Leo Houlding nearly a decade later, curious once more about how he might fare, he chose to sleep without it. In 1922 it was the innovative Australian climber George Finch who first championed sleeping with oxygen. Not only did it reduce the risk of frostbite by keeping the extremities supplied with oxygenated blood, it also allowed a more restful night. Some thought Finch's claims preposterous. That night, as Houlding drifted off to sleep, he found that Finch was right.

The climbers of the Altitude Everest Expedition were alone when they crossed the invisible line into the Death Zone the following morning, 13 June, strung far apart from one another along the fixed lines. Each man was climbing with just his own thoughts for company as he made for their final stop before the summit, the 27,000 ft of Camp IV. Leaving Camp III earlier in the day, Leo Houlding had traced a line down from the apex of the mountain. The Second Step was in plain view, as was the daunting prelude to it, the short, technical traverse that took climbers to the base of the cliff. Below, there yawned 8,000 ft of fresh air – almost the entire North Face of the mountain. The rope Houlding pulled on was the same one that would soon guide him across another line of transition, from Everest's North-East Ridge to the adjoining plane of the North Face. Houlding let the rope lead him, and came eventually to a series of small gullies. Sheltered by their low, rocky walls, he was pleased to be out of the wind.

'High altitude is like putting your head inside a plastic bag and running up a ski slope,' he had remarked when he first sampled the delights of rarefied air. But the supplementary oxygen was much to his liking. The climb to high camp, a gain in elevation of 1,400 ft, was one which took many climbers as much as six or seven hours. A strong climber like Houlding, well acclimatized and 'pulling on gas', could make it in three. High above, the sky offered a suggestion of blustery conditions, but as he wound his way ever higher Houlding was beginning to think that 'Death Zone' might be another of those overly portentous monikers that climbers were wont to indulge in.

In the distance, he thought he could see one of his teammates squatting down in the snow to take a break. His first reaction was to wonder why his colleague had chosen this, of all places, to stop. The bright yellow boots worn by all the members of the Altitude team were clearly visible against the snow, and through his goggles he looked intently to see if he could make out who it was. Whoever it was, he had drawn his legs up close to his chest, presumably in an effort to keep warm.

It was only as Houlding trudged closer, the rush of his breath issuing back and forth through his oxygen mask, that he realized it wasn't one of his own teammates at all. The boots were the same, but this was a climber whose summit bid had long since ended. In the dry, freezing atmosphere, the dead man's body was perfectly preserved. The rate of deterioration of a corpse stranded high on Everest is measured in years rather than months – the body of George Mallory, still in remarkable condition after the best part of a century, was proof of that. Once skin had been bleached and desiccated by the parched, frozen atmosphere, it could prove difficult to tell a climber who had died ten years ago from one who had died a decade before that. As Conrad Anker could testify, it was often a climber's clothing that provided the best guide.

Houlding approached the body; as doses of sobriety went, the measures didn't come much larger. 'I had been moving well,' he said, 'feeling really strong, and suddenly there was a dead guy, just sitting there, right beside me on the trail.' In that moment he realized something else: in the Death Zone, a climber is only ever on borrowed time. His nearest teammate was hundreds of yards away, so there was no opportunity to share the moment, no chance for a sympathetic word in honour of this poor, fallen soul. He left the fallen climber where he would remain indefinitely, and moved on.

The next member of the Altitude team to pass the body was Gerry Moffatt. At first, Moffatt did his best to look the other way, to offer a shred of dignity to a dead man destined to prove a macabre curiosity for the climbers who would pass in the seasons to come. But, with the body lying directly next to the trail, it was all but impossible. 'It had been a long day,' Moffatt remembered. 'Even with help of oxygen, I had been moving slowly. Then I noticed someone lying down in the snow.' As Houlding had before him, Moffatt thought the man was simply taking a break. His face told a different story. 'The expression was set,' Moffatt recalled – 'a death mask, I suppose you'd call it. It was entirely frozen but at the same time also badly burnt by the sun.'

The Scotsman was surprised by the reaction it provoked: he just didn't have time to be shocked. 'At that altitude you're operating in a different reality,' Moffatt said. 'It's as if your consciousness changes. Everything you have left is focused on reaching that tent.' He too moved on, leaving it to one of the Sherpas to try to scrape a covering of snow over the man's remains.

The lack of level ground on Everest's upper slopes means that, much like Camp III which precedes it, Camp IV is, during the pre-monsoon season, made up of a number of smaller campsites cut into the loose scree that exists below the Yellow Band. From it, both the First Step and the Second Step are clearly visible. Gerry Moffatt took a good deal longer than he would have liked before he reached the sanctuary of his own tent, once he had finally moved clear of the fallen climber's body.

Conrad Anker had been the first to reach the team's high camp, but, despite the effort it had taken him to get there, he didn't wait around to welcome his teammates in. Instead, he headed off immediately on business of a nature as unique as it was personal. Accompanied by Mark Woodward, one of Russell Brice's two guides who had joined the summit party at the eleventh hour, Anker set off on a small act of pilgrimage. With their ascent of the Second Step just hours away, he hoped to re-create another small historical moment – to try to find again the last resting place of George Leigh Mallory.

Inside his tent, Leo Houlding began to melt snow, aware that, when Anker returned, his teammate would be tired, dehydrated and in need of refreshment. When Houlding had first hauled himself in, zipping shut the doors against the bitter wind that shook the tent indignantly, he discovered that the sleeping bag he normally used to get warm after a hard climb had been misplaced. It was left to the ever-reliable Ming Ma, the Sherpa who had rubbed life back into his feet after the freezing shoot on the North Col, to find it. When it arrived, Houlding discovered to his dismay that it was wet and the zip was frozen to the hood. He spent the next hour drying it out on the stove, chipping off the ice where he could, a task as tedious as it was unwelcome. It had been, Houlding thought, a day of hugely conflicting emotions. The oxygen mask and down suit excepted, the climb to Camp IV felt at first like a regular day in the mountains, and the views were breathtaking. But the corpse on the trail was a stark reminder of the price some people were willing to pay for such a vista, and he wondered if less experienced climbers ever fully appreciated the risks. The dead body also brought home one of the grim truisms of high-altitude mountaineering: that fallen climbers were simply too far from rescue. Anyone who made it this far was operating pretty much at his limit. Expecting him to have the strength to carry a 70- even a 60-kg man back down the mountain was almost nil. If you fell, that's where you stayed. The thought unnerved him. He checked on the snow on the stove, watching as it gradually reduced, the angular crystals being slowly submerged as they changed from one state to another.

From camp, Anker and Woodward headed west, towards the catchment bowl where Anker had made his great discovery eight years earlier. Now he wanted to pay his respects at the makeshift grave that he and his earlier team mates had fashioned for Mallory. That chance encounter had changed his life; the expedition that he was now on had consumed him during three years of planning. Now it would come down to a 90-ft stretch of rock in just a few hours' time. The American had always considered Mount Everest a fitting place for George Mallory to be buried. If he had succeeded in making the summit and had returned home a conquering hero, he would have been knighted and would now lie in a prominent plot in an important graveyard. Instead, he was laid to rest on a Buddhist mountain far from England. It was, after a fashion, what Buddhists called a 'sky burial', a traditional ceremony in which monks break up a corpse to feed the squadrons of vultures circling overhead. The birds congregate over the smoke from a signal fire built specifically for the purpose. As a ritual designed to signify the impermanence of human life, it is hard to argue with. The two climbers reached the bowl in which

Anker knew Mallory to be, and began sweeping back and forth, looking for signs of the grave.

For the next hour they moved across the rocky slope, but conditions turned against them. There was far more snow this time than there had been on Anker's previous visit, and the poor light from an overcast sky made distinguishing one feature from another extremely difficult. There was, as Noel Odell had indicated in the wake of his own desperate search following Mallory's disappearance, no trace. It soon dawned on Anker that his meeting with Mallory of nearly a decade ago, when an unknown rock climber from California had discovered one of the greatest legends of English exploration, would be his last. Just as the mountain had claimed Mallory before, so it had now done so again.

In 1999 he and his teammates had performed a small committal service over the body, a brief but dignified act of remembrance. Anker's teammate Andy Politz had read a passage from the Bible. Pulling a small Bible of his own from inside his down suit, it was Conrad Anker who now began to read that same passage requested by the family of Sandy Irvine, Psalm 103: 'Bless the Lord ... who redeemeth thy life from destruction; who crowneth thee with loving kindness and tender mercies; who satisfieth thy mouth with good things; so that thy youth is renewed like the eagle's ...' It was an emotional moment, and he broke off from the reading repeatedly. He confided in Woodward that the efforts of recent weeks had taken their toll; he even wondered out loud whether he had the energy for the climb of the Second Step.

When Anker at last fell into the tent alongside Leo Houlding he was, in the words of his young teammate, 'pretty fucked'. It was the first time he had displayed tiredness so openly, and it wasn't until he switched to supplementary oxygen – the first time he had done so since arriving on the mountain – that he began to feel better. For all Anker's experience and preparation, he realized he should have done it sooner. In his desire to find Mallory's body, he had descended much further down the mountain than planned. As a consequence he had given himself a more strenuous return leg – a huge effort given the 1,400-ft climb he'd made earlier in the day. Under different circumstances he would take it easy the following morning, but, with an early start being crucial for their assault on the Second Step, it was a luxury he didn't have.

II

The Second Step

As CONRAD ANKER roused himself from half-sleep to consciousness, the sound that had been growing steadily louder
outside his tent began to clarify until, finally, it became a voice.
He strained to identify the owner against the monotonous rush
of air through his oxygen apparatus, the relentless advance and
retreat of his own breath. It was Phurba Tashe. The head Sherpa
was banging something – a saucepan by the sound of it – and
hollering with noticeably muted enthusiasm to rouse the team.
This was Phurba's third time on the mountain, and he was perfectly aware that few, if any of them, had been granted the luxury
of deep slumber. Standing on the ridge, alone in the mountain
night, it was, for those few brief minutes, the loneliest job in the
world.

In the sleeping bag next to Anker Leo Houlding was already
awake. As an occasional shrill blast of wind blew through the
camp, an alarm clock sounded close by, then another, then more
Sherpas could be heard, confident and strong as they moved from
tent to tent to ensure the stoves were firing. Houlding had slept
well and he felt good. Even now, three days after he first 'pulled
on gas', he marvelled at how, even on a low flow rate, the dull
aching cold could be forced from his body, down legs and along
arms, to be finally expelled from the ends of fingers and toes.
Sleeping with the mask on took some getting used to, but he
reckoned the mild claustrophobia was more than a fair trade for
keeping warm.

When they had settled down the previous evening, as early as

6 p.m., Houlding's excitement had been palpable. Whatever he had said or felt about Everest before this point, it seemed now that a dose of 'summit fever', even a small one, was going to be hard to avoid. Anker was grateful for his enthusiasm, for in it he thought he glimpsed what it must have been like on that June morning in 1924. The night had seen Mallory's tent buffeted relentlessly, a small canvas boat holding fast against the squall, anchored to an ocean of ice and rock. But the morning had brought calm weather, and with it the sun, and the summit, clear and tantalizingly close. Anker and Houlding split a cup of instant soup. In recent days they had struggled to keep much down at all, and as they drained their cups they congratulated each other on their 'hearty meal'.

Houlding had never liked 'alpine starts', waking in that peculiar nylon light, condensation dripping from the ceiling of the tent. On his usual beat it was never long before the sun was up, and he could bounce out into the morning to let it warm his muscles as he stretched out in preparation for the hard climbing that lay ahead. On Everest, when the sun rose it often seemed to do so with intent, rising high in the sky to set about baking the mountain slowly and relentlessly. He checked his watch: 1.30 a.m. – the earliest he had risen in years. He clicked on the beam of his headlamp and sat up, peering at the pan of snow on the stove. The flame licked gingerly at its base, labouring timidly in the reduced oxygen as if being asked to melt the Rongbuk Glacier itself. But speed, or rather the lack of, was to be their watchword for the day. It was a tactic partly chosen to ensure they didn't expend valuable energy, but one mostly forced upon them by the 'silent menace' of the Death Zone.

In an adjacent tent, Kevin Thaw tore open a sachet of instant coffee and watched as the barely boiling water turned to thin, brown liquid. It was hardly the rocket fuel they enjoyed at Base Camp, so heavily laced with caffeine that it didn't so much stimulate the synapses as detonate them, but he was pleased he had packed it nonetheless.

Anker watched from the door of his tent as the other members of the team began to emerge, pairs of boots visible beneath the sharply edged fans of light thrown by their headlamps as they secured their crampons. Leo Houlding spent a full thirty minutes arranging his footwear, checking his 'sock system', smoothing the heated boot liners as, all the while, Anker's near-constant reminder played in his head: 'Remember the margins.' When their lamp beams occasionally fell across each other faces, the glances they exchanged told them they were all thinking the same thing: 'We're going.' A radio crackled into life. Down at Base Camp, Russell Brice had woken moments earlier and looked out to find it snowing. For all his digital omnipotence, the sophisticated computer technology that allowed him so accurately to monitor the approaching monsoon, he suddenly wondered if they had left it too late. Anker reassured him. It had snowed briefly, but above the cloud line it was beginning to clear.

Anker and Phurba made their final checks. In the weeks that the two men had known each other, they had forged a strong bond, an easy and natural understanding such that their trust in each other was now absolute. The previous afternoon they had discussed plans for the summit departure, taking the measure of the team and carefully sequencing the order in which the climbers were to make the ascent. Houlding would go first. The fixed lines would plot his course, but Anker was still asking him to lead the team, into the darkness and on unfamiliar terrain, shutting out any thought of the precipitous drops that ran, deep and invisible, on either side. It was some compliment.

Now, as they had done on each of the other mornings of their summit push, Anker and Phurba stationed themselves at the camp's exit point – 'the gatekeepers' as the rest of the team had come to refer to them. The climbers passed through in single file, the sirdar checking the Sherpas, Anker the 'Westies', ensuring crampons were attached correctly, that the belt on a climbing harness was doubled back to prevent it coming loose. When they tested the oxygen systems, it was to see not only that were they secure, but that they were working. The last check was perhaps the most important of all; a look into each man's eyes for long enough to guarantee that he was with them in mind as well as body. As Houlding moved through the 'gate', Phurba held out his hand, offering to carry the young climber's water. He declined, politely. Everest wasn't his sort of mountain, but he wasn't about to start being a passenger now.

When Anker and Phurba had talked the previous day, it was the American who noted the tendency for the team to run at least thirty minutes behind schedule. Lower down the mountain it had become a habit, the result of their busy schedule. Worryingly, it was a habit that had endured well into their summit push. Anker's 'official' departure time, 2.30 a.m., was therefore a cheat, a minor but significant one. If indeed it had been Irvine's last-minute tinkering with the oxygen that had delayed his and Mallory's departure, he was going to ensure that nothing similar happened on his watch. When Houlding struck out from high camp it was 3 a.m. precisely; Anker and Phurba nodded knowingly to one another.

Houlding eased his way across the slabs, the treacherously angled rocks that Edward Norton had compared to 'the sloping tiles of a roof', and disappeared into the dark, following the beam of his headlamp, the intermittent bounce on the fixed rope indicating when another man was making his way up the line. Their oxygen masks induced an isolation not dissimilar to that experienced by scuba divers, and it wasn't long before they were far enough apart to be discernible only by their headlamps, a string of fairy lights being pulled towards the sky.

Among the numerous advances to come to the aid of mountaineers and climbers in recent decades, the humble headlamp has improved survival rates considerably, extending climbing time well beyond the hours of daylight. Of those lamps now winking and bobbing behind him, Houlding noted that just four, belonged to the original summit team. They were fortunate 'it was as many as that. Kevin Thaw had developed a fever the previous week, but it had failed to morph into something more serious. The relish with which viruses had set about members of the team, with so little regard for the rules that encumbered other organisms at altitude, was worrying. Gerry Moffatt too was restored, the panic that had visited him at the North Col now left on that icy plateau. While he was the least experienced of the climbers, his recovery spoke volumes for his credentials as an outdoorsman and the countless hours of additional climbing preparation put in back in Idaho. He had 'trained his arse off', and now he was glad of it.

When he reached the Yellow Band, Leo Houlding scanned left and right, noting the countless remnants of old fixed-rope lines as they zigzagged their way upward. When at last he reached the top of the cliffs, picking his way through the narrow gullies that climbers called the 'exit cracks', Houlding felt the mountain open up around him. An hour and a quarter after setting out, he was on the North-East Ridge for the first time.

As Conrad Anker made his way through the Yellow Band behind him, small banks of questions began to gather in his head. In 1924 Edward Norton chose his route below the Yellow Band in order to avoid the Second Step altogether. Mallory's route had indeed been 'climbed' by countless summiteers since, but not by the method they were now about to use. The entire expedition was now funnelling down to the hour or so they were about to spend on that rocky ledge at around 28,000 ft. Would he have enough strength left? Would the rope be long enough? Did he even have the right gear? He focused on the task in hand, reminding himself what he had told Houlding repeatedly during those nights in their tent. Break it down, one hold at a time: the Second Step was just another crag crowned by 15 to 20 ft of moderately challenging climbing.

At the head of the line, Houlding was beginning to revel in the terrain. Compared with what they had encountered so far it was reasonably testing, and he found himself crossing knife-edged ridges or traversing single-track paths that plunged away violently. These were parts of the mountain where the exposure was so great that a less experienced climber could only find them terrifying. To Houlding, it was like walking along a beach on a summer's evening. The snow had been good this year, and was tamped down by the hundreds of climbers who had gone before them that season; his crampons therefore bit firmly, one foot following the other. For a supreme rock technician like him, who usually made ascents with a dizzying mix of speed and precision, this *was* high-altitude walking.

Approaching a prow of rock, he recognized the two grey limestone bands instantly from Anker's description: the First Step. The fixed line to which he was now attached soon took him clear of the small rock buttress. By the time he reached Mushroom Rock, the large, mushroom-shaped boulder that all climbers used as a point of reference, he found he had built a significant lead on the others. It was here in 1999 that Conrad Anker saw his summit team rapidly dwindle as he and Dave Hahn, his fellow American, pushed on to the Second Step alone. The rock was covered now in half an inch of haw frost.

Houlding watched as dawn began to break. There was just ambient light at first, but then, as the sun began to edge higher, sunlight raced towards him, revealing a sea of cloud below and, rising like sentinels through the vapours, great peaks in every direction. He had seen privileged views of the earth before – a meteor shower in Patagonia; a golden eagle climbing to meet him on a high wall on a bright-red Yosemite morning – and this was up there with the best of them. He reproached himself for his nerves lower down the mountain, realizing that this was the part of the trip he should have been looking forward to.

From the cache of oxygen cylinders that Brice's Sherpa team had stashed the previous day, Houlding took a fresh canister, popping the valve on the rapidly emptying old one and screwing the new one firmly in place. Down at Base Camp, the New Zealander monitored their ascent, keeping in touch through regular checks on the radio. For all the countless teams he had seen come and go, there was something rather special about one attempting to free climb the Second Step.

Last to arrive at Mushroom Rock was Gerry Moffatt, ably accompanied by Sonam Dorje, a patient and experienced Sherpa. The Scotsman's eyes, Houlding thought, looked as though they were on stalks. Moffatt sat down, breathing hard into his mask before relaxing enough to speak. 'Fucking hell,' he said, 'I am so far out of my element.' Houlding checked his watch again: 5.30 a.m.

With Mushroom Rock sheltered from the wind and with the sun continuing to rise, Anker began to rack up for the assault, attaching to his harness the things he would need for the ascent. First he hooked on three 'camming devices', metal pegs with retractable arms. Anker planned to push these at intervals into gaps in the rock, to secure the rope in the event of a fall. Next came the rope itself, an 8-mm-thick 'dynamic' type, which, if he did fall, would stretch and offer vital shock absorption. Last of all came a small wooden wedge or 'stacking block', designed to reduce the size of any cracks for which the cams proved too small.

By the time they were ready to move, Gerry Moffatt had recovered his composure. Keen to get on with things, he clipped in behind Houlding, breaking the sequence in which they would attempt the climb. Dean Staples and Mark Woodward, Russell Brice's two Kiwi guides, offered a rebuke. It was an innocent mistake, but, as the New Zealanders prepared to move off in advance to help release the ladder, Moffatt 'parked' himself off to one side to allow them past. Though the incident was over in a moment, it suggested that Anker's anxiety was filtering down to the rest of the team.

By the time they reached the Second Step, the ladder detail was already at the top. The familiar dihedral of the two plane faces opened up before them, but the ladder itself was nowhere to be seen, now stowed flat on the ledge above. It had come to represent many things: a leg-up for the technically incompetent; an affront to some of the most basic principles about how man should test himself against the extremes of the planet. It had put up a reasonable fight, requiring some hefty chopping to release it. Now it was gone, Anker thought the rock looked naked – like the face of friend you had previously seen only wearing glasses. At the top of the step, Mark Woodward sat poised to film the ascent.

The short, tricky traverse to the base of the cliff was a daunting one, as the vast acreage of the mountain's North Face opened its jaws below them. Checking his rig, Anker realized this was one of those 'life moments', the rare occasions that cast everything into a different perspective. Dropping down into the snow alongside Mallory eight years ago had been another, although he could never have known what he had started on that morning in May. Free climbing the Second Step restored to something approaching its raw state would allow him to move on and obsess about something else.

They gained the first part of the face unroped, scrambling over a sheet of rock about 10 ft in height via a natural ramp. Here they built a belay, to allow Houlding to arrest Anker's drop if he fell. The Englishman clipped on to a karabiner coupling attached to the rock. He slipped the end of Anker's lead rope through the belay's figure-of-eight device, doubling it back on itself before spooling out the slack, throwing great loops of rope in a metronomic rhythm and with a flourish that had long ago become automatic. Watching Anker go first felt strange: he couldn't remember the last time he had seconded on such a high-profile climb. At least he could be thankful it wasn't cold. Minus 20 °C was hardly balmy, but it could have been so much worse.

Between their belay and the main wall of the step lay an incline of snow roughly 30 ft in height. Anker scaled it easily, kicking in the front points of his crampons with measured force. At the top, he removed his oxygen apparatus. Climbing with the extra bulk of boots, he would need to be able to see his feet, just as he had on his previous visit, and he stuffed the canister and mask into his pack before depositing the bag on the ledge beside him. He clipped off a piece of old rope that was hanging free. The mountain was covered with them – loose threads in countless summit stories. Perhaps this one had concluded with some unfortunate climber being sent to an unscheduled appointment with the glacier below. As Anker prepared to climb, Houlding met his glance with a nod, his red down suit sharply in focus in the morning sunshine. Anker was 'on belay'. It was a phrase as familiar as ordering a cup of coffee. Amid the chatter of conversation nearby, Moffatt's soft Scottish burr could be heard: 'Here he goes. Come on baby.'

Unlike Houlding, Anker wasn't known for unbridled speed, but he could still shift when the need arose. His previous attempt on the Second Step had taught him that this was no place to hang around. At sea level, tired arms would eventually experience a build-up of lactic acid. The involuntary response from many climbers was to lift their elbows, as the body sought to transfer the effort to the larger muscle groups of the back – a sure sign that a climber was tiring. At extreme altitude, with muscles already deprived of oxygen, disabling levels of lactic acid could develop all too quickly.

Anker started to climb, placing protective equipment and surveying the face as he went. Two routes presented themselves. The first ran along a wide or 'off-width' crack. Offering the shortest route, it lay to the right of the ladder site, but the presence of loose rock suggested it might be less than safe. A far better option seemed to be a larger fissure to the left, which, crucially, ran all the way to the top. It was the line he had attempted in 1999, when the close proximity of the ladder had caused him to fail. One of the more common techniques used to negotiate very large cracks is 'chimneying', literally climbing inside the crack while bracing against its interior walls. The fissure fell between two stools: on the one hand it was too narrow to chimney, while on the other it was too wide for the largest of the cams he now carried with him. He reached for the stacking block, easing in to narrow the gap, before sliding a cam in alongside it. It wasn't a perfect fit, but it would have to do. He clipped his rope to the cam and continued on.

As Houlding watched Anker preparing the stack, he recognized it for what it was: what climbers euphemistically refer to as 'psychological protection'. Fall, and there was a good chance that if weighted fully and suddenly – an effect known in climbing parlance as 'shock loading' – the cam would come loose. The principal function of such protection was to make you feel better.

Even so, Houlding knew that Anker had several things in his favour: not only was he a cautious climber, but he was one who had come within a hair's breadth of free climbing the step already. Such was Houlding's confidence in his man that he decided to record the moment for posterity. As he rummaged for his camera in the pockets of his down suit, Anker moved across the face, locating his foot on a small ledge. In the rock shoes in which he normally climbed he would have felt it almost tenderly, caressing its edges through the thin rubber soles to gauge if it was good. To wear rock shoes at 28,000 feet, however, you had to be prepared to leave your toes behind. When he weighted his foot, the crampon's spikes skittered along the ledge – until it ran out.

After three years of preparation, not to mention how close they had come to aborting the expedition just days earlier, he fell in a moment. Those watching saw only a flurry of snow, heard only an anguished cry, but in that split second Anker's climbing instincts kicked in. As he fell, his hand shot out and his fist closed around the rope. He bounced downward, the toes of his boots peppering the rock as he went, praying that the improvised piece of gear would hold when loaded by his weight. If it failed, the next point at which his fall might be checked was another 15 ft below that. A 30- to 40-ft fall in total, and on to uneven terrain, meant a sprained ankle at best. But, as the rope snapped against the cam, he jerked abruptly to a stop. The protection, crude and low-tech, held fast. Houlding broke out into a toothy grin, then started to laugh. He saw what Anker had been trying to do: climb wide of the precarious stacking block to minimize the risk of knocking it out if he fell – it hadn't occurred to him for a moment that he might fall. The smile hid Houlding's surprise, but also a little embarrassment. Since Anker had grabbed the rope himself, he hadn't needed Houlding to arrest his fall on the belay. Even so, taking a photograph had been a foolish thing to do, and he chided himself for being so complacent.

He also realized something else. In grabbing the rope and arresting his fall, Anker had used the gear he had placed only to protect himself. Had he used it to haul himself up, to 'aid progress', he would at that point have turned his free ascent into what climbers called an aided one – just as climbing the step with the ladder would have been. It was a technicality, but a vital one. A free ascent was still on.

On the ledge at the base of the step's main wall, Anker sat into his harness as he figured out his next move. One minute became five, became ten, became twenty. To Houlding it seemed like an eternity. As the younger man waited, it began to occur to him that the fall had disturbed Anker more than he realized. Houlding knew only too well that, however much the American wanted to honour George Mallory, however much he wanted to nail the Second Step, Anker wasn't prepared to risk his own safety, his family's future, for the sake of 'freeing' one small section of rock. What if that was what Anker was weighing up now? In the shakedown, the fall was a minor one, but, if the protection had come loose, anything more than a basic injury would have constituted a genuine emergency. The monsoon was snapping at their heels, and Russell Brice had given them until today to summit. If they couldn't, they were going home.

When he looked again, he was relieved to see Anker's head tracking left and right, reappraising the rock. Falls, or rather the reaction to them, said much about a climber's heart. For some they offered just the excuse they were looking for. As Anker put it, 'they were free to cash in their chips and rappel down.' Many had the ability to continue, but refused to see reason. Regardless of what protective equipment they had in place, they preferred to retire, believing the limit of their ability had been breached. Like Houlding, Anker was the other kind: a climber for whom falling was merely a setback. Provided it wasn't terminal, it was simply part of the process that helped to refine technique. As Kevin Thaw put it, most climbers perform at the limit of their powers only in the moment before a fall takes place.

Suddenly Anker began to climb again, varying his line slightly to increase the number of available holds. A direct climb of the cliff had proved impossible in 1999, but now, with the ladder gone, Anker found he could make moves in quick succession. His hands were beginning to get cold now, and he paused intermittently to blow on them, each breath warming them a little.

At last he approached the most difficult part of the climb – that section known as the 'crux'. It was a small overhang, and he was beginning to feel his fuel gauge dipping into the red. He'd put in his last two pieces of protective gear and, with his arms beginning to ache, he wouldn't be able hold on for much longer. With his full weight now on his arms, he prepared to swing round the overhang, his crampons scratching at the rock beneath him. He would have to go for it. The hush that followed was suitably pregnant, as if a long-called-for quiet had arrived at last. Only Anker could be heard, struggling to finish the job. Houlding could barely breathe. Was this the line George Mallory might have chosen, his fluid elegance guiding him to the top as his energy began to ebb away? Houlding reckoned it was five, maybe six, minutes until, with one great last effort, Anker pulled himself over the ledge and into the fog created by his own desperate breathing.

If Noel Odell had indeed been watching in 1924 when first Mallory and then Irvine had surmounted the Second Step, his claim that they had done so easily bore little relation to how hard

Anker found himself blowing. One by one the Sherpas who had made up the ladder detail shuffled across to congratulate him, before spontaneously bursting into song. Down at Base Camp, the radio being used by Brice to monitor the climb erupted with noise. Either Anker had made a free ascent of the Second Step or he'd fallen to the glacier below – it was hard to tell which.

From the top of the ledge, Anker peered down as he waited for his partner to follow him. The American was sure the technical nature of the climb would give an accomplished 'stone monkey' like Houlding little difficulty. But this stone monkey had other problems. More specifically, Leo Houlding had literally cold feet. Watching Anker make the climb, Houlding had been aware of standing in a small apron of sunlight. It spread steadily as the sun rose higher in the sky, but what Houlding had failed to notice as the drama played out above him was the ledge, roughly waist height, that kept the lower half of his body in constant shade. Leaning into his climbing harness as he watched Anker climb had only made matters worse, restricting the circulation to his legs. Now, as he set himself to go, he found his toes were completely numb. For all the warnings about Everest's hazards he had been given by seasoned campaigners, for all his experience in period costume on the North Col, he had simply forgotten to follow one of the basic rules: keep your toes moving. Since arriving on the mountain, he had worried more about losing toes than about losing his life. As he began to imagine all manner of hideously blackened extremities, the thought began to freak him out. The only place with sufficient sunlight to warm his feet lay 90 ft above him. There were times when it paid to be a speed climber, and this was one of them. It was no longer a question of *if* he could make the climb, just of how quickly. There was no time to lose.

He whipped off the oxygen set and stared at his feet, unfamiliar in the heavy mountaineering boots. The rock shoes he normally wore balled his toes into 'fists', his digits coming together as one to detect subtle nuances in the rock as he moved from hold to hold. He ran his eye over the face above him. There was certainly merit in the route that Anker had taken, but, when the moment came to commit to the most difficult move, his crampons had caused his foot to skate sideways. Reading the face, Houlding was certain there had to be another way.

Despite Anker's reservations, his eye was drawn to the off-width crack. Anker's earlier reluctance, Houlding reassured himself, came from concern for the gear, knowing it might easily be displaced if he attempted to secure it in less than solid rock. Climbing second, Houlding had the added security of a top rope running above him. Provided he kept some tension in the line, this meant that, should he fall, it wouldn't be far. Most importantly, the route represented his quickest path to the top. He began to climb out along the crack.

The further out to the right he climbed, the further the rope ran to the side of him. If he did fall now, the drop might be a short one, but he was likely to swing or 'pendulum'. If he bounced off the rock it would be painful, but more importantly it would delay his getting into the sun. Though the boots felt awkward, as he climbed he found he was able to compensate for the reduced sensation, transferring his weight to other parts of his body.

Looking up to the small series of moves that had inconvenienced Anker, Houlding saw that they centred around the small overhang it had taken the American several minutes to negotiate. Desperate to be delayed as little as possible on the obstacle himself, as Houlding neared the most testing part of his chosen line – a pitch of 15 ft or so of genuinely technical climbing – the thinness of the air began to tell. The slowing of a climber's technique and thought processes was something Anker likened to an old computer, its processor struggling to deal with a surfeit of commands. As Houlding inched toward the overhang, working on his arms, he did so 'anaerobically', holding his breath as climbers often did on a complex manoeuvre. Even at sea level, climbing anaerobically could create a modest oxygen debt.

When Houlding eventually transferred his weight back to his feet he tried sucking in a breath – it wasn't nearly enough. At 28,000 ft, fearing that he might be racing the mountain in order to save his toes, it felt as if that plastic bag had been pulled over his head once again.

Questions began to float down to him from the other side of the overhang. Was he OK? Did he need a hand? To Houlding, it was as if he had sprinted several hundred yards and was now being asked to conduct an interview. As the oxygen began to return, however, he found he could breathe more easily, and it wasn't long before he made the final few moves to the top. There was a full thirty minutes before the blood flow returned, Houlding wiggling and shaking his feet all the while. When the familiar pinpricks of oxygenated blood began spreading through them once more, he was overjoyed.

With Houlding at the top, the free climb was a double success. Anker and Phurba now began helping the other Sherpas to rig the new ladder that Russell Brice had supplied specifically for the occasion. At Base Camp they had referred to this light-heartedly as 'housekeeping', but, as he felt the new ladder in his hands, for a moment Anker contemplated throwing it off the mountain altogether, leaving the Second Step in its natural state. But he knew what the repercussions of such a unilateral decision would be: for one thing he'd be a pariah in the climbing community; for another, he'd have some serious explaining to do at Base Camp.

It was only when they had finished securing the new ladder that Phurba pointed to Anker's pack. It contained the oxygen he would need for the rest of climb, only now it lay at the bottom of the cliff. It was the least the Sherpa could do to retrieve it for him. Anker thought now would be a good time to show his friend an old trick he used regularly when he climbed in the Yosemite valley. Reaching for the rope he had attached to the pack before starting the ascent, a 'haul line', all he now needed to do was to pull it up after him. But the sirdar wouldn't hear of it, telling Anker that techniques that worked on the big walls of Yosemite simply wouldn't cut it on Everest. The two men continued their discussion for several minutes. It was only when the Sherpa neared the top of the ladder carrying both packs that Anker saw Phurba's offer for what it was. There weren't many ways he could help an experienced climber like Anker on this mountain; this small and gracious act was one of them.

With a ladder back in place, the rest of the team soon followed. For an experienced climber like Kevin Thaw, coping with the vast exposure of the Second Step was straightforward. For Gerry Moffatt, on the other hand, by far the least accomplished climber, the traverse to the base of cliff might all too easily have been an experience verging on trauma. In the event, however, as Moffatt made the short but dangerous crossing to the foot of the ladder, his feeling was one of euphoria rather than terror, a rush of excitement so huge as to be almost abstract.

As the team now trained its sights on the summit, from inside his pack Anker pulled out the satellite phone he was carrying and turned it on. The signal bar edged its way up the side of the display, indicating there was reception. With the fourteen-hour time difference, it would be around 7.30 in the evening back in Bozeman, and getting dark. He dialled Jenni's number. They had last spoken following the departures of two of the team's senior members, Jimmy Chin and Ken Sauls, when Anker had understandably been concerned about what lay ahead. Now, when she answered the phone, Anker found it hard to contain his excitement. With his mind a blur of emotion, he settled for just three words: 'We made it.' Even down a crackling line from the roof of the world, her husband's overwhelming sense of relief was palpable. From the outset, his wife had known how much a free climb of the Second Step meant to him – far more, in fact, than the summit. After all, this was what the entire expedition had been about. In proving it was possible to scale the Second Step as George Mallory and Sandy Irvine had encountered it, they had unlocked one of the great secrets of exploration. And Conrad

Anker had achieved something else. In bringing to a conclusion a chain of events that had started on that May morning in 1999, he had finally freed himself of a burden he had been carrying for the past eight years.

As Anker pulled his oxygen mask back on, he wondered what Mallory might have thought had he succeeded on an obstacle which, even in 1924, was recognized as holding the key to his chosen summit route. He and Irvine would have arrived at this point tired and dehydrated. Mallory had, in a display of typical clumsiness, sent the stove which was their only means of melting snow tumbling down the mountain. He would have made the climb with no prior knowledge of the rest of the ascent, and with none of the physical or mental preparation that had given Anker a considerable advantage. If he had made it to the top, his joy would have been brief, tempered by the realization that this short climb was about to present Irvine with the sternest of challenges. He knew his young friend was both strong and courageous – it was part of the reason he had chosen Irvine to accompany him. But if Mallory had looked down from the ledge and seen the North Face plunging away beneath Irvine's feet, he must have wondered how the young rower would cope. They had survived the treatment meted out by the weather early in the expedition, and made it through the interminable delays and changes to their plans. Mallory had finally got his opportunity to climb with the 'superman' of whom he had written to Geoffrey Young. But now his superman was fading, his sunburn so severe that his skin was coming away in great sheets. If the climb was beyond Irvine, the alternatives were hardly much better. Should Mallory leave him there and make a dash for the top alone, or try and haul his young friend up on a rope, one hand over the other? It would have required an effort of almost superhuman strength. Whatever the scenario, it only increased Anker's admiration for the iconic Englishman.

When he at last turned to follow his own team, Anker's relief at conquering the Second Step ensured that the remainder of the ascent felt like a reward. They made good time, climbing strongly as, beneath a fast-rising sun, monstrous peaks glinted all around them. As Houlding had done at Mushroom Rock, Anker gazed at the great mountains now before him. He could identify many of them by name: Pumori, Gaurisankar, Cho Oyu. It was a period of the day he would later describe as 'ninety minutes of joy'. But, as he climbed, he knew that above the Second Step the challenge for Mallory and Irvine would have just been beginning.

Of the various theories on what might have happened on that June morning, one by the climber and author Tom Holzel (who had himself searched for evidence of the two men in 1986) offers an illustration of the dilemma that might now have faced the Englishmen. Holzel pointed out that from the top of the Second Step the snowfield that remains to be crossed before reaching what appears to be the summit of Everest suggests a climb of about an hour, possibly two. If, based on checks by Irvine, they calculated that they had sufficient oxygen to reach the summit, they might well have continued. But the view from the top of the Second Step is deceptive, for what appears to be the summit is in fact merely the shoulder of a far larger summit pyramid. Only when you reach this shoulder does it become clear that the summit lies still another hour away – sixty or so minutes of fairly difficult climbing.

If they had pressed on, it wouldn't have taken Mallory and Irvine long to realize their error. At some point, with considerably further to go than they had allowed for, their oxygen would have expired. Complete though his conversion to oxygen usage was, what Mallory could not have known was that above 27,000 ft, in the so-called Death Zone, the deterioration in the body's performance accelerates even more rapidly than lower down. If their oxygen had run out, it is something they would have discovered all too quickly.

Some thought Holzel's theory fanciful, based on a spiral of ever-increasing speculation, but it nevertheless illustrated the challenge. Anker was of the view that, as an accomplished mountaineer,

Mallory might well have taken the decision to turn back much sooner. As the climbing leader, his primary responsibility was returning Irvine safely back to camp. Yet, with the summit so close, such a decision would have been incredibly difficult.

When the Altitude team began to close on the summit themselves, it was 7½ hours since they had left their high camp, and as they wound their way ever upward the final summit triangle revealed itself as no more than a patch of white. It was the Sherpas who were given the honour of being first to the top. For them this was a holy place, Chomolungma, Goddess Mother of the World, and the moment they reached it they began chanting, dancing and singing in a display of unbridled joy. One by one, the Altitude team took their place alongside them. Kevin Thaw noted the reams of prayer flags and scarves draped over a small statue of the Buddha, while Gerry Moffatt was as wide-eyed as he had been at any point that morning. The view was beyond spectacular: below them an undulating carpet of clouds; above, a suffused band of blue merging into a deep purple.

Last of all came Conrad Anker and Leo Houlding. With their period clothing now far below them, it was Anker who suggested that they make the final 100 ft of the ascent without oxygen – a mark of respect to the two Englishmen whose historic climb they had re-created. On his previous plodding steps, Houlding had been climbing in a world far removed from 1924, but as he took off his mask it didn't take long to be reminded that the exacting realities of life at high altitude are timeless. The elevation came rushing up to meet him. Almost immediately he found himself breathing hard. He began to feel light-headed, and both he and Anker were glad when they finally stepped on to the summit and were able to turn their oxygen systems back on. At precisely 10.45 that morning, Dean Staples radioed down to Russell Brice to give him the good news: the Altitude team were all safely on the summit.

Leo Houlding took the opportunity to break his communications embargo for the second time on the expedition. He called his wife, Jessica. It was the briefest of conversations, no more than two minutes. He told her that he loved her and that, quite literally, he was on top of the world. Next he phoned his parents, before laying some photographs of his loved ones in the snow. He thanked Anker for his help over the previous month and a half, realizing at the same time that it was an experience he was unlikely to repeat.

Anker, too, thought it probably his last visit to the summit of Everest. In recognition of the fact, he took the opportunity to set down some mementos of his own. The first was a small camera, a Kodak vest-pocket model identical to that loaned to Irvine by his colleague Howard Somervell before he and Mallory left the North Col for the final time, on 6 June 1924. Anker had purchased it some years before in a Buenos Aires flea market. From the moment he saw it, he vowed that, were he ever to return to the summit of the mountain, he would take it with him. Perhaps, somewhere below, a similar camera lay on the frozen slopes. Perhaps it contained photographs of the two climbers in their final hours, or even an image of them on the summit. From inside his down suit, Anker retrieved his final memento. It was a photograph of George and Ruth Mallory. The absence of a similar picture on her father's body brought much comfort to Mallory's daughter, Clare, in her old age. Now Anker set his picture down carefully in the snow.

Against a background of excited chatter from the Sherpas, Gerry Moffatt sat down to record some footage for the behind-the-scenes film of the expedition he was making. He had been shooting for only a few minutes when the scene in the camera viewfinder disappeared in a squall of snow. The radio crackled into life once more. It was Russell Brice. The monsoon had arrived. It had been four days since the New Zealander had delivered his ultimatum for them to reach the summit. He had tracked the monsoon tirelessly as it made its way up from the Indian subcontinent – the very weather system which had caused Jenni Lowe-Anker such concern as, far away in Montana, she had followed the expedition's progress. In the end, Brice's prediction had been accurate to the day.

Leo Houlding was used to the rapid changes in conditions that could occur in the mountains, but the speed with which the bad weather arrived caught him off guard. There he was, looking down as the entire world stretched away before him, the tops of the clouds bathed in sunlight. Then suddenly it had gone, the thick cloak of a storm obscuring it so completely that he found he could barely see his hand in front of his face. Hanging around in such conditions was inviting disaster, walking dangerously close to the fine line that existed at high altitude between being in control and being hopelessly out of it. It was time to go. But, as the rest of the team started to file off the summit, Houlding chose to remain for a few minutes more. The last man of the final expedition of the season, he wanted just one moment to himself, one climber and one mountain, the expedition reduced to terms he understood.

Anker had already gone before him. Before he went, he picked up a small stone from the final summit triangle and quietly slipped it into his pocket.

12

Between Earth and Heaven

As sir edmund Hillary famously observed, the summit of Mount Everest is effectively only halfway. One of the more uncomfortable realities of climbing on the world's highest mountain is those deaths that occur when climbers are descending. Though such fatalities are relatively few, two of the four deaths that had taken place following the Altitude team's arrival had happened once the climbers in question had reached the top. With adrenalin, even raw ambition, no longer drawing a person upward, exhaustion could soon take over, the end being rapidly hastened through hypothermia, oedema or a fall. For all the celebrations that followed the successful free climb of the Second Step, once they reached the summit no one on the Altitude team was foolish enough to regard the job as over.

With the monsoon arriving on the very day they achieved their goal, it seemed Jenni Lowe-Anker's sense of foreboding had been more prescient. When the call came from Russell Brice to start their descent, Gerry Moffatt, who had been plagued by nerves for much of the climb, didn't need telling twice. Accompanied by Sonam Dorje, a strong Sherpa with whom he was paired for the summit day, Moffatt promptly clipped his harness to the fixed lines that ran from the summit to Crampon Point and began making his way down.

The descent didn't start well. For one thing, the storm gave the route they had followed on the way up an entirely different complexion. 'The snow covered our tracks completely,' Moffatt recalled, 'in every direction, there was nothing that looked the same.' As Noel Odell had waited for his friends in the small tent at Camp VI on the afternoon of 8 June 1924, descending in a whiteout was a hazard that Mallory and Irvine had experienced for themselves. For Moffatt, things went from bad to worse. As he was making his way along the ridge above the Second Step, he was forced to watch in horror as, without warning, Sonam fell, engulfed in a powder slough, a small avalanche that knocked him from his feet. The Sherpa gathered speed, sliding down the mountain in a blur of powder, and it was only when he struck a ledge that his fall came to an end. Moffatt spent the rest of the descent in a state of high anxiety. On reaching Mushroom Rock, he was joined by Leo Houlding. With the monsoon snows falling in earnest, the two men looked at each other as if to say, 'Let's get out of here.' Houlding had no desire to be stuck in a blizzard high on Everest either.

They spent the rest of the descent in ever deteriorating conditions as the snowstorm intensified. Eventually, visibility became so compromised that they had little choice but to trust entirely to the fixed lines to guide them down. The slack in the ropes that caused them to lie against the mountainside meant the lines were soon buried in the snow. As the climbers pulled them out, the poor visibility made the rope ahead promptly disappear into the storm, often as little as 10 yards in front of them. If they had planned for their expedition to replicate the final experience on Everest of George Mallory, the weather was doing its best to help.

As he made his way down, Leo Houlding peered through the snow in search of the top of the Yellow Band, the route back through the 'exit cracks' which they had climbed so easily in clear weather that morning. He wondered how on earth Mallory and Irvine might have coped on the unstable terrain, the blizzard raging around them as their hobnails scratched for purchase. Without any fixed lines to guide them, they would have found locating the gullies that led to the lower reaches of the mountain a serious challenge. It even occurred to Houlding that the point at which they had fallen was probably near where he was now standing. It was enough to focus his concentration, and it wasn't long before he found what he was looking for: the point at which the fixed lines dropped down into the cliffs of the Yellow Band.

Seven hours after reaching the summit, the Altitude team began drifting into Advanced Base Camp, tired but exhilarated. Moffatt was physically and emotionally spent. The effort and concentration required for the descent, combined with the unrelenting effects of life at high altitude, meant that the moment he was handed a cup of tea he broke down in tears. Leo Houlding's return was rather less emotional. Tossing his bag into the corner of the mess tent, he proceeded to tell anyone within earshot that he never wanted to see a heavy pack again: he was done with high-altitude walking. Kevin Thaw announced his arrival in typically idiosyncratic manner: in his opinion it had been 'a fine day out'. That evening, they all celebrated with a few beers.

The next morning Thaw was less cheerful as he endured the minor ignominy of being helped around camp by Leo Houlding. During the night he had developed a bad case of snow blindness, a consequence of dispensing with his goggles on the final stages of their descent. It was an error of judgement similar to that displayed by Edward Norton during 1924 expedition. If Leo Houlding occasionally now left it late when warning of imminent obstacles, he undoubtedly recalled Thaw's endless jarring steps in 2002 when their attempt on the Patagonian peak of Cerro Torre had ended in similarly undignified circumstances, after a fall and one broken foot.

For Conrad Anker, his achievement on the Second Step was the fulfilment of a long-held dream, and during the next few days he reflected on how the summit push had gone. Given the challenge it had presented, he revised the Second Step's technical rating. Instead of the 5.5 he had awarded it in 1999, he and Houlding now thought more likely to be a climb of 5.9. Houlding had coped with it well. Anker had always suspected he would, and he was greatly impressed with how the young Englishman had adapted to life at high altitude. It was a sign of his real climbing pedigree. That he had maintained himself in good condition (Gerry Moffatt, in contrast, had lost 20 lb) had given him a significant advantage. A career like Houlding's, which routinely called for long days in the field, racking up climbs of 24, 36 or even 72 hours at a time, with only the briefest episodes of sleep, inevitably led to a depletion of a climber's physical reserves. With practice, however, it also taught the body to regenerate. For non-climbers, exercise was something that took you out of the house for an hour at a time, maybe two. It was great for staying in shape, but it didn't teach the body to cope with continuous exposure to the elements in the way that climbing expeditions did.

Such long days had paid dividends for Houlding, hardening both his mind and his body for the unique test that Everest provided. Even as a schoolboy, George Mallory was used to seventeen-hour days in the Alps. The mental fortitude developed was common among the members of the early Everest expeditions, marching their way across the Tibetan plateau, the prize of the great mountain looming closer with each passing day. In 1924 Sandy Irvine had impressed his fellows hugely, even with his face ravaged by extreme sunburn. Now that he had seen the upper mountain for himself, Houlding found Irvine's achievements all the more remarkable. He might have been an outstanding rower and an accomplished athlete, but on the North-East Ridge of Everest his limited technical ability would have left him at a considerable disadvantage. It had been his performance on the expedition to Spitsbergen led by Noel Odell in 1923 that had first alerted the Mount Everest Committee to his potential. Nevertheless, Houlding reasoned, it was hardly a solid preparation for the harshest mountain environment in the world. And yet a year later he had risen to the challenge magnificently. It had been the coldest season yet seen on Everest, and not only had Irvine performed his basic duties well, he had been an effective and enthusiastic engineer to boot, tinkering endlessly with the oxygen apparatus in the evenings, as well as experimenting with a range of improvements to clothing and equipment.

By the time Mallory came to make his final, fatal summit bid, he believed he had chosen Irvine over the far more experienced Odell for good reason. Just as Geoffrey Winthrop Young had been a guiding influence throughout Mallory's own climbing career, Mallory doubtless felt a sense of obligation that he too should act as some sort of mentor. That it was an obligation to be fulfilled on the grandest scale suggests it was a decision inspired as much by idealism as by common sense. Anker knew perfectly well that Leo Houlding was too talented to need his hand held on the Second Step. Mallory's trust in his badly sunburnt and inexperienced young companion, on the other hand, was an act of faith, prompted by Irvine's wizardry with the oxygen apparatus. In spite of this, and whether or not they had reached the summit, they had climbed higher on the mountain than anyone before them, with none of the benefits, unreliable oxygen excepted, enjoyed by their modern counterparts.

Houlding knew that he and Anker had effectively turned with their tails between their legs, giving up their period clothing as early as the North Col. It was an act of self-preservation, in the interests of their future livelihoods. Yet the members of the 1924 expedition were evidently a tough old breed. Perhaps this toughness had stood Mallory and Irvine in better stead than many previously assumed.

So what were the chances they had completed the climb? In 1924, any ascent of the Second Step would almost certainly have been shortened by the heavy snowfalls of that year. If Mallory and Irvine had managed to scramble up the initial snow ramp – which might have stretched around 15 ft – they might then have been able to launch their assault using 'combined tactics', one standing on the shoulders of the other to reach the better holds that existed higher up the wall. Given Mallory's superior experience, it is only reasonable to assume that he would have gone first, leaving Irvine to negotiate the ascent in on his own – either that or be hauled up by Mallory from above, an unlikely scenario given the effort required. Even giving them the benefit of the doubt, Houlding guessed they would almost certainly have had just one attempt to get it right. If they had succeeded, the snowfield above the Second Step would have soon revealed its true nature: not the short climb they might have envisaged, but an undulating expanse that called for more oxygen than the 'two cylinders' that Mallory had mentioned in his note to Odell.

When Leo Houlding had made his way along the North-East Ridge, he had been sure to stop at roughly the location at which Noel Odell had caught that final, fleeting glimpse of Mallory and Irvine at 12.50 p.m. on 8 June 1924. Odell was convinced he had seen the two men arrive at the Second Step and that, having got there, they 'shortly emerged at the top'. But his view had come through a break in the clouds at a time of day when pre-monsoon conditions obscured the majority of the upper mountain. Houlding, in contrast, had taken in the same view when conditions were perfectly clear. Even then, with an eye well practised at setting distance against elevation, he found it extremely difficult to identify the Second Step at all. How could Odell be certain it was this he had seen the two men climb? In the years following Mallory and Irvine's disappearance, Odell vacillated, swayed by the experiences of later climbers who reported the much easier climbs that existed on the steps both above and below that second rocky outcrop.

Before evacuating their Base Camp on the Rongbuk Glacier, Edward Norton had called a meeting of the expedition team in an attempt to ascertain what might have happened to their two friends. Most thought one or other must have slipped on the snow-covered, angled slabs that made the upper slopes of the mountain so treacherous. Only Odell clung to the notion that they had died of exposure. If they had reached the summit, by Odell's estimate they would have arrived at around 3 p.m. On their descent, given the hours of daylight left to them, Odell concluded they could have reached no lower than Camp V, around 25,500 ft, before nightfall forced them to stop. Yet, on a night clear enough to bathe the mountain in moonlight, neither Odell or Norton had seen a light as they had watched from below for signs of life.

For Mallory to continue with an ascent knowing that they would have to descend in the dark would have meant endangering Irvine's life as well as his own. But Noel Odell was among those who thought the summit might just have proved too much of a temptation. 'Who of us that has wrestled with some Alpine giant in the teeth of a gale,' he later wrote, 'or in a race with the darkness, would hold back when such a victory, such a triumph of human endeavour, was within our grasp?' It was a sentiment endorsed by Geoffrey Winthrop Young, who added that, 'Difficult as it would have been for any mountaineer to turn back with the only difficulty [the Second Step] past, for Mallory it would have been an impossibility.'

Conrad Anker was far from convinced that George Mallory would have chosen a death-or-glory finale. Like Roald Amundsen and Ernest Shackleton before him, Mallory knew that to be regarded as a 'great explorer' meant great rewards, the promise of a comfortable life and elevated social status. What was a little hardship in the field if it meant a glamorous career beyond humble teaching? Everest was the ideal vehicle for realizing that dream. But, to claim the prize, you had to get back in one piece. Whether they were above or below the Second Step when the clouds moved in, Mallory would soon have come to the crushing realization that they would have to turn around – that glory would have to wait for another day. 'That moment when he turned his back on the summit and gave the order to descend', wrote Herbert Carr, the editor of Sandy Irvine's diary, '[was] a mental agony very hard to endure ... May not the bitterness of disappointment have accelerated the onset of fatigue?'

As an experienced climber, Anker regarded any decision to turn around less as a failure and more as a testament to Mallory's mountaincraft. Descending through the Yellow Band in rapidly deteriorating conditions would have been extremely difficult, but had they done so they would have been encouraged. It was at some point after this, Anker believed, that the fatal slip occurred, one of them falling and pulling the other with him. In Anker's opinion, Mallory probably fell for around 700 ft. The bruising he found around Mallory's midriff seemed to confirm that at some point the rope had tightened, exerting considerable force before snapping. From his experience in mountain rescue, he also believed that Mallory was still conscious when he came to a stop. That Mallory's unbroken left leg was crossed over the broken right had always suggested to Anker a conscious attempt to protect a damaged limb. The absence of frostbite in his fingers, however, seemed to repudiate Odell's theory, or rather his hope, that Mallory and Irvine had survived a night in the open before waking and falling the morning following. Crucially, Mallory's gloveless hands exhibited no sign of 'blebs', the waxy, fluid-filled blisters that form at the end of the fingers as frostbite takes hold. That they do so only in living tissue suggests that Mallory had indeed died on 8 June.

What, if anything, Mallory might have been thinking as he lay there, high on the mountain, Anker could only guess. Perhaps, cocooned by the onset of shock, he had imagined he might still walk off the mountain, that Noel Odell would come and administer some restoring hot tea before guiding him down to Base Camp. Then on to Darjeeling, Bombay and home. Instead, he had been left alone, inadvertently condemned to a form of sky burial, the role of the vultures being taken by the goraks that would peck at the cavities in his torso. Anker had even come wonder whether the hole in Mallory's forehead might have been caused by a gorak, before the body ended up in the position in which he had found it, rather than as a result of striking the mountain.

Of all the members of the Everest expedition of 1924, only Sandy Irvine has not been formally laid to rest. To this day he remains somewhere on the mountain, either entombed up high or, if he fell from the North Face, cast adrift on the Rongbuk Glacier beneath. As a footnote to Irvine's story, following the discovery of Mallory's body in 1999, two members of that expedition, Jochen Hemmleb and Eric Simonson, travelled to Beijing to meet the surviving members of the Chinese expedition of 1960 that had first summitted via the North-East Ridge. Among those they met was the deputy leader of the team, a climber by the name of Xu Jing. It was during colourful accounts of Jing's team's battle with the Second Step that the veteran climber made a startling confession. Finding himself lagging off the pace those thirty-nine years previously, Jing had been climbing at around 27,000 ft when he came across the body of a climber in period clothing. Unlike George Mallory, found in a final act of prostration, the body Jing happened upon was lying on its back and wrapped in something that looked like an early sleeping bag. Had this been the body of Sandy Irvine? Until the corpse is found again it is impossible to confirm Jing's claims.

As for the latter-day Mallorys and Irvines, in the days following the successful free climb of the Second Step, the members of the Altitude Everest Expedition 2007 began to think about heading out. Most would be heading for a well-earned holiday – less gruelling adventures in warmer climes, designed to act as a fillip after the hardships of Everest. Gerry Moffatt planned to spend the coming weeks kite-surfing between the atolls of Bora Bora in the Pacific Ocean; Leo Houlding was headed for a surfing trip to Indonesia.

As he prepared to leave the mountain – thinking it unlikely he would ever return – Houlding's strongest impression of the trip had been made by the Sherpas with whom he had climbed. Since childhood, he had developed an unshakeable belief that his was a head, to say nothing of a heart, able to operate at great heights. On the highest slopes of Everest, however, the Sherpas had operated to a different set of rules entirely. Being born above 5,000 m would always provide a physiological head start, but the speed and strength with which the Sherpas manoeuvred at high altitude was something he found extraordinary. Houlding consoled himself with the fact that most of them were happiest when climbing on fixed lines, that the intricacies of his brand of technical climbing still required a particular type of guts and guile. All the same, he had to acknowledge that men like Phurba Tashe were accomplished and powerful climbers in their own right.

The relationship between Sherpas and Western climbers had come a long way since the days of Mallory and Irvine – a time when those bearing heavy loads had been deemed unable to work without 'European' supervision, being 'like children in our care', as Mallory put it. Today they enjoyed bonds of mutual respect and dependence. Thanks to projects such as Anker's Khumbu Climbing School, Sherpas had the opportunity to develop a wide range of technical skills. Houlding even thought it likely that the next round of pioneering Himalayan ascents – certainly those demanding high levels of endurance – would be made by Sherpa climbers.

Conrad Anker would be heading home. In 1999, his discovery of Mallory's body had made headlines around the world, and the furore that had come with them had caught him by surprise. In the eight years since, not a day had gone by without him reflecting on whether he had done the right thing: if, in drawing the attention of the world to his find and in his team's subsequent search for artefacts, he might have trespassed on consecrated ground. It was a nagging question that proved hard to shake, and was only compounded when the Himalayas claimed the life of his dear friend Alex Lowe. The great discovery of Mallory was his, but the awful cost that enabled it had been borne by others. Five months later it was a burden he experienced for himself. In the years that followed Lowe's death, he managed to pick up his life again, knowing that, in adopting Lowe's sons and bringing them up, he was also picking up Alex's on his behalf. Coming back to climb Everest again, to free climb the Second Step, somehow had closed the circle.

A few months after his return, Anker took his family to Washington. He had been invited to meet the Dalai Lama, the spiritual leader of Tibet, who was to be awarded the Congressional Medal of Honor at an official reception at the White House. It was the third time Anker had been invited to Washington, but climbing commitments had previously made him unable to attend. This time he promised the boys the trip. Among all the handshakes thrust at the holy man that day, the one from Conrad Anker contained a small, flat stone. It was the rock he had slipped into his pocket as he started his descent from the summit of Everest, the holiest mountain in Buddhism. In the intervening months, Anker had asked a Tibetan friend to carve into it a single word: 'Chomolungma'. When the Lama read it, he broke into a broad grin.

Almost eighty-three years to the day before Anker carried the small stone from the highest point on earth, Colonel Edward Norton and the surviving members of the 1924 Everest expedition left Base Camp. News of the deaths of Mallory and Irvine was met with an outpouring of public grief back in Britain. There was a day of national mourning for the fallen climbers, and memorials to them were numerous. A bronze memorial plaque at Shewsbury School, where Sandy Irvine had been a pupil, was dedicated to the two men. It read:

> They are rightly reputed valiant
> Who, though they perfectly apprehend
> Both what is dangerous and what is easie [*sic*]
> Are never the more thereby
> Diverted from adventuring.

And in the small church of St Wilfrid's in the village of Mobberley in Cheshire, where Mallory's father has once been rector, a stained-glass window was created in honour of the man destined to become Mobberley's most famous son. 'All his life he sought after whatsoever things are Pure and High and Eternal.

At last in the flower of his perfect manhood he was lost to human sight between Earth and Heaven on the topmost Peak of Mount Everest,' it declared. Later in 1924, on 17 October, a memorial service for George Mallory and Sandy Irvine was held in St Paul's Cathedral. That same evening, a joint meeting was held by the Alpine Club and the Royal Geographical Society. Edward Norton said of Mallory that 'a fire burnt in him and it made him one of the two most formidable antagonists Everest has ever had. He was absolutely determined to conquer the mountain and no one knows better than I do how for several months this year he devoted his whole mind and will to this project.' Later, it was left to another friend, the poet Robert Graves, to sum up the relationship between a very gifted climber and the most daunting of challenges: 'So like George', Graves wrote, 'to choose the highest and most dangerous mountain in the world.'

Ruth Mallory had got to hear of her husband's passing eleven days after the event, on 19 June, following a coded telegram from Norton informing his superiors in London of the tragedy. It was early evening when the news arrived at the house in Cambridge, and their three children, Claire, Beridge and John, were by now asleep. Not wishing to disturb their slumbers, their mother waited until the next morning to tell them what had happened. When they awoke, she gathered them into her bed and gave them the awful news: their father was gone.

Ruth and the children moved back in with her parents, to the house at Westbrook in Godalming. In the garden there she would read *The Spirit of Man*, the same anthology of poetry that Mallory had used to fortify his teammates when the mountain had checked their ambitions at the beginning of May 1924. Mallory's daughter, Clare, recalled that one piece of verse her mother had a particular affection for was entitled 'I rise from dreams of thee' – presumably Shelley's 'Lines to an Indian Air', which begins:

> I rise from dreams of thee
> In the first sweet sleep of night,

When the winds are breathing low,
And the stars are shining bright . . .

For all Ruth's public displays of stoicism, Mallory's mother, Annie, saw her suffering more keenly. 'She reminds me of a stately lily,' she wrote later, 'with its head broken and hanging down.' She also saw how the greatly the tragedy affected Irvine's family. 'They were', she noted, 'terribly broken down. I don't think they had in the least realized how great the risk was.'

Eventually, Ruth would marry again, to a close friend of her husband's – Will Arnold-Foster. It was to Arnold-Foster that Mallory had first revealed his love for the woman destined to be a wife to both of them. For the time being, however, she was left alone with her grief.

In the early years of their friendship, Geoffrey Winthrop Young was one of those to have likened Mallory to Sir Galahad, for his idealistic zeal. A knight of the Round Table in the court of King Arthur, it was Galahad who, according to legend, was destined to find the Holy Grail. It cost him his life.

When Ruth and George had courted as young lovers, poetry, literature and romance illuminated their relationship. Now she was forced to live the cold, prosaic reality of his loss. 'Whether he got to the top of the mountain or did not . . . makes no difference to my admiration of him', Ruth later wrote to Geoffrey Young, 'I have got the pain separate. There is so much of it, and it will go on for so long.'

Selected Bibliography

Anker, Conrad, and Roberts, David, *The Lost Explorer: Finding Mallory on Mount Everest* (Touchstone, 2001)

Ashcroft, Frances, *Life at the Extremes: The Science of Survival* (HarperCollins, 2000)

Breashears, David and Salkeld, Audrey, *Last Climb, The Legendary Everest Expeditions of George Mallory* (National Geographic Society, 1999)

Bruce, C. G., et al., *The Assault of Mount Everest: 1922* (Edward Arnold, 1923)

Carr, Herbert (ed.), *The Irvine Diaries* (Gaston–West Col Publications, 1979)

Coffey, Maria, *Where the Mountain Casts its Shadow: The Personal Costs of Climbing* (Arrow, 2004)

Connor, Jeff, *Dougal Haston: The Philosophy of Risk* (Canongate, 2002)

Firstbrook, Peter, *Lost on Everest: The Search for Mallory & Irvine* (BBC Worldwide, 1999)

Gillman, Peter (ed.), *Everest: Eighty Years of Triumph and Tragedy* (Little, Brown, 2001)

Gillman, Peter and Leni, *The Wildest Dream* (Headline, 2000)

Graves, Robert, *Goodbye to All That* (Jonathan Cape, 1929)

Green, Dudley, *Because It's There: The Life of George Mallory* (Tempus, 2005)

Green, Dudley, *Mallory of Everest* (Faust, 1991)

Hemmleb, Jochen, Johnson, Larry, and Simonson, Eric, *Ghosts of Everest* (Macmillan, 1999)

Hill, Lynn, *Climbing Free: My Life in the Vertical World* (HarperCollins, 2003)

Howard-Bury, Charles, *Mount Everest: The Reconnaissance, 1921* (Edward Arnold, 1922)

Holzel, Tom, and Salkeld, Audrey, *The Mystery of Mallory and Irvine* (Pimlico, 1999)

Keynes, Geoffrey, *The Gates of Memory* (Clarendon Press, 1981)

SELECTED BIBLIOGRAPHY

Krakauer, John, *Into Thin Air* (Macmillan, 1997)

Lowe-Anker, Jennifer, *Forget Me Not* (The Mountaineers Books, 2008)

Macfarlane, Robert, *Mountains of the Mind: A History of a Fascination* (Granta, 2003)

Noel, John, *Through Tibet to Everest* (Edward Arnold, 1927)

Noel, Sandra, *Everest Pioneer: The Photographs of Captain John Noel* (Sutton Publishing Limited, 2003)

Norton, E. F., *The Fight for Everest* (Edward Arnold, 1925)

Ortner, Sherry B., *Life And Death on Mt. Everest: Sherpas and Himalayan Mountaineering* (Princeton University, 1999)

Parsons, Mike, and Rose, Mary B., *Invisible on Everest: Innovation and the Gear Makers* (Northern Liberties Press, 2000)

Pye, David, *George Leigh Mallory: A Memoir* (Oxford University Press, 1927)

Robertson, David, *George Mallory* (Faber, 1969)

Salkeld, Audrey, *Mystery on Everest: A Photobiography of George Mallory* (National Geographic Society, 2000)

Somervell, Howard, *After Everest: The Experiences of a Mountaineer and Medical Missionary* (Hodder & Stoughton, 1936)

Summers, Julie, *Fearless on Everest: The Quest for Sandy Irvine* (Weidenfeld & Nicolson, 2000)

Unsworth, Walt, *Everest: The Mountaineering History* (Baton Wicks Publications, 2000)

Young, Geoffrey Winthrop, *On High Hills: Memories of the Alps* (Methuen, 1927)

Younghusband, Sir Francis, *The Epic of Mount Everest* (Edward Arnold, 1926)

Acknowledgements

In writing this book, I must pay tribute to the two principals of the story, George Leigh Mallory and Andrew Comyn Irvine, without whose unquenchable spirit of adventure the history of exploration would be much the poorer. The majority of Mallory's letters quoted in this work come from the collection at Magdalene College, Cambridge; the rest are held by the Mallory and Irvine families and by the relatives of other members of the 1924 expedition to Mount Everest. Other documents, including some of the letters between Mallory and his friends and colleagues, are in the care of the Royal Geographical Society's Everest Archive. I am grateful to them all.

The 'voice' of Sandy Irvine as it appears here is drawn mainly from *The Irvine Diaries*, the edition of his journal published in 1979 and prepared with such aplomb by Herbert Carr, whose own informed conclusions on the fate of the two men also appears in part.

Mallory's legacy has benefited from a number of exceptional biographies. David Pye's personal and touching account of his good friend's life and times, *George Leigh Mallory: A Memoir* (1927), cannot be recommended highly enough. The same applies to David Robertson's excellent *George Mallory* (1969). Grateful as I am to both Pye and Robertson, however, the inspiration for the chapters on Mallory and Irvine comes from more recent accounts of their exploits.

Given the passion and professionalism with which modern biographers have chronicled their lives, it is inevitable that any new history of such iconic figures as George Mallory and Sandy Irvine will be largely an amalgam of previous works. Of the accounts to appear in recent years, three, in my opinion, stand out. The first of these – they are in no particular order – is *The Mystery of Mallory and Irvine*, by Audrey Salkeld, co-written with Tom Holzel. Its research is meticulous, and the forensic detail with which it reconstructs Mallory's final days on Everest exceptional. Next comes Peter and Leni Gillman's account, *The Wildest Dream*. Compelling from start to finish, no other book on Mallory better captures the spirit of the great man's age and the cost to his and Irvine's friends and family in the wake of his disappearance. Last but by no means least is Dudley Green's *Because It's There: The Life of George Mallory*, which conveys complex information in a manner that is both accessible and informative. I have relied on these three books, and have endeavoured to represent their authors' work honestly and faithfully.

While biographies on George Mallory are numerous, those on Sandy Irvine are less so. Too long regarded simply as Mallory's humble sidekick, he was at last done justice in print with the publication in 2000 of a biography written by his great-niece, Julie Summers. *Fearless on Everest: The Quest for Sandy Irvine*, goes some way to redressing the balance, and I am grateful for the colour it breathes into Irvine's brief, though eventful, life.

Of the modern dramatis personae, my thanks must first go to Conrad Anker whom, thanks to the internet, I joined for morning coffee in his study in Montana on numerous occasions. He was always a gracious host, putting up with endless questions with good humour. I am also grateful to him for *The Lost Explorer*, his published account of finding Mallory on Everest. Its vivid recollections of finding Mallory's body and of Anker's first attempt at a free climb of the Second Step form the basis of my own, and I thank both him and his co-author, the excellent climbing writer, David Roberts.

Thanks must go, of course, to Altitude Films, without whom

this book would not have been possible, and to Anthony Geffen, James Taylor, Mimi Gilligan, James McNeile and Kate Fraser in particular. As well as organising the opportunity for me to join the expedition team at Base Camp, they made available a wealth of background information and gave me access to transcripts from the exhaustive interviews conducted meticulously for the film which have proved a rich source of material. I would also like to thank Leo Houlding, Kevin Thaw and Gerry Moffatt.

I am indebted to countless journalists and writers not directly connected with the 2007 expedition but whose work it was a pleasure to read during my research. They are too numerous to list in their entirety here; however, I would like to single out Ed Douglas, one of Britain's finest climbing writers, whose articles, principally in *Observer Sport Monthly,* have been a particular inspiration. Thanks also to Seb Morton-Clark, whose account in *The Times* of Leo Houlding's climb of Cerro Torre in 2001 bolstered my own research. In the US, I would like to thank the journalists and editors of *Outside* magazine, and also the *Outside* contributor and author Maria Coffey. Her compelling book *Where the Mountain Casts its Shadow* conveys the personal cost of climbing in discomfiting detail.

Some of the accounts of modern expeditions that appear in this work were written when the participants could not be contacted – an occupational hazard even for the modern climber despite the wonders of modern telecommunications. Nevertheless, the details have been corroborated as thoroughly possible.

I would also like to thank my agent, Jessica Woollard, for her hard work and perseverance, as well as Paul Marsh and all at the Marsh Agency. At John Murray, I would like to thank my two editors, Rowan Yapp and Helen Hawksfield, and also Roland Philipps, for his ongoing courtesy and patience.

A number of thanks are also due to friends and family: in particular to Mum and Dad for helping out, and to Yvonne Constance for 'HQ'. Lastly and most importantly of all, I would like to thank Amanda, William and Honor. I love you very much.